COLLECTOR'S REFERENCE & VALUE GUIDE TO

THE LONE RANGER

LEE FELBINGER

COLLECTOR BOOKS
A Division of Schroeder Publishing Co., Inc.

Searching For A Publisher?

We are always looking for knowledgeable people considered to be experts within their fields. If you feel that there is a real need for a book on your collectible subject and have a large comprehensive collection, contact Collector Books.

Cover design by: Beth Summers
Book design by: Mary Ann Dorris
Illustrations by: Lee Felbinger

Additional copies of this book may be ordered from:

COLLECTOR BOOKS
P.O. Box 3009
Paducah, Kentucky 42002-3009

@$18.95. Add $2.00 for postage and handling.

Contents

HI-YO Silver A-WA-A-A-Y!

On the following pages you will wander through a pictorial scrapbook of a radio and television legend America took to its heart. Included are never before published photos, clippings, toys, games, comic books, cards, advertisements, comic strips, buttons, movie ads, books, and all those wonderful radio premiums you had — and could never forget!

Although this book is primarily a hobby project, utilizing my own collection of Lone Ranger memorabilia, I have also included prices in the collectibles portion of the book. However, it is my hope that it will be much more than that to my fellow collectors, that it will provide enjoyment and information to all those interested in the Lone Ranger, whether it be Brace Beemer or Clayton Moore. I have tried to include a comprehensive scrapbook; however, I'm sure that there are items I have missed. I would appreciate hearing from collectors with additional information or corrections.

The prices shown were averaged out by checking with collectors, catalogs, flea markets, conventions, etc. These figures can only serve as a guide, as prices range widely on many items and the condition of the collectible influences the price.

Have fun...read...look...enjoy! Return to those thrilling days of yesteryear and to those happy times when ten cents and a box top could buy a world of dreams.

Lee J. Felbinger
Green Lane, PA

Acknowledgments

"A tip of the white hat" and a gracious, "thank you" to the following individuals who were kind enough to contribute information and help in making this third book a reality.

First and foremost a special thanks to Mrs. Leta Beemer Peterson and Bob Beemer who have given the author permission to use the photographs of Brace Beemer (original photographs are a part of the Burton Historical Collection, Detroit Public Library). Mrs. Peterson also was kind enough to send the author a few choice Brace Beemer items for his collection of Lone Ranger memorabilia, for which I will forever remain greatful. Thanks also to Richard Beemer; the Wrather Corporation; George W. Trendel Jr.; Fred Flowerday; WXYZ Incorporated; The Detroit Free Press; The Detroit News; and also Clayton Moore; Tom Gill; Marj High; Palladium Media Enterprizes, Incorporated; Bill Mays; American Bakeries; Jean Toll and Evelyn Wilson; General Mills Incorporated; J.J. King; Amoco Oil Company; Fran Striker, Jr.; and Irvin Romig.

Special thanks to the following collectors who have contributed information and photographs — Dick Fuss, Karl Rommel, Bob Cauler, Jim Scancarelli, Jerry Cook, Jim Rosch, Anita and Rick Senkow, Bob Beemer, Dave Holland, Clint Kueker, Joseph Gura, Jr., Eugene Smith, Harry Matetsky, Terry Klepey, John Fawcett, and Jim Pfleiger. Color photography by Edward F. Cunnally.

Dedication

To my Aunt Sis, Aunt Annie, and Uncle Herman who raised me after my mother died and never threw away my childhood mementos of my hero, The Lone Ranger. My boyhood room in Pittsburgh remained the same until I was an adult and returned to reclaim many of the items in this book.

To my dad, who taught me his love of horses and how to say "Hi-Yo Silver Away." My biggest thrill as a child was the day my dad let me drive the red produce wagon and Nellie (a draft horse) from the Pittsburgh produce yards to the stable after a long day's work. (Of course Nellie knew the way home by herself and needed little direction from a small boy yelling "Hi-Yo Silver" to her.)

Last, but not least, to my wife, Suzanne, who has put up with my hobby and interests over the years.

About the Author

Lee Felbinger is a long-time collector of Lone Ranger memorabilia and has one of the largest collections in the country today. He has appeared on numerous radio and television programs and has written articles for *Antique Trader*, *Collectibles Illustrated*, *Collectors News*, *Inside Collector*, *Today's Collector*, and other publications.

The white German shepherd shown with him is his trusted companion named "Silver" who was born in, of all places, Silverdale, Pennsylvania.

Foreword

by Richard Beemer
Son of radio's Lone Ranger

"Who was that masked man? That was the Lone Ranger!"

Hundreds of episodes of possibly the most enjoyed radio drama ever to air ended with those two lines. There were as many answers to the question as there were people glued to their radios. That was the beauty of the Lone Ranger. For he lived in the imaginations of millions of children, and, yes, adults. A line in an old movie haunts the answer — it went something like this: "He's what every boy wants to be when he grows up and what every old man wishes he had been."

Lee's *Collector's Reference and Value Guide to the Lone Ranger* illustrates the immortality of the Lone Ranger. There is a longing within many to remember the principles represented by the Lone Ranger and, in so doing, give new life to the basic values of truth, honesty, and courage whenever we allow our minds to "return to those thrilling days of yesteryear — the Lone Ranger rides again!"

The subject I have been asked to address is embodied in the question, "Who was Brace Beemer?" My father, Brace Beemer, was one of the most complex men I have ever known, and yet there was a basic simplicity in the manner in which he approached life. He did so with truth, honesty, and courage. When he believed in something, he was relentless in fighting for his cause. He loved America with a passion, first demonstrated when, at 14 years of age, as a member of the famed Rainbow Division, he fought in the trenches of France during many of the fiercest campaigns of World War I. My grandmother spared no effort to retrieve her "baby." When the MPs would enter the company area to "return the boy to his mother," the troops would hide Dad until the MPs finally gave up and left the area.

Dad believed in the inherent goodness of man. In his philosophy, beliefs had to be backed up by actions. If you believed in the goodness of man, then you had to serve mankind with whatever talents God bestowed upon you. This he did with fervor. Yes, Brace Beemer could ride a horse and shoot with the best of them. He also had a tender, caring side. Dad loved children. Countless hours were devoted to children's hospitals, schools, clubs, any place where a child in need might be found — all without fanfare.

Many years ago, while visiting the children's ward of a large eastern metropolitan hospital, Dad was introduced to a paralyzed 12-year-old boy. The doctors said they had been unable to find any "physical explanation" for the boy's paralysis. Dad, in full costume, spoke quietly to the bedridden child. No one, other than the child, heard his words. He turned and walked several feet down the ward away from the little boy's bed. Turning back to face the child, Dad knelt down and held out a silver bullet. In the voice so well known to millions, he said simply, "If you want this silver bullet, walk over here and take it." The young lad struggled awkwardly out of bed, took the several steps to where Dad was kneeling, and with a big grin on his face, fell into Dad's arms grasping the silver bullet. Other than the grinning boy, there wasn't a dry eye on the ward, including the Lone Ranger's.

The out-of-doors was one of his greatest loves, as was poetry, which he read and collected in great abundance. Having gone to war at a tender age, he lacked a formal education. An insatiable reader, he mastered the English language and taught himself Latin. He became versed in both history and current events. In our home, education was held in high regard. Once, when I was a student at Michigan State, my brother, Bob, got me the opportunity to read for the part of a jet fighter pilot in a show to be produced by a local TV station. I was thrilled with the idea and went home that weekend to "discuss" it with Dad. He was sitting on the porch reading when I approached him with the idea. Without looking up, he said simply, "finish school." So much for "discussion." No child ever came to the door of the farmhouse to meet the Lone Ranger who didn't hear the words, "finish school."

My father would have been proud to have personally met each and every one of you reading Lee's book and collecting, or simply remembering with fondness, those mementos which symbolize the history of the Lone Ranger. His greatest pride would be to know that the principles embodied in the Lone Ranger have survived with such strength as we embark into a new century. Perhaps that is because there is a measure of the Lone Ranger in every caring person. "Out of the past come the thundering hoofbeats of the great horse Silver, the Lone Ranger rides again!"

Richard Beemer
November 1996

Where Have All the Heroes Gone?

The youth of America need heroes...good guys in white hats, or whatever words you may choose to describe them!

Call it corny, call it old fashioned, but in the days of my youth, we had heroes we could look up to, pattern ourselves after, and aspire to, and we were better for those actions. Heroes were everywhere in those days. On the football field there was Doc Blanchard and Glen Davis — Mr. Inside and Outside were on the Saturday sport pages every week. Baseball had Jackie Robinson, Gil Hodges, Ralph Kiner, Johnny Mize, Micky Mantle, Joe DiMaggio, and Bob Feller. Out in the West we had Gene Autry, Roy Rogers, Hopalong Cassidy, and a posse of other western heroes.

This book is a pictorial and written tribute to a fictional character from those days and to Brace Beemer and Clayton Moore, the men who made, molded, and developed him into a hero who has been a legend for generations of fans that were thrilled by their performances in the title of the Lone Ranger.

It seems like only yesterday that I was back in the smoky twilight of Pittsburgh, Pennsylvania, in the early forties, watching for the street lights to come on at dusk. This was the signal for me and my buddies that it was time to run home and get a seat in front of the family radio. I always sat in front and could see with my vivid imagination, the Lone Ranger and Silver, galloping out of the mesh speaker of our trusty Philco.

Fred Foy's exciting, unbeatable voice announcing once again that classic, polished opening... "Hi-Yo Silver, a fiery horse with a speed of light, a cloud of dust and hearty Hi-Yo Silver — The Lone Ranger."

No matter where I was or what I was doing, I always made sure that I was home in time to thrill to that classic opening of gunshots, hoofbeats, and the William Tell Overture! For the next 30 minutes, the voice of Brace Beemer cast a spell over me that no one could interrupt.

With his faithful Indian companion, Tonto, the daring and resourceful masked rider of the plains led the fight for law and order in the early days of the West. Return with us now to those thrilling days of yesteryear. The Lone Ranger rides again!

I can still recall the time my father took me to the Pittsburgh Police Circus to see the Lone Ranger and Silver. The thrill of seeing and hearing Brace Beemer's cry of Hi-Yo Silver echo throughout the packed stands of Forbes Field remains with me now if I close my eyes. My disappointment at not getting to shake his hand as he circled the stands and was mobbed by both young and old fans who could afford those more expensive seats down in front was noticed by my father. As a consolation prize, he bought me a Lone Ranger felt pennant souvenir of our trip to see my hero. To this day, I have this pennant in my Lone Ranger collection of memorabilia. It means a great deal to me and reminds me of that long ago trip with my father to see my boyhood idol.

The whole country suffers from a lack of heroes today especially with Watergate, drugs in all aspects of the country, and leaders in government, business, media, show business, etc. being exposed in shady deals, criminal acts, and immorality. We have a desperate need in America for heroes — for our youth and for ourselves of the older generation. There is a need to create the fine virtues and values that we need and should strive for in ourselves, family, and friends. I, personally, would like to to see more ap pie, flag waving, and a return to a faith in Ameri its leaders, and in ourselves. Let's stop emphasizing the negative and start shouting out the positive side of American life and values. Let's bring back the heroes in the white hats to center stage and push the "bad guys" of today and their standards into the wings for good.

Mourning the death of a hero and the Wild West, a boy weeps in a *Boston Record* cartoon, Jan. 15, 1917.

The success of any fictional character or hero depends on countless intangibles that can neither be foreseen nor considered. A great many characters are created, developed, and presented to the public but through the years, only a few remain as established heroes of fiction.

The Lone Ranger, with his ringing cry of "Hi-Yo Silver!" has become an American institution ranking with the top heroes of folklore and legend. The Lone Ranger is a hero born of radio and aired by a Detroit showman, George W. Trendle, who was truly a twentieth century pioneer.

Trendle, a pioneer in motion picture distribution and exhibition, and his associates turned a single nickelodeon into a chain of Detroit movie theaters. In 1928 they decided to sell the chain of theaters to Paramount; however, Trendle stayed as active head of the United Detroit Theatres.

In 1930, he became interested in radio and sold his associates on the idea of establishing station WXYZ in Detroit and WOOD in Grand Rapids. Again, Trendle established a statewide network, with station WXYZ as the keystone for the Michigan radio network.

When the station terminated all affiliations with Columbia Broadcasting System, Trendle faced the challenge of assembling a schedule of high caliber programming to meet the stiff competition of famous radio stars and bands. He organized a dramatic stock company and began searching for suitable radio scripts. A Buffalo, New York, writer, Fran Striker, was asked to supply scripts. Striker responded with one program a week for Trendle's dramatic group.

Trendle found an outlet for his many years of experience in the theatre in radio drama. He watched over his own productions, as well as those of his competition, and decided that most shows were being designed for adult listening. His decision was to create a program for the vast youth audience, one which would be interesting, exciting, inspirational, and educational. His aim was to entertain, and at the same time to instruct and inspire, with a program that would appeal to children and adults alike.

Trendle recalled that during his motion picture days the pictures that received the least criticism were the westerns, and they were always very popular with fans of all ages. A western story would be the best type program, he decided. A radio series that would tell about the hardships endured by our pioneers and the resulting character traits and principles that became our American heritage.

During the winter of the Great Depression, Trendle considered and rejected dozens of program possibilities. He finally decided that his main character would be a rider visualized as a lone operator. He would be a man of mystery — one who, for some reason, concealed his identity. This "Lone" operator who would ride on the side of right and justice was implied to have been a Texas Ranger.

When Trendle mentally put together the bare bones of this "Lone Ranger" character, he called on Fran Striker to sculpt the flesh and blood. Striker wrote and rewrote the first trial script.

The first broadcast of this trial script was late at night, without any advance publicity. The staff of WXYZ was enthusiastic, but Trendle objected to Striker's conception of the Lone Ranger as a somewhat lighthearted hero, who laughed when he trounced over evil villainy. The Lone Ranger, Trendle declared, should be the "embodiment of granted prayer." Every day, there were suggestions from Trendle such as, "The Lone Ranger must not shoot to kill" "Action, more action!" "Watch the logic; don't become farfetched." "Be fair to all racial and religious groups." "Good grammar, when the Lone Ranger speaks." Story after story went to Trendle for study and personal revision.

Finally, Striker assembled 12 scripts and evolving from these scripts were Tonto, the Lone Ranger's Indian companion, and the now famous phrase, "Hi-Yo Silver, A-Wa-a-ay!"

On January 30, 1933, the Lone Ranger first launched his silver bullets over station WXYZ and became a regular fixture in the program lineup. Trendle was torn with the doubts and uncertainties of an

expectant father. Was anyone out in radioland listening to the Lone Ranger? Had youngsters taken him to heart as a hero?

A startling reply came in mid-May, when the Lone Ranger offered a free pop-gun to the first 300 children who applied to the station. Twenty-five thousand letters poured into WXYZ. Trendle had his ideal program.

In July of that same year, the Detroit Department of Recreation innocently announced the Lone Ranger would make a personal appearance at the annual school field day on Belle Isle. Seventy thousand screaming kids packed the Isle. Emergency squadrons of police had to quiet the crowds to avert a near panic. Trendle was now confident that he had struck the bonanza of radio broadcasting — he had a hit show.

Brace Beemer, the radio Ranger, was heard on hundreds of radio broadcasts and seen at countless personal appearances astride the great horse, Silver.

The triweekly production of the Lone Ranger was an expensive undertaking, even in those days of low prices and salaries. For a solution to his budgeting problems, Trendle turned to H. Allen Campbell, a brilliant advertising salesman for the Hearst organization.

Campbell accepted the challenge and assured the continuation of the Lone Ranger program by selling it to a baking company for broadcast, not only in Detroit, but also in Chicago and New York City.

Unabashed by the countless difficulties involved in the three station outlets, Mr. Campbell helped establish a three-station hook-up, with WXYZ feeding the Lone Ranger program to the nationally famous stations, WGN and WOR. This hookup was called the Mutual Broadcasting System. Campbell also arranged for sponsorship on a number of New England stations, and later the stations of the West Coast-based Don Lee Broadcasting System. With the two ends of the nation linked for the broadcast of the Lone Ranger, the Mutual Broadcast System became a coast-to-coast network and an important voice in radio. Then eventually there was General Mills sponsorship in 40 northern states also.

With his financial problems behind him, and his favorite hero successful, Trendle learned that imitation, although flattering, may well be costly. Many imitators began to appear, hoping to cash in on the success of the Lone Ranger. Again, Trendle knew just where to find the man he needed. Raymond J. Meurer, a young attorney who was on the path to becoming one of the "big names in the law profession" was made the legal representative of the Lone Ranger. Meurer was convinced that the Lone Ranger could be a big factor in the teaching of Americanism...something that must be preserved and protected against cheap imitators and carefully guarded at all times. There must never be any unfavorable publicity about the program or any individuals connected with the program that could disillusion the millions of boys and girls who idolized the masked hero. Throughout the years, Meurer traveled to every part of the country to put down imposters, block copyright infringements, and guard against misrepresentation in publicity or advertising.

During the run of the radio series, the Lone Ranger and Tonto traveled the country from Texas to the Dakotas, from the Mississippi to the Pacific, dispensing justice and silver bullets. Stops were made along the Rio Grande, the Panhandle on the Barbary Coast at the Redwood Timber Grab, the Chisholm Trail, the Canadian Northwest Border. Bad men, who had it coming to them, got it on riverboats, in gold rushes, in copper and silver mines, and in the Indian Wars. Stagecoaches, covered wagons, the pony express...all played their parts. Famous names, like Buffalo Bill, Wild Bill Hickok, Billy the Kid, Geronimo, General Custer, and Samuel Colt have also been skillfully worked into the radio episodes.

The Lone Ranger, Silver, and Tonto did their part during World War II, from a war dispatch: "Whenever we approached an output in our speedy jeep, the driver sang out the American password of the day, "Hi-Yo Silver," and in reply came the guard's leather lunged reply, "A-Wa-a-y!"

From another dispatch, "They have named Mosquito pilots the 'Lone Rangers' of this war." From *Radio Daily*, December 24, 1943, "The seventh annual nationwide poll of writers-critics, shows the Lone Ranger tied for first place in Children's Shows. The Ranger has been either first or tied for the last three years." The Ranger program didn't stop there, but continued to win awards and other recognition over the years.

There was always a "set" opening for every live broadcast. It was always heralded by the William Tell Overture, then, over the music, "A fiery horse with the the speed of light, a cloud of dust, a hearty Hi-Yo Silver — The Lone Ranger." Next the commercial and, "Return with us to those thrilling days of yesteryear...From out of the past come the thundering hoofs of the great horse Silver — The Lone Ranger rides again."

The close of the show was just "Hi-Yo, Silver — A-Wa-a-y!"

The Lone Ranger property continued to grow and prosper under the guidance of George W. Trendle. America found a special place in her heart for the Lone Ranger, the original good guy in the white hat!

He was a mystery — everyone was curious as to who he was. He even had to wear his mask in the studios of WXYZ and at all appearances. But he was America's hero, he never shot to kill, he was always on the side of the law, he always told the complete truth. Best of all, because he had an Indian as his faithful companion, he was shown to be free of prejudice.

Several times a year, the program would make a special premium offer for a Lone Ranger item costing no more than ten or fifteen cents, along with a box top (of course) from Cheerios, Kix, or Wheaties. Upon sending the proper ante to Michigan or Minnesota, the weeks would be full of anticipation as kids across the country waited for their brown package that contained a Lone Ranger premium — a bargain at any price!

The ultimate radio premium, Frontier Town, which was basically a 4½ foot square sheet of paper in four separate sections, depicting a map of a complete western town, with 72 models of buildings, bridges, trains, wagons, etc. Once you had the four sections and purchased the extra boxes of Cheerios (17 of these models were on the backs of special packages), you could follow the adventures of the Lone Ranger and Tonto in Frontier Town for an entire year.

Although George W. Trendle is given the bulk of the credit for both creating and enhancing the Lone Ranger idea, it was the voice of Brace Beemer that carried this successful radio program for its 21 most-listened-to years on radio.

The Lone Ranger Western Adventure

Cast:
The Lone Ranger — John Reid:
George Seaton
Jack Deeds
Earle Graser
Brace Beemer
Tonto:
John Todd
Dan Reid, the Lone Ranger's nephew:
Ernie Stanley
James Lipton
Dick Beals
Butch Cavendish:
Jay Michael
Thunder Martin:
Paul Hughes
Announcer-Narrator:
Harold True
Brace Beemer
Harry Golder
Charles Woods
Bob Hite
Fred Foy
Also:
Rollon Parker
John Hodiak
Jack Petruzzi
Herschel Mayal
Ted Johnstone
Amos Jacobs (later known as Danny Thomas)
Bob Maxell
Frank Russell
Elaine Alpert
Creators:
George W. Trendle
Fran Striker
Producer-Director-Writer:
James Jewell
Directors:
Al Hodge
Charles Livingstone
Chief Writer and Story Editor:
Fran Striker
Writers:
Felix Holt
Bob Green
Shelley Stark
Bob Shaw
Dan Beatty
Tom Dougall
Gibson Scott Fox
Theme:
William Tell Overture by Rossini
Bridge Music:
Les Préludes by Liszt

Opening:
Music. Theme up full and under...
Sound. Hoofbeats fade in...
Ranger. Hi-Yo Silver!!!
Sound. Gunshots and hoofbeats...
Announcer. With his faithful Indian companion, Tonto, the daring and resourceful masked rider of the plains led the fight for law and order in the early western United States. Nowhere in the pages of history can one find a greater champion of justice. Return with us now to those thrilling days of yesteryear.
Sound. Hoofbeats fade in....
Announcer. From out of the past come the thundering hoofbeats of the great horse Silver. The Lone Ranger rides again!!!
Ranger. Come on, Silver! Let's go, big fellow! Hi-yo Silver! Away!
Music. Theme up full...

In 1954, the Lone Ranger, Inc. was sold by the Campbell Trendle Agency in Detroit to a wealthy Texas oilman, Jack Wrather, for $3 million — a record sale up to that date.

What is the reason for the Lone Ranger's long-lasting appeal and loyalty? It is best expressed by the words of Wrather, as quoted in *Screen Thrills Illustrated Magazine*: "The Lone Ranger is a composite of every man who stands for law and order, always stresses the fact that young people of America owe much to their ancestors, and to pay this debt, they must maintain their heritage and pass it on to their descendants."

"All those things teach something. They teach patriotism, fairness, tolerance, sympathy, religion. And, yet, they don't preach, these lessons, once learned, will never be forgotten."

And neither will the Lone Ranger — Hi-Yo Silver, A-Wa-a-y!

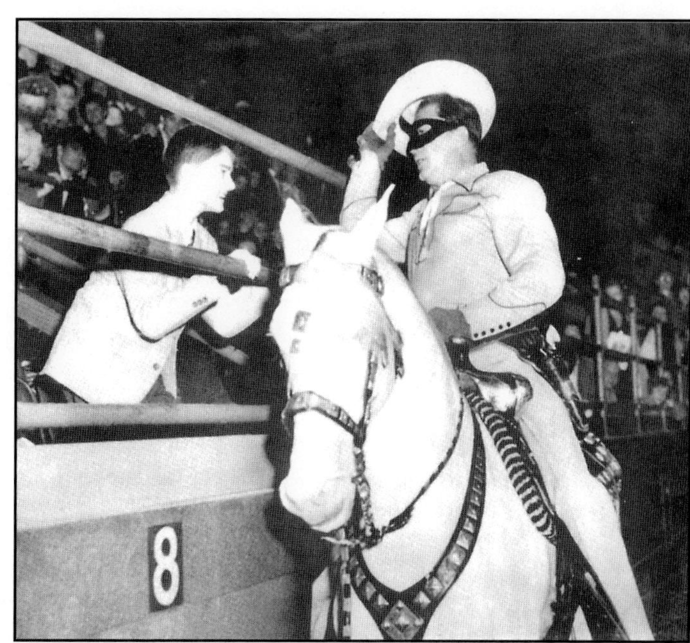

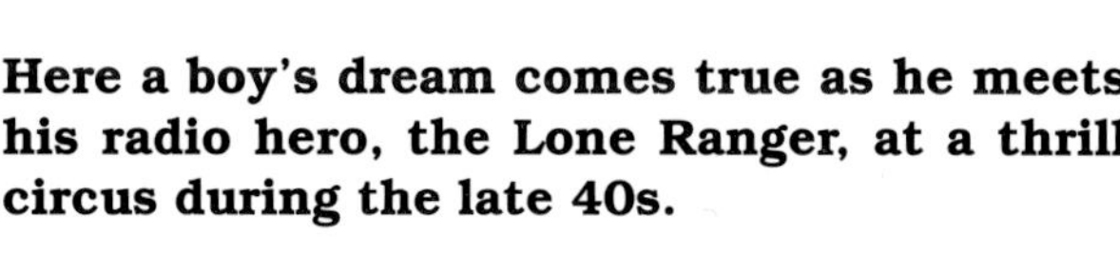

Here a boy's dream comes true as he meets his radio hero, the Lone Ranger, at a thrill circus during the late 40s.

Brace Beemer introduces an admiring young fan to Silver during a 1940 personal appearance. Note the boy's Lone Ranger cowboy hat with Lone Ranger logo, a highly desirable collectible today.

WEST INTERMEDIATE

Circus

THUR. and FRI.
MARCH 22--23

28
BIG ACTS

Hi-Yo-Silver

OF RADIO FAME

Trained Ponies and Dogs

FREE Live Bull Pup Given Away At
Thursday Matinee at 3:45 p. m.

Matinee 15c Evenings 25c 8 p. m.

Circus poster promoting "Hi-Yo Silver" of radio fame as a feature attraction. This was the first Silver that was used before Trendle bought his own white horse for personal appearances. Carl A. Romig is shown on the horse that he owned, trained, and rented to WXYZ for Lone Ranger personal appearances.

As the popularity of the radio show increased in the 40s, so did the merchandising of the Lone Ranger character from an adult radio (pilot), books, toys, gum cards, and cereal premiums.

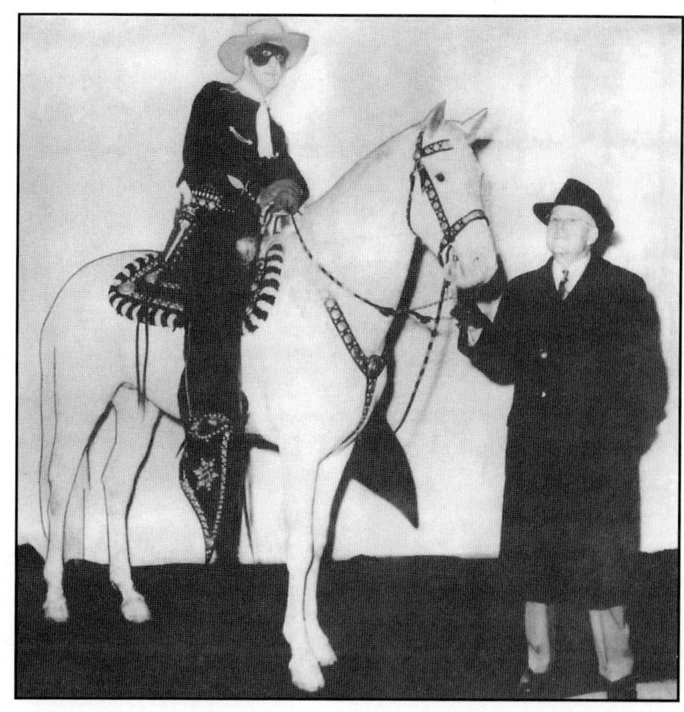

Very early photo of Brace Beemer astride Silver; that's Lone Ranger creator George W. Trendle at right. (Note holster and mask — both were changed or improved for personal appearances.)

Brace Beemer in early Lone Ranger publicity photo (taken by a Detroit photographer 1933 – 35).

Radio's Lone Ranger, Brace Beemer, admiring Silver's beautiful saddle in early 1941.

A little girl accepting a silver bullet from Brace Beemer at a local personal appearance.

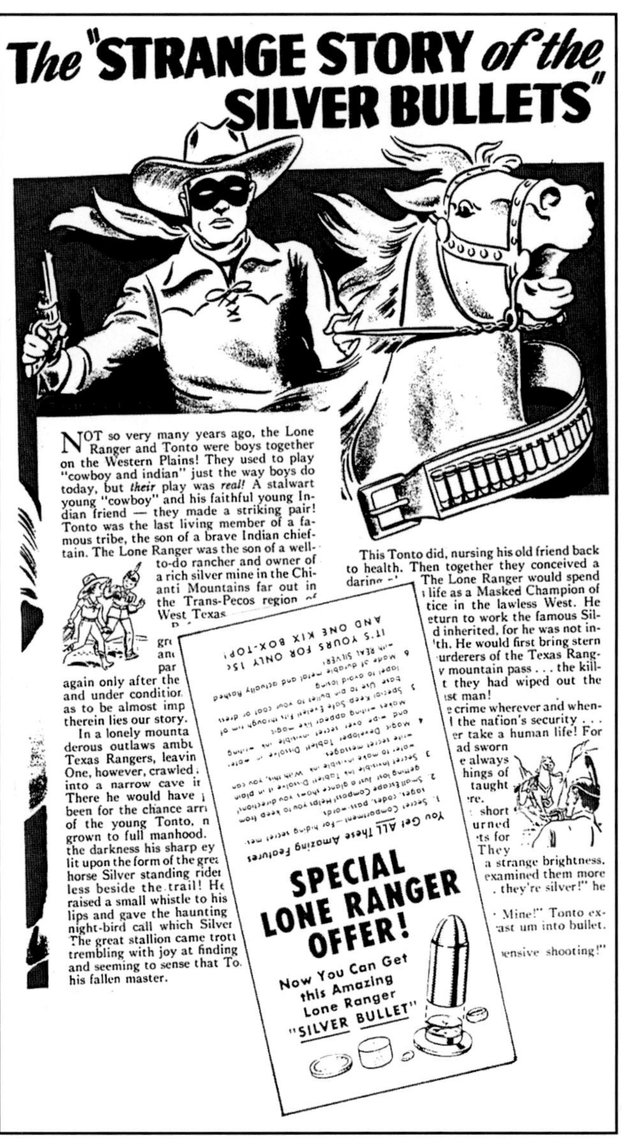

The "STRANGE STORY of the SILVER BULLETS"
NOT so very many years ago, the Lone Ranger and Tonto were boys together on the Western Plains! They used to play "cowboy and indian" just the way boys do today, but their play was real! A stalwart young "cowboy" and his faithful young Indian friend — they made a striking pair! Tonto was the last living member of a famous tribe, the son of a brave Indian chieftain. The Lone Ranger was the son of a well-to-do rancher and owner of a rich silver mine in the Chi-anti Mountains far out in the Trans-Pecos region of West Texas
again only after the
and under condition
as to be almost imp
therein lies our story.
In a lonely mounta
derous outlaws ambu
Texas Rangers, leavin
One, however, crawled
into a narrow cave ir
There he would have
been for the chance arri
of the young Tonto, n
grown to full manhood.
the darkness his sharp ey
lit upon the form of the grea
horse Silver standing rider
less beside the trail! He
raised a small whistle to his
lips and gave the haunting
night-bird call which Silver
The great stallion came trott
trembling with joy at finding
and seeming to sense that To.
his fallen master.
This Tonto did, nursing his old friend back to health. Then together they conceived a
The Lone Ranger would spend
life as a Masked Champion of
tice in the lawless West. He
eturn to work the famous Sil-
d inherited, for he was not in-
th. He would first bring stern
urderers of the Texas Rang-
mountain pass . . . the kill-
t they had wiped out the
st man!
crime wherever and when-
the nation's security . . .
er take a human life! For
a strange brightness.
examined them more
. they're silver!" he
Mine!" Tonto ex-
ast um into bullet.
ensive shooting!"
SPECIAL LONE RANGER OFFER!
Now You Can Get this Amazing Lone Ranger "SILVER BULLET"
You Get ALL These Amazing Features
IT'S YOURS FOR ONLY 15¢ AND ONE KIX BOX-TOP!

As the show became more popular so did the silver bullets the Ranger used. Over the years many premiums would be some type of silver bullet.

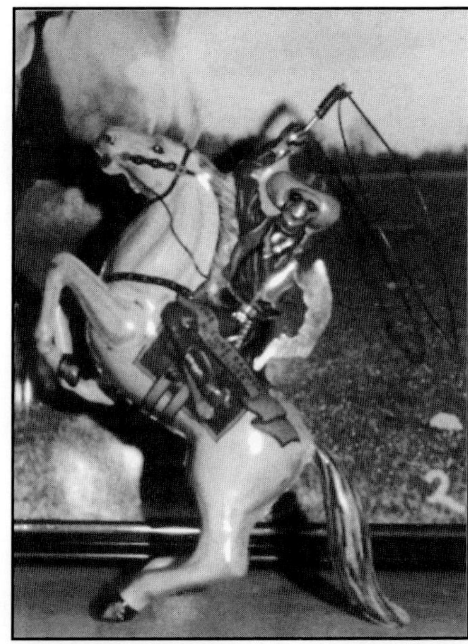

s the radio Ranger's popularity grew, so did the merchandising of the show. Many of the items shown bove are highly collectible today.

You had to dress the part to act the part...even on radio. Proof is this photo of Brace Beemer and the entire cast which participated in the old radio programs. Beemer had to wear the mask every time he entered the public. Photo courtesy of Mrs. Brace (Leta) Beemer.

While on promotional tours Brace Beemer did not forget to make appearances with some of the neighborly tribes of his companion and faithful friend, Tonto.

Here honorary blood brother Brace Beemer holds a pow-wow with the tribal chief on one of his many personal appearances.

During a rehearsal of Duffy's Tavern, Brace Beemer demonstrates his Colt Revolver to Ed Gardner (Archie, the bartender). Brace was a guest on the show February 2, 1943.

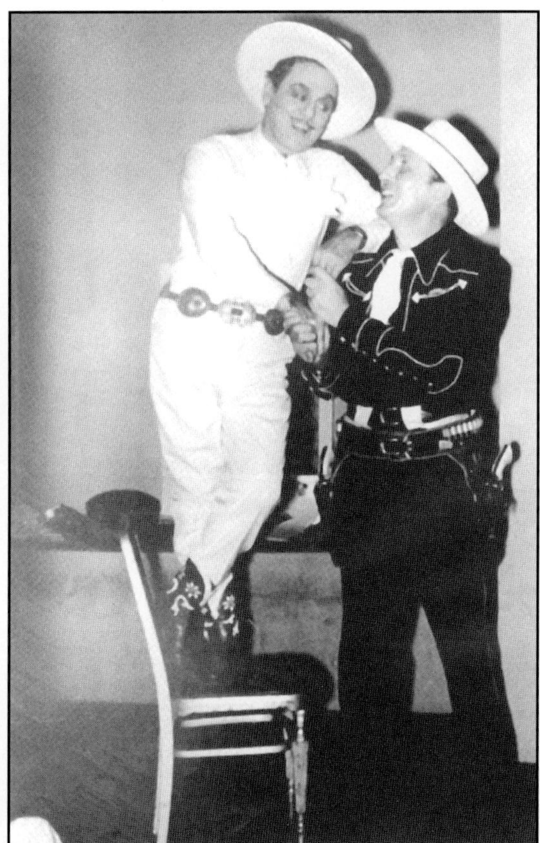

Brace Beemer (sans mask) clowns it up with popular Leo Carillo, television's Pancho on the Cisco Kid Show.

Brace Beemer birthday party at radio station WXYZ. At the extreme right is John Todd who played Tonto.

Brace Beemer signing autograph for a proud Lone Ranger Safety Club member.

Here a Boy Scout Jamboree admire their special guest heroes Lone Ranger (Brace Beemer) and Tonto (Jay Silverheels T.V.'s Tonto).

The 1938 serial, The Lone Ranger. was first shown in Detroit at the popular Palms Movie Theatre.

Boys-Girls
HEAR THE
LONE RANGER

The Modern Robin Hood
And His Famous Horse, "Silver"

Tune in this mysterious masked rider who gallops from place to place, helping the downtrodden and bringing outlaws to justice. His heavy guns shoot silver bullets —but he never shoots to kill. He is the fastest rider on the fastest horse in all the West. With his Indian friend, Tonto, he speeds from one thrilling adventure to another. Don't miss a single broadcast. Each one is filled with surprises for YOU.

AMERICA'S MOST FAMOUS RADIO SERIAL—
Clean, Thrilling Entertainment for the Entire Family

Adventures of the Exciting Frontier Days!

Fair play and courage triumph in this great radio serial — against the colorful background of the old, hard riding West. Hear every broadcast.

His Indian Friend, Tonto

Tune in
WCBS
7:30 P.M.
MONDAY
WEDNESDAY
FRIDAY

Remind Mother to Order
Butter-Nut Bread
Dolly Madison Cakes

Butter-Nut bread advertising the Lone Ranger radio show. This is some of the very early advertising for the bread company in 1938.

THE DETROIT NEWS, THURSDAY, DECEMBER 15, 1938

The Lone Ranger Show Has Come to

KERN'S

WOODWARD AT GRATIOT
OPEN 9 TO 9

SEE the lifelike scene at the Secret Silver Forge, where the Lone Ranger's silver bullets are made.

SEE the stagecoach's perilous fall over the cliff — all in miniature.

SEE the true-to-life capture of the desperadoes, by the Lone Ranger and Tonto.

SEE the Redman's Cascade. Hear the splash of waterfall and paddle.

SEE "Hi-Yo" Silver Away" — the triumphant finale!

"Lone Ranger" Surprise Packages

Price includes admission to the Lone Ranger cave, with its wonderful sights. And what surprise packages! Holly-gay boxes of Christmas thrills, selected to delight boys and girls of every age. Exchange privileges insure satisfaction. Truly . . . experienced Santa Claus that we are . . . , we've never seen a finer variety.......... **25¢**

Lone Ranger Toy Village—Ninth Floor

Advertisement from *Detroit News* dated December 15, 1938, promoting Kern's department stores' Lone Ranger show. Fred Foy as a young man was hired as an elevator operator and dressed as the Lone Ranger took kids to Lone Ranger Toy Village. This was years before he would win fame as the most remembered announcer for the radio show.

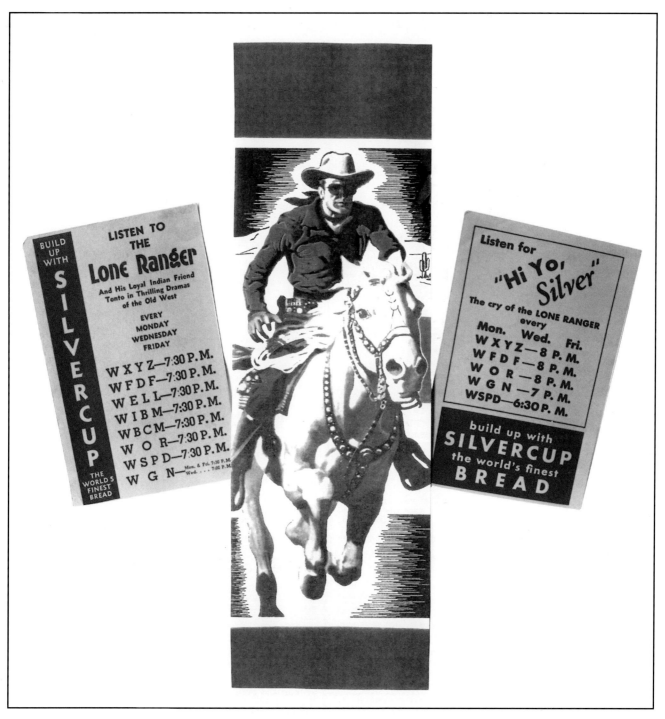

Early Silvercup giveaway cards listing the radio stations carrying the radio show in their marketing areas. Silvercup was one of the earliest sponsors of the show.

DETROIT TIMES

TUESDAY, JUNE 1, 1943 PAGE 15

Jack Pickering

Here and Now

HI-YO, SILVER!

Just yell "Hi-Yo, Silver," or whistle the theme song "Buddy-up-buddy-up-buddy-up - up - up," and 50,000,000 adventure fans know who you mean. It's the Lone Ranger.

THE RANGER

Maybe it's more than 50,000,000. It might be 10 times that many, because, in 10 years, his fame has spread all over the world, and his adventures are printed in French, Spanish and a few other languages.

But who created him? Who is the real Lone Ranger? He's a fellow Detroiter, and it's high time you met him.

* * *

His name appears in this and scores of other newspapers, every day of the week. But, without skipping back to the comic page, can you remember his name?

Oh, you can, eh? That's right. Fran Striker.

* * *

Going home from a late movie some night, you might meet him in Grand Circus Park, going to work at midnight.

An energetic young man, somewhere along in his 30's, he isn't given to the temperamental quirks usually attributed to authors, but he has a few peculiarities, and one of them is going to work in the middle of the night.

How he started doing it, he doesn't exactly know. He got used to working nights, and now, when he can work pretty much when he pleases, he finds he can do his best work from midnight to 5 or 5:30 a. m. Besides, it's quiet then, and there's nobody to bother him.

So, every night around midnight, he leaves his Grosse Pointe home and goes down to his office in the Stroh Building and figures out what the next adventure of the Lone Ranger will be.

Along about daybreak, he goes homes, catches a nap, gets up to have breakfast when his family (his wife, Janet, and three little Rangers, Bob, 12, Don, 10, and Francis Jr., 5) are having lunch.

In the afternoon he goes downtown again to answer fan mail, and have conferences with other writers who have been added from time to time to help him with the daily flood of fiction that he produces.

He gets home again in the latter part of the afternoon, tinkers around the house, reads, plays with the children and has supper. Sometimes he goes to sleep again in the evening but not always. And at midnight it's time for a cup of coffee before he goes to work.

* * *

"They're unusual hours," Striker admits, "but I see as much of my family as most men do, and probably more."

* * *

The Lone Ranger began as a radio serial. George W. Trendle, of WXYZ, was sparring with one of the big networks, and got Striker, then in Buffalo, to create a character "like Zane Grey's Lone Star Ranger."

From there on in Striker took it and created the world's best known gun-totin' rider of the west.

Now the Lone Ranger gallops through comic strips, comic books, novels and movies.

"Some of his colloquial language, translated into other languages, sounds pretty funny sometimes," Striker says. **"Boy, it must be a job, translating."**

* * *

Writing that much would be enough to wring most men dry in a few weeks. Not Striker. He not only has kept the Lone Ranger going for 10 years, in all its various fictional forms, but has added some others along with it—the Green Hornet, Ned Jordan, Federal Ace, the Crimson Fang, and Thrills of the Secret Service. He also supervises the Challenge of the Yukon.

He writes seven days a week, year in and year out, and for a big part of the time he was turning out 50,000 to 60,000 words a week. A good many novels are less than 50,000 words; the Bible is 733,000, so Striker was doing the equivalent of four books a year the size of the Bible.

All this was in addition to supervising movies, hunting up new ideas, helping his three sons with their hobbies and tending to his own (making fireworks; taking photographs, both still and motion pictures, some in color) and tinkering around the house, which he enjoys.

PROGRAMMING

for

SALES MILEAGE

The Mutual Network covers America's richest market—that 40% of the nation's area from the Mississippi Valley to the Atlantic Seaboard which yields 80% of the nation's retail business.

The super-powered stations that now form Mutual were individually strong in program-popularity from the start. In network combination, their audience-building power has grown steadily through such outstanding programs as those pictured above.

In the past 10 months, 48 advertisers have proven their conviction of Mutual's effectiveness and economy by an investment of more than $1,500,000 *for time alone.*

The *only* network deliberately *"made to order"*, Mutual is planned to provide intensive coverage of this rich Number 1 territory without costly and wasteful overlapping. Its low cost is fairly represented by the following basic *Sales Mileage* figures:

One ¼ hour, 1 *night* a week, 52 weeks $90,000 — One ¼ hour, daytime, 5 days a week, 26 weeks $75,000

One ¼ hour, 3 *nights* a week, 13 weeks 50,000 — One ¼ hour, 1 *night* a week, 13 weeks 25,000

(Additional stations are available for special emphasis or market extension, without wire charges.)

The United States as it looks to a sales manager — distorted according to sales. 40% of the area does 80% of the business. The black section is Mutual territory, covered by Mutual's basic super-powered stations: WGN, WLW, WOR and CKLW

MUTUAL BROADCASTING SYSTEM

OFFICES: CHICAGO, TRIBUNE TOWER—WGN • CINCINNATI, RADIO STATION WLW • NEW YORK, 1440 BROADWAY—WOR
DETROIT-WINDSOR, RADIO STATION CKLW • BOSTON, YANKEE NETWORK • PITTSBURGH, RADIO STATION WCAE

One of the first advertisements for the new Mutual Broadcasting System. The Lone Ranger program was the key radio show of the new network.

DAILY NEWS, FRIDAY, NOVEMBER 24, 1939

GIMBELS

33rd Street and Broadway

COME ONE!

COME ALL!

IT'S FREE!

THE Lone Ranger

PRESENTS

THE CAVALCADE OF THE WEST

THRILLING LIFE-SIZE TABLEAUX—AT GIMBELS!

See the Lone Ranger and Silver—as big as life!
See Buffalo Bill bringing down the huge buffalo!
See Davy Crockett leading the Texans to the Alamo!
See General Custer's Last Stand against the Indians!
See Annie Oakley saving the Plainsman from the buffalo!
See Chief Sitting Bull and his Braves in War Council!
See Daniel Boone warning the settlers of an Indian attack!

LET'S GO TO GIMBELS—SIXTH FLOOR

OPEN FRIDAY 'TIL 9 P. M.

The year 1939 was a big year and was the start of country wide merchandising of the Lone Ranger. Samples of Gimbel's promotion of Christmas 1939 are sought by collectors around the country.

Special Offer to Lone Ranger Club Members:

BOYS! GIRLS! Have a special picture of yourself taken with the Lone Ranger and Silver at the Lone Ranger Exhibit in Gimbels, 33rd Street and Broadway, New York City.

ONLY 15¢

REGULAR PRICE 25c

This offer good beginning May 1st

When you go to Gimbels take this notice for proof you're entitled to the Special Lone Ranger price.

©T. L. R. 1939

YOU ARE INVITED TO VISIT GIMBELS LONE RANGER SHOW

Thrill to a trip through Gimbels Lone Ranger Hidden Canyon, marvel at the five animated life-like scenes taken right from the heart of the Lone Ranger drama! See the Lone Ranger's helper casting his silver bullets! The Stagecoach's perilous fall over the cliffs! The amazing capture of the desperadoes by the Lone Ranger and his faithful friend, Tonto! Yes, we even have a life-size model of the famous masked man and his rearing steed!

GIMBELS 33rd Street & Broadway New York

Pittsburgh, Philadelphia, Milwaukee, New York

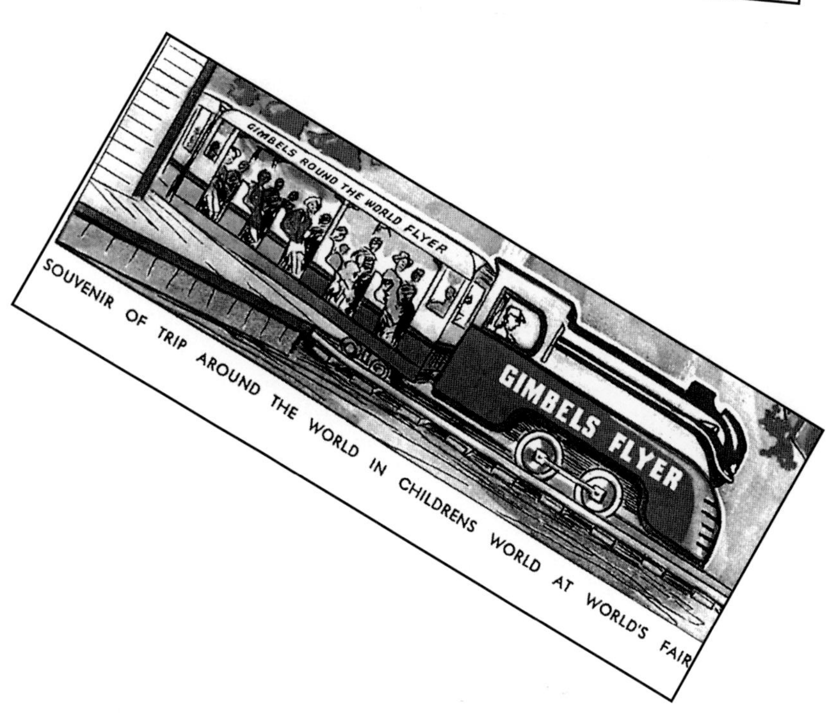

Charles Livingstone, producer and director of radio's 'Lone Ranger'

DETROIT (AP) — Charles D. Livingstone, 83, who produced and directed "The Green Hornet," "The Lone Ranger" and "Sgt. Preston of the Yukon" for live radio from 1938 to 1954, died Monday in a nursing home in Sarasota, Fla.

A University of Michigan graduate, he joined Detroit radio station WXYZ in 1933, playing minor roles in "Warner Lester" and "The Lone Ranger" and a major part in "Thrills of the Secret Service."

His first directing assignment came that year in "Dr. Fang," where he was credited with improving the timing of live radio broadcasts.

Livingstone was named the station's dramatic director in 1938 and remained there overseeing the nationally broadcast shows until 1954, when he went to Hollywood to help supervise filming of "The Lone Ranger" for television.

Brace Beemer Dies; Radio's 'Lone Ranger'

Oxford, Mich., March 1—(AP)—Brace Beemer, 62, who played "The Lone Ranger" on radio in the 1930s and 1940s, died today at his home here.

He had been playing bridge with friends when he was stricken with a heart attack.

"The Lone Ranger" show's trademarks of the William Tell Overture and Beemer's "Hi yo, Silver, away," were familiar to a generation of radio adventure story fans.

Traffic Crash Ends Epic of 'Lone Ranger'

The voice of the "Lone Ranger," a hero to countless thousands of radio listeners, was stilled Tuesday by the very hazard he sought to curb—highway traffc.

Earle W. Graser, 32 years old, was killed in front of the Farmington Methodist Church in suburban Detroit when his automobile hurtled out of control into the rear of a parked trailer. The accident occurred at 5 a. m. For months, Graser, in personal messages to the "Friends of the Lone Ranger" had used his program and his voice to promote traffic safety.

APR 9 1941

Program to Continue

The "Lone Ranger" will still be heard on WXYZ, key of the 140-station network which broadcasts the program. Brace Beemer, the original voice of the "Lone Ranger" for a few months at the program's start nearly 10 years ago, will resume his old role. Beemer is now the narrator for the program.

In contrast to his adventures on the air, Graser in private life was quiet and studious—even standoffish, his neighbors said. But if he was standoffish it was only to carry through the aura of mystery which surrounded him on his program. He lived in Farmington in a quaint farmhouse built in 1842, with his wife and one-year-old daughter.

On the air his real identity was shrouded in secrecy, and in private life only an intimate few knew him as the "Lone Ranger."

Graser had played the role of enforcer of justice for almost nine years, and the network over which the program was carried, WXYZ officials said, was the largest of any radio program.

Until 10:30 a. m. Thursday Graser's body will be at the Spencer J. Heeney Funeral Home, 23720 N. Farmington Road, Farmington. Services will be held at 2 p. m. Thursday in the German Evangelical Church in Farmington.

Gone Is the Mask

'Lone Ranger' Leads the Lutheran Hour

The Lone Ranger is back on radio in Detroit where he held forth for more than 20 years.

The voice of Brace Beemer radio's "Hi-yo Silver" man, is the narrator for a religious program at 6 to 6:15 p.m. Sundays over CKLW

Beemer, now a real estate developer, near Oxford, emcees the new Missouri Synod program, "Detroit Lutherans Present."

It's much like a job he had 30 years ago when he was announcer and narrator of the original "Lutheran Hour" that originated here with the Rev. Walter Maier.

DEC 7 .1963

BEEMER SAID there was never any conflict between introducing preachers and pretending to ride about with a mask

"The content of the Lone Ranger program was good for Sunday schoolers and was consistent with Sunday school teachings he said.

"It is preaching, but not preaching," he said. "The Lone Ranger never preached as such."

* * *

NOW BEEMER leaves the preaching to men like W. Harry Krieger, president of the Michigan District of the Missouri Synod Lutherans, in the new program.

Beemer still gets about speaking to his many admirers.

Recently after speaking in a little church in Kentucky a gray haired little woman came up to him and wanted to know if he really were the Lone Ranger.

"Can you hit a penny in the air with a Colt .45," the little old lady asked.

"I can come close," the great Lone Ranger told her.

"Oh, I'm so disappointed," the little lady said, "Buffalo Bill used to be able to hit it."

* * *

WHEN HE comes on the air now the Lutheran Lone Ranger puts out more stately fare, than the moral achieved with violence some years back.

He signs off with a poem.

"There is an hour of peaceful rest, Mourning wanderers give, There is a joy for souls distress, A balm for every wounded breast, 'Tis found above in heaven."

Death: Livingston

AP

LIVINGSTON: Lone Ranger unmasked

Cowboy film star **Robert Livingston**, 83, who once removed his mask while playing the Lone Ranger, died Monday at his home in Tarzana, Calif., after a career that spanned more than 45 years.

The brief mask removal came in the 1939 movie *The Lone Ranger Rides Again*. Republic Pictures thought that would endear him to viewers as the Ranger, preventing other movie studios from duplicating the character. 3-9-88 – USA Today

Deaths Elsewhere

MARCH, 1965

Brace Beemer, 62, the radio voice of the legendary "Lone Ranger" that thrilled millions of listeners from coast to coast for many years, in Oxford, Mich.

The half-hour weekly radio program originated in Detroit in 1933 over station WXYZ and was aired from coast to coast. Mr. Beemer originated the role in the first few months on the air.

BRACE BEEMER LONE RANGER

Then the late Earl Graser took over as the voice of the legendary hero of the west and continued in the role until his death in 1941. Mr. Beemer again took over the role and was the Lone Ranger until the program went off the air in 1955.

During its heyday in the '30s and '40s, the program was one of the most popular on the air, enjoyed by adults as well as children. The names of the Lone Ranger, his horse, Silver, and his faithful Indian companion, Tonto, were household words.

Especially familiar was the introduction, a wild version of the William Tell Overture, the hoofbeats of horses and the cry, "A fiery horse with the speed of light, a cloud of dust, a hearty 'Hi-Yo Silver, Away'—the Lone Ranger."

Following the death of the radio program in 1955, Mr. Beemer slipped into relative oblivion. He had nothing to do with the movie or television versions of the Lone Ranger. Clayton Moore was the television voice.

Mr. Beemer retired to a "ranch" near Detroit. He raised thoroughbred horses and dabbled in land as a sub-divider.

Herald CHICAGO American
AN AMERICAN PAPER FOR THE AMERICAN PEOPLE
THURSDAY—AUGUST 31—1944
DAILY 4 Cents

Lone Ranger Dies in Pacific Battle

LONE RANGER (Lee Powell) AND WIFE, NORMA
When they wed in Chicago.

LONG BEACH, Calif., Aug. 30. —(AP)—Sgt. Lee Powell, 35, of the United States Marine corps, who as the red-masked Lone Ranger rode his white stallion through 15 episodes of a motion picture serial, has been killed in action, his widow, Mrs. Norma Powell, said today.

With the marines in the South Pacific since November, 1942, Powell fought at Tarawa and Saipan. Mrs. Powell said she was not informed where he met his death.

Powell attended the University of Montana, where he was a football and track star. He toured the United States and Canada with Wallace Brothers circus in his Lone Ranger character.

Powell was married in Chicago Jan. 7, 1940, to Norma Rogers of York, S. C. Their marriage culminated a romance that started when they met while playing in the Shrine Winter Circus. She was a bareback rider and Powell did cowboy stunts.'

The character he portrayed on the screen is known to thousands of Chicago children from the comic strip, "The Lone Ranger," appearing in the Chicago Herald-American.

Report FDR to See Churchill

NEW YORK, Aug. 30. —(AP)— The BBC said in a broadcast to Europe heard by NBC monitors tonight it was predicted that Prime Minister Churchill will confer with President Roosevelt soon on German armistice terms and the Asiatic military situation.

Obituaries 6/29/79

George Seaton, 68, '34th Street' director

BEVERLY HILLS, Calif. — Moviemaker George Seaton, who wrote and directed "Miracle on 34th Street," "Airport" and several other memorable Hollywood films, died in his sleep at his Beverly Hills home yesterday. He was 68.

Mr. Seaton had been suffering from cancer for about two years, said Alan Rivkin of the Writers Guild of America, West.

During a 40-year film career, Mr. Seaton won two Academy Awards for his screenwriting and was beloved by actors and actresses for his soft-spoken "human quality" as a director.

Lean and hawk-nosed with a low radio-trained voice, Mr. Seaton had put a personal stamp on performing history even before coming to Hollywood. As the title character's voice of the original "Lone Ranger" show at a radio station in his hometown of Detroit in the early 1930s, the 20-year-old Seaton shouted, "Hi Ho Silverrrr" and beat his chest with coconut shells to give the sound effect of Silver galloping off.

His biggest commercial success was as writer and director of "Airport" for producer Ross Hunter in 1969. "Airport' grossed $45 million in film rentals in the United States and Canada and was the biggest moneymaker in Universal Pictures history until "Jaws."

Death Strikes 'Lone Ranger' Cast Again

For the second time in a year, death, which the characters of the "Lone Ranger" program "shrugged off" in radio dramas from week to week, has come to the cast.

On April 9, a year ago, the familiar voice of the "Lone Ranger" himself, Earl W. Grazer, was stilled by his death in an automobile accident.

Saturday, the equally well-known "gravelly" voice of "the sheriff," John Fred Reto, was stilled.

Reto, a member of the cast of the broadcasts heard from coast to coast, died in Harper Hospital following a five-week illness. For nine years, almost the length of time the series of western dramas has been unfolded, Reto was in "The Lone Ranger."

Before he came to Station WXYZ, the fifty-seven-year-old Reto was a veteran of the stock companies.

His body will be at the Wood Funeral Home, 8450 Plymouth, until Sunday night when it will be taken to Butler, Pa., for burial.

Tuesday, July 16, 1957—THE DETROIT NEWS—31

Voice of 'Tonto' Stilled as Actor Todd Dies at 80

The radio voice of Tonto on the Lone Ranger for 21 years, John Todd, 80, will be buried in Crossingville, Pa., Thursday.

Mr. Todd, who was born Frederick McCarthy in Erie County, Pa., died Sunday night at Henry Ford Hospital after a three-week illness. He had taught dramatics for 16 years at the Detroit Conservatory of Music and recently appeared on several Detroit television programs.

While playing the radio role of Tonto, Mr. Todd also acted in the Green Hornet, another radio thriller popular in the 1930's and 1940's.

Mr. Todd came to Detroit in 1933 to begin his career here as Tonto. He continued in this with only brief vacation interruptions until 1954.

Before World War I, Mr. Todd played in musicals and stock companies in Chicago, Omaha, Neb., where Harold Lloyd was one of his friends, the South and New York.

Discharged from the Marines in 1919, Mr. Todd was in a play on Broadway with Eva LeGallienne and was on the old Orpheum circuit for seven years. He also did radio work in St. Paul and Cleveland before coming to Detroit.

The rosary will be said for Mr. Todd at 8 o'clock tonight at the William R. Hamilton Co., 3975 Cass.

Surviving is one daughter, Mrs. Mary Dorcas Cadenhead, of Salem, Mass., one grandchild, and a brother. Mr. Todd lived at the Strathmore Hotel.

Harold L. Neal Jr., 55, a former president of the ABC radio network, died Thursday at his home in Darien, Conn., after suffering a heart attack.

Mr. Neal, who became president of ABC radio in 1972, resigned last March.

He joined ABC in Detroit in 1943 as a staff announcer for WXYZ on such popular network programs as "The Lone Ranger," The Green Hornet" and "Sergeant Preston of the Yukon," all produced at WXYZ.

3/14/80

Farewell to Tonto

The Lone Ranger said good-by to Tonto at a memorial service Wednesday at the First Presbyterian Church of Hollywood. **Clayton Moore**, who played the famous masked man with the silver bullets, was among the 300 persons who attended the service for **Jay Silverheels**, the actor who portrayed Tonto, the Lone Ranger's faithful Indian sidekick. Silverheels, a Mohawk Indian, died at 62 last week in the Motion Picture Hospital. "I thought of him as a brother," said Moore. "I loved him very much. I'll miss him. He was my kemo sabe, which we all know means faithful friend." Moore and Silverheels were friends on and off the screen. "Jay was a fighter for the Indian people," said Moore. "The Indian cause was utmost in his mind at all times."

Died. George W. Trendle, 87, creator of *The Lone Ranger* radio serial; of a heart attack; in Grosse Pointe, Mich. A vaudeville-house owner who switched to radio at the start of the Depression, Trendle sought to turn his struggling Detroit station into a moneymaker with a program that would be "good, clean and long-lived." Hence his Masked Rider of the Plains didn't smoke, swear, drink, fool with women or even kill the bad guys; he did endure and make a fortune for Trendle. *The Lone Ranger* lasted 20 first-run years on radio and twelve on television, and the show's popularity inspired Trendle to create two more true-blue heroes: *The Green Hornet* and *Sergeant Preston of the Yukon.*

TIME, MAY 22, 1972

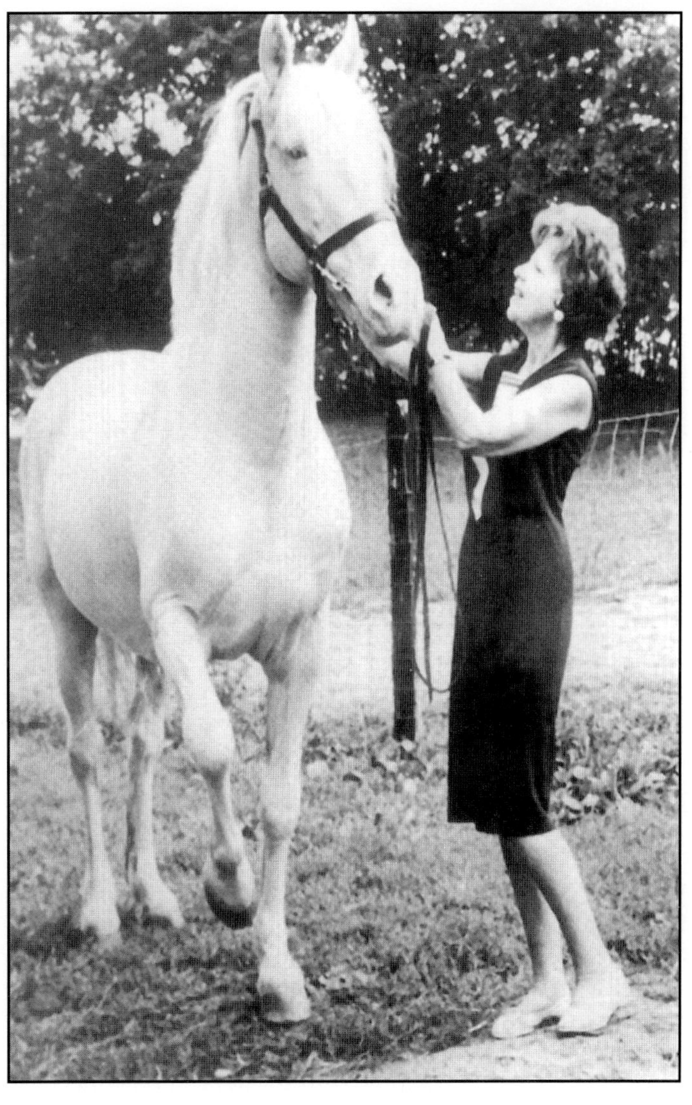

Hi-Yo, Silver is Safe — The Lone Ranger's horse Silver, standing high and proud, seems to realize that he is not headed for a glue factory but will spend his days on the Oxford, Michigan, farm of Mrs. Brace Beemer — who also looks happy about it all. Mrs. Beemer is the widow of the masked Lone Ranger.

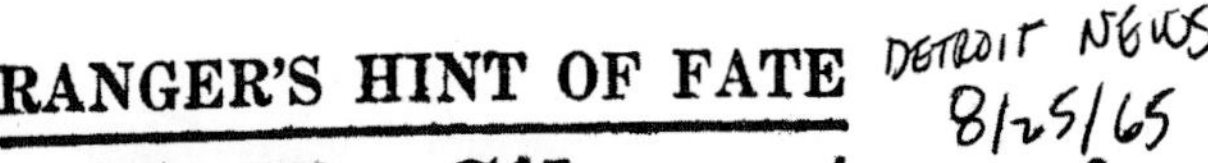

RANGER'S HINT OF FATE

DETROIT NEWS 8/25/65

Hi-Ho Silver–Away! No Takers for 2 Steeds

AUG 25 1965

Is the Lone Ranger's horse Silver out to pasture for good?

Or will the big white stallion thrill today's youngsters the way it did their parents in their youth?

Silver, portrayed in TV series by horses now 27 and 14 years old, is not wanted by the Detroit zoo, the Department of Parks and Recreation or the Detroit Police Department's Mounted Division.

GRAZING ON FARM

The horses have been grazing incognito at the farm of Mrs. Brace Beemer in Oxford, Mich.

Her husband was the original Lone Ranger — the old West's epitome of goodness who inevitably triumphed over stereotyped badness to the delight of millions.

He died in March, leaving the famed stallions among his possessions. He wanted children to be given a chance to enjoy them, his wife said

Frank McInnis, director of the Detroit Zoo, said, "I don't think today's kids know about the Lone Ranger or Silver. If we displayed them it would be mostly for their parents.

'NOT TOO GENTLE'

"But we handle wild animals. We don't have a stable or exercizing grounds ~~for horses~~.

"Mayor Cavanagh asked us to take a look at the horses and see if we could house them. They're beautiful animals, but stallions sometimes are not too gentle. We don't know how they would be around children."

Parks and Recreation officials have expressed similar doubts. And Detroit police can not use the Lone Ranger's horses in its mounted division

Ranger fans might wonder if the animals' future lies in the famous cry of the departing masked rider—"Hi-Ho, Silver—away."

Television Days

The Lone Ranger made the transition from radio to television in late 1949. Although it was a well known fact that Brace Beemer wanted to do the television show, as well as the radio program, he was not given the part by Trendle. Instead, the Lone Ranger was portrayed by veteran actor-stuntman, Clayton Moore. Moore had performed in many of the top serials produced by Republic Pictures and also in many western features.

A great many fans of the radio program were disappointed when Beemer was not cast in the part. Most of them had followed the career of Clayton Moore at Republic and other studios and had to admit that he earned his spurs and was a good second choice as the Ranger on television.

However, because television was still a relatively new medium, the Lone Ranger show's initial production values were far less satisfying than they should have been.

After several years of low production values (although the show was extremely popular), Jack Wrather acquired the Lone Ranger copyright. The action then moved away from the crowded, poorly matched sets to beautiful, spacious outdoor locations. Wrather continued to improve the show, and in the final years, the television productions were outstanding in every respect. Many of these shows were filmed in color, with original scripting and fairly large casts.

After the first season, Moore decided he needed more money to portray the masked rider. Trendle, always careful with a buck, decided to find another Lone Ranger. He also felt that he wanted a taller, heavier Lone Ranger. Moore, of average height, had suffered initially in comparison with Beemer's great radio voice and the audience's imagination of a taller Lone Ranger.

It was about this time that the movies' Jack Armstrong became television's Lone Ranger. George Trendle decided to cast John Hart, who appeared in the movie serials of *Captain Africa* and *Jack Armstrong, the All American Boy.*

Hart was tall and well built... a good looking hero. However, for some reason he was very stiff and wooden in the Lone Ranger part. And, after 52 episodes (one season) of the show, Hart was removed from the part and replaced by the man he had replaced, Clayton Moore. Today, both the Hart and Moore versions appear on television in syndicated packages.

After Clayton Moore's recall by Trendle, new programs were produced. Moore climbed into the silver saddle and made the Lone Ranger role his greatest part, one with which he will always be associated. He could ride, handle the action, and was a top notch actor to boot! He rode across the television screen with Jay Silverheels as Tonto from the beginning of the series in 1948 until it ended in 1961.

Clayton Moore, the man behind the mask and a myriad of disguises, is known to millions of fans as the intrepid hero of the old West in The Lone Ranger.

Born and educated in Chicago, Illinois, Moore served in the Army Air Corps during World War II and worked at a variety of occupations, including circus trapeze artist and Robert Powers model in New York, before heading west to California and a successful acting career.

Moore worked originally under contract to Republic Studios, where he soon became known as the "King of the Serials" because of the quanity of such films he made. Subsequently he also worked for Warner Bros., MGM, and Edward Small Productions until 1949, when he was cast in th title role of the Lone Ranger.

Moore starred as the Texas Ranger left for dead after being ambushed by the notorious Cavendish gang. Nursed back to health by Tonto, an Indian he had befriended many years before, the Ranger donned a mask to conceal his identity in order to apprehend the killers of his fellow Rangers. When he was successful in this mission, he decided to retain the mask and dedicate his life to aiding the settlers of the lawless West.

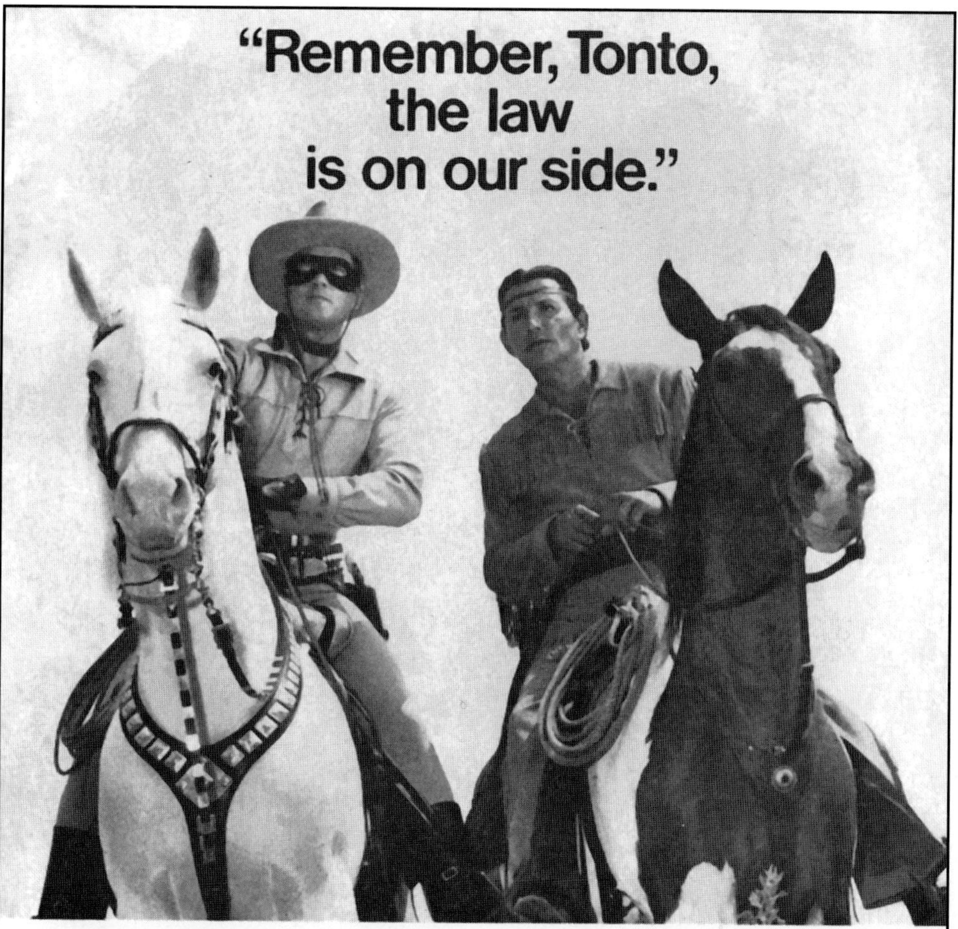

"Remember, Tonto, the law is on our side."

We should let everyone know that Wrather Corporation owns The Lone Ranger®, and that his name, likeness and certain characters and expressions associated with him (Tonto,® "Hi Yo, Silver,®" and "Kemo Sabay®") cannot be used without our permission, and we won't tolerate any rustlers. Wrather Corporation. The company behind the man behind the mask.

© COPYRIGHT 1970 WRATHER CORPORATION

The Lone Ranger®
The Lone Ranger Food Systems, Inc.®
Disneyland Hotel
Lassie
Muzak®

Sergeant Preston of the Yukon
Vacationland
Andersen's Animal Park
The Queen Mary—A Flagship Hotel
(A Sky Chefs-Wrather Joint Venture)

Wrather Corporation

Corporate Headquarters: 270 North Canon Drive, Beverly Hills, California 90210, (213) 274-8521

Lone Ranger's Sold for 3 Million

The Lone Ranger was sold Monday for three million dollars in cash.

Tonto and Silver were included in the transaction.

George W. Trendle, who created the Lone Ranger as a radio program 22 years ago on WXYZ and parlayed it into a multimillion-dollar radio, television, comic book and record property, announced the sale.

He said all stock in The Lone Ranger, Inc., has been sold to Jack Wrather and Mrs. Mazie Wrather, Los Angeles and Dallas oil operators and television station owners, and John L. Loeb and Associates, of New York City.

The new owners issued hasty assurances that the Lone Ranger's war on the lawless villains of the Old West will continue.

This will come as good news to millions of small fry who watch their idol every week on 50 television stations.

And also to Mom and Pop who get a secret boot out of the make-believe world where justice always triumphs.

The Lone Ranger's exploits also are carried three times a week on 249 radio stations. The radio shows have been originating "live" at WXYZ. But starting in Setpember, transcriptions of previous programs will be used for an indefinite period.

Trendle said the three million dollars was the highest cash sum ever paid for a radio-television property. The Lone Ranger stock was owned by Trendle, H. Allen Campbell and Raymond J. Meuerer.

Though Moore became known as the "mysterious masked man," his skills in American dialects and foreign accents constantly came in handy when the Ranger was permitted to doff his mask in favor of disguises. He appeared disguised as a Shakespearean actor portraying Othello in the episode titled, "Outlaws in Grease Paint," and as a Swedish laundryman in "The Letter Bride." In "The Wooden Rifle," he was seen as a goateed patent medicine salesman, and even Tonto joined in the act in "Wanted: The Lone Ranger," when the twosome appeared as circus clowns. Perhaps the biggest challenge to Moore's versatility came in "The Return of Don Pedro O'Sullivan," in which he appeared as the Ranger, a Mexican killer, and a red-headed Irish-Mexican patriot.

In the 12 years Moore played the masked man, he starred in almost 200 half-hour episodes of the series and 15 full-length color features, thrilling and delighting children all over the world. Today Moore lives in California and spends time fishing, training horses, and collecting antiques.

Known to millions as Tonto, the faithful Indian friend to the mysterious masked man of the old West, Jay Silverheels can be seen co-starring in The Lone Ranger.

Born on the Six Nations Indian Reservation in Ontario, Canada, Silverheels, a full-blooded Mohawk, grew up in a family of seven brothers and sisters. As a youngster he exhibited a sizeable talent for athletics, and it was this ability which eventually gave him an opportunity to pursue a career in Hollywood.

His father worked with him in several sports, and he first achieved success in wrestling, taking the middleweight wrestling championship of the Niagara district for two consecutive years. As a boxer he then won the Eastern Square finals of the Golden Gloves championship in Madison Square Garden and went on to become a runner-up in the nationals. But it was in the Indian sport of lacrosse that he truly excelled. By the age of 17, he left school to pursue the sport professionally, and within a short time he became Canada's highest paid and highest scoring professional in the nation's history.

Silverheels came to Hollywood in 1933 as a member of a touring lacrosse team. Veteran actor-sportsman Joe E. Brown saw him star in a game and convinced the young man to try for an acting career. Brown arranged introductions and helped him get work until his career was established. Silverheels then appeared in a succession of Westerns and Indian pictures, among them *Broken Arrow, Geronimo,* and *Battle of Apache Pass.*

Though he found steady work in films for some years, it was not until 1949, when he was cast as the Lone Ranger's "faithful Indian companion," that Silverheels was propelled into national prominence. Starring opposite Clayton Moore's mysterious masked man for 12 years, Silverheels appeared in almost 200 episodes of the series and 15 full-color features portraying the boyhood friend who saved the Ranger when he lay dying from an ambush by the notorious Cavendish gang. When the Ranger recovers and dedicates his life to the preservation of law and order, Tonto vows to remain at his side and assist in the fight for justice.

Photo of Clayton Moore and Jay Silverheels — TV's Lone Ranger and Tonto, 1950.

The original good guy in the white hat, Clayton Moore astride Silver.

One of the most popular movie stills of the Lone Ranger and Silver. This was taken during the filming of the *Lone Ranger* feature film in 1956.

THE LONE RANGER, INC.
9363 WILSHIRE BLVD. • BEVERLY HILLS • CALIF.

September 14, 1955

Mr. Donald Wilson
1942 Lincoln St., N. E.
Minneapolis, Minn.

Dear Mr. Wilson:

Thank you very much for your card and your interest in The Lone Ranger. It is always a pleasure to hear from our listeners.

There aren't many secrets left in business, but I suppose every firm has a few things that it just doesn't talk about. In our case, we are particularly proud of the special production techniques employed, including the use of musical underscorings which we own, and we are sorry that it is not possible to share them with others. It has been the policy of this company and the sponsors since the inception of the program. Under the circumstances, I am sorry that it is not possible to render the information you requested in your letter.

I do hope, however, that you will continue to listen to and enjoy our Lone Ranger programs, both radio and television.

Sincerely,
THE LONE RANGER, INC.
Jack Wrather
JACK WRATHER

JW:sk

CLAYTON MOORE
P. O. Box 3797
Incline Village, Nevada 89450

August 30, 1974

Mr. Lee J. Felbinger
Badman Road
Green Lane, Pennsylvania 18054

Dear Lee:

It was a pleasure to hear from you and I would be most happy to assist you in any way that I possibly can.

First of all, may I thank you for being such an ardent follower of those early days of yesteryear when Clayton Moore rode for Republic serials and "The Lone Ranger". Speaking of serials, they certainly helped prepare me for my portrayal of "The Lone Ranger" character.

As a young man, I never thought that I would have the opportunity of portraying "The Lone Ranger" on television. It seems as though some dreams do come true.

I am very proud to say that over the past 25 years I have been able to bring a part of Americana to the youngsters of our nation, together with a fine upstanding American as my partner, Mr. Jay Silverheels, who played the role of "Tonto".

Let me wish you great success in the writing of your book!

Kindest personal regards.

Sincerely yours,
Clayton Moore
Clayton Moore
THE LONE RANGER

CM:rs

Here T.V.'s Lone Ranger and Tonto (Clayton Moore and Jay Silverheels) pause before taking action in a popular T.V. episode of the radio hero.

Clayton Moore and Silver take a bow during a personal appearance.

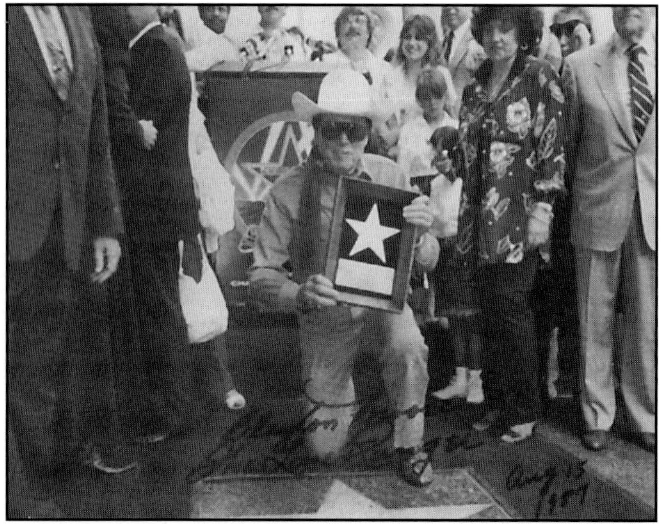

Lone Ranger (Clayton Moore) and Jay Silverheels (Tonto) honored with stars on Hollywood's Walk of Fame.

Star for Lone Ranger

The nation's most famous masked man, the Lone Ranger, finally got his own star along Hollywood's Walk of Fame. **Clayton Moore,** the actor who played the popular Western television hero until 1958, claimed the 1,848th gold-colored star to be embedded in the famous sidewalk. Moore, 72, wore his trademark black mask, white hat, a Western-style suit and snakeskin boots at ceremonies Friday. A number of the fans who gathered along Hollywood Boulevard also wore black masks. Moore's star comes eight years after actor **Jay Silverheels,** who played the Lone Ranger's faithful sidekick, Tonto, received his star. Silverheels was honored less than eight months before he died.

Clayton Moore

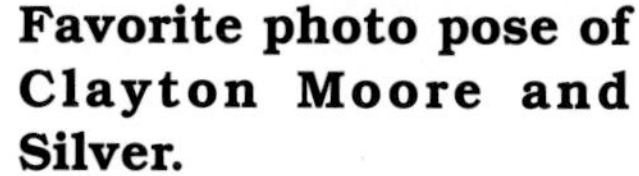
Favorite photo pose of Clayton Moore and Silver.

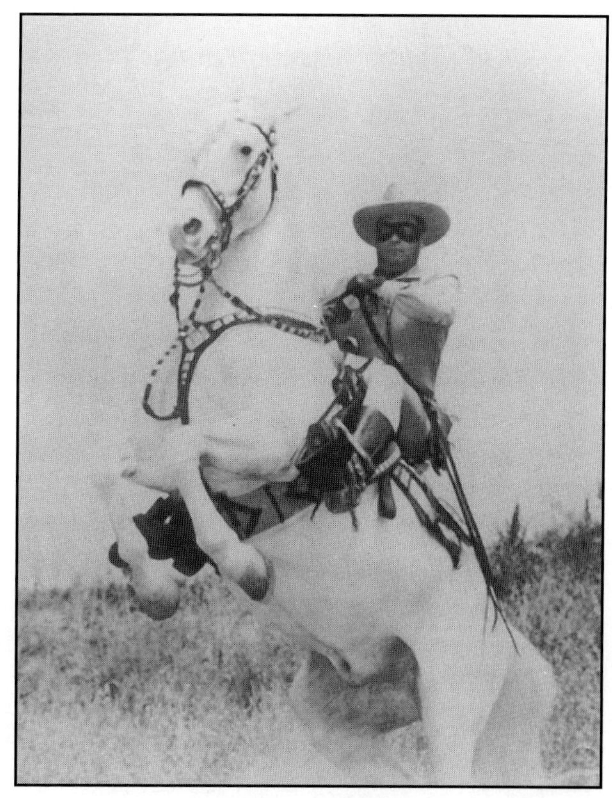
Classic Lone Ranger and Silver pose.

Next to Brace Beemer, Clayton Moore is the actor most identified with the Lone Ranger as the star of the television series and two major motion pictures. Like Brace Beemer he was ideally suited for the part and was a good selection for the TV image of the radio hero.

Clayton Moore, long-time serial action star and actor was top notch, not only during filming of the T.V. series, but also in both Wrather produced motion pictures. Currently still under contract, he does make personal appearances (with mask of course) and is in excellent shape and still enjoys the Lone Ranger role.

Who was that masked man? None other than **Clayton Moore,** back behind the mask again. Moore, 70, who played the legend-ridden Ranger in the long-running television series, had been forced to bite the silver bullet and trade in his black mask for sunglasses in 1979. The Wrather Corp., which owns the Lone Ranger (yes, even the Lone Ranger can be owned), had decided to replace Moore for the 1981 Ranger movie and did not want him out making personal appearances wearing the trademark mask. A restraining order was issued, and of course the Ranger always obeys the

Moore: back in the saddle

law. But Moore says that a million signatures were collected on his behalf, and now the company has voluntarily agreed to lift the restraint. "I'm extremely happy and pleased for my fans," Moore says. "I will continue wearing the white hat and black mask until I ride up into the big ranch in the sky." Hi-ho, Silver, away! —*By Guy D. Garcia*

SILVER

TRENDLE - CAMPBELL - MEURER. INC.

TRENDLE-CAMPBELL BROADCASTING CORPORATION
WTAC FLINT, MICH. (N. B. C. AFFILIATE)
THE LONE RANGER, INC
THE GREEN HORNET, INC
SERGEANT PRESTON OF THE YUKON, INC
THE AMERICAN AGENT, INC.

DETROIT 26, MICHIGAN
WOODWARD 2-9184

Executive Offices
1800-1810 MUTUAL BUILDING
28 WEST ADAMS AVENUE

GEO W. TRENDLE, PRESIDENT & TREASURER
H. ALLEN CAMPBELL, VICE PRES. & GEN MGR
RAYMOND J. MEURER, SEC. & GEN COUNSEL
GEO. W. TRENDLE, JR., ASSISTANT SECRETARY

February 18, 1953.

Miss Evelyn Wilson
General Mills, Inc.
623 Marquette Avenue
Minneapolis, Minnesota.

My dear Miss Wilson:

Attached are the letters and replies you requested returned to you.

For your information, I own the stallion, Hi-Yo Silver ; there are not two horses. We shipped the horse to California to make all of the television pictures, and it is the same horse that was in Minneapolis two years ago at the Aquatennial . When TV pictures are being made, there are no personal appearances scheduled.

Sincerely,

Geo. W. Trendle,
President.

Letter from George Trendle stating that the same horse is used for filming and personal appearances, and he owns the horse Hi-Yo Silver.

TRENDLE - CAMPBELL - MEURER. INC.

TRENDLE-CAMPBELL BROADCASTING CORPORATION
WTAC FLINT, MICH. (N. B. C. AFFILIATE)
THE LONE RANGER, INC
THE GREEN HORNET, INC
SERGEANT PRESTON OF THE YUKON, INC
THE AMERICAN AGENT, INC.

DETROIT 26, MICHIGAN
WOODWARD 2-9184

Executive Offices
1800-1810 MUTUAL BUILDING
28 WEST ADAMS AVENUE

GEO W. TRENDLE, PRESIDENT & TREASURER
H. ALLEN CAMPBELL, VICE PRES. & GEN MGR
RAYMOND J. MEURER, SEC. & GEN COUNSEL
GEO. W. TRENDLE, JR., ASSISTANT SECRETARY

December 1, 1952

Miss Evelyn Wilson
General Mills, Inc.
623 Marquette Avenue
Minneapolis 2, Minnesota

Dear Miss Wilson:

I was delighted to hear from you, although I, of course, feel badly about the letters you have been getting regarding John Hart. However, I note that most of these just ask "why" and they still listen to the program.

The last couple of television shows, with the new man, were darn good, I thought.

It will take time for the old man to wear off. I had them send me a half dozen of the early films made by Clayton Moore which we are running off this week, and I know they will be just as bad as the first half dozen John Hart films. However, that doesn't help the situation any.

I am more than pleased to know that the rating continues to stay up where it should be, which is the main thing.

I am answering the letters which you forwarded and am sending you copies of my replies.

Incidentally, did you have a nice Thanksgiving?

Sincerely,
THE LONE RANGER, INC.

Geo. W. Trendle, President

Letter from George W. Trendle to General Mills explaining his opinion of the new Lone Ranger, John Hart. Interestingly, he calls Clayton Moore the old man and makes it clear that he feels John Hart will win over fans of the program. Unfortunately, this did not happen and he brought Clayton Moore back as the Lone Ranger for the remainder of the TV series and two feature movies.

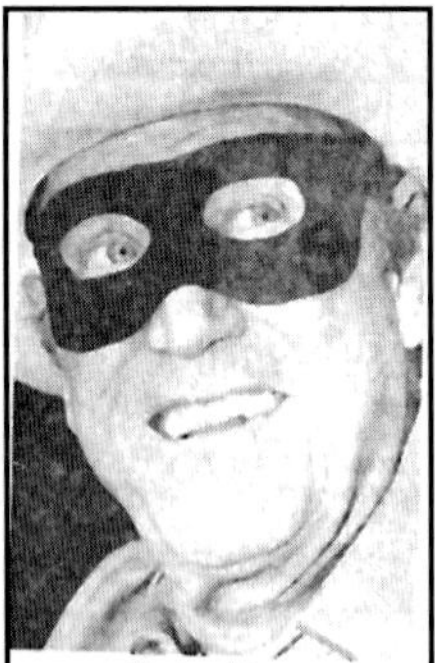

Clayton Moore

Who was that . . .?

To the rescue: **Clayton Moore**, 73, who starred in the long-running *Lone Ranger* television series, had starred in a fire-safety program for children on Saturday night and was returning to his motel in Spartanburg, S.C., when he came upon the scene of a hit-and-run accident. "He got out [of his car] and asked me how I was doing and tried to make me comfortable," said motorcyclist **Robert Pat Humphries**, 22, a volunteer firefighter injured in the accident. "I was still kind of out of it at the time." Moore, dressed in mask and Western garb, began directing traffic and helping emergency personnel. "People were just stopping on the side of the road and couldn't believe it," said **Dixie Hopper**, a publicist for the show in which Moore had starred. "People will think we staged the whole thing, but we didn't." Humphries was taken to a Spartanburg hospital, treated for cuts and a badly bruised leg, and released. "I think we all were Lone Ranger fans at one time or another," the cyclist said. "I know I am." Moore promised to give him, as a memento, a silver bullet.

Theft of Lone Ranger's guns nets $5,000 fine

United Press International

HOUSTON — A former airline baggage handler who swiped the Lone Ranger's two Colt .45 pistols and a holster has been placed on 10 years' probation and fined $5,000.

Edward Louis Young III, who could have been sentenced to 10 years in prison, also was ordered to repay actor Clayton Moore for two Lone Ranger costumes and some "silver" bullets still missing from a suitcase stolen Christmas Eve at Hobby Airport.

Young, 43, of Missouri City, is a former baggage handler for Continental Airlines. He was found guilty of theft Tuesday after testifying that he bought the holster and guns for $200 from a man who was trying to pawn them. He later sold the items to a gun collector, he said.

The collector, Jack Hendlmyer, testified earlier that he bought the pistols from Young. Hendlmyer returned the pistols to Moore after learning they were his.

Moore, 72, testified that he began using the gear when the Lone Ranger television series first aired in 1955. Moore, dressed in a powder blue suit and white cowboy hat, testified that the guns and holster were priceless.

Defense attorney Ealy Bennett said he will appeal Young's conviction because it was based only on circumstantial evidence.

"If this had been a regular theft case, they [prosecutors] would have offered probation" for Young during plea bargaining, Bennett said. "They asked me, 'Don't you want an opportunity to cross-examine the Lone Ranger?'"

Looking back over the years, the Lone Ranger dispensed his first silver bullet on January 30, 1933, in a program that would be in the regular lineup of WXYZ for more than 21 years. Although numerous actors have played the role, the essential character of the Masked Rider of the Plains has remained unchanged, capturing the hearts and imaginations of fans of all ages for over 65 years.

For the first six broadcasts, an actor named Jack Deeds played the role. He was replaced by George Stenius, later famous as movie producer George Seaton, who continued in this role for three months. When Stenius quit, Brace Beemer, then WXYZ station manager, was selected to play the Lone Ranger, but Beemer left after a few months to open his own advertising agency. Another actor, Earl W. Graser, took over the role and developed an easy-going naturalness that provided a strong identification for listeners, glued to their Philcos for the program that aired three times a week at 7:30 p.m. But Graser was killed suddenly in an automobile accident on April 8, 1941, and producers, baffled as to a replacement, had to improvise the next few episodes by having the Lone Ranger critically wounded and unconscious, with no dialogue except for some heavy breathing, thus shifting the plot to the faithful Indian companion, Tonto. You may not remember when Earl Graser died, but if you're over 50 years old, you probably remember when the Lone Ranger's voice changed.

The casting dilemma was resolved when Brace Beemer returned to the role to which he would become closely attached in future years. Beemer's sonorous voice would make him the most famous of the radio Rangers, and he played the part until the final live broadcast on September 4, 1954.

On radio, the character of Tonto was a model of stability compared to the Lone Ranger. Former Shakespearian actor John Todd, who took the part when he was over 60 years old, played the Indian sidekick for all of the 3,000 half-hour episodes broadcast.

The popularity of the radio program led to the production of two movie serials in 1938 and 1939. The Lone Ranger was played by actors Lee Powell and Bob Livingston. Tonto was played by Chief Thundercloud (Victor Daniels) in both of the successful serials titled, *The Lone Ranger*, and *The Lone Ranger Rides Again.*

The hero proved that he was capable of adapting to technological innovations on September 15, 1949, when the television show, The Lone Ranger, premiered. Clayton Moore played the title role until its last season in September 1961. Jay Silverheels, a Mohawk Indian by birth, gained considerable notoriety as Tonto.

Because of the popularity of the TV series, the Lone Ranger rode across the silver screen in 1956 in a Warner Brothers technicolor movie called fittingly, *The Lone Ranger*, starring Moore and Silverheels. In 1958, a second feature-length film, featuring the same pair, was released by United Artists under the title, *The Lone Ranger and the Lost City of Gold.*

In 1966, animators brought the Masked Rider back to television in the form of a cartoon series that ran in the prime-time Saturday morning slot. Michael Rye was the voice of the Lone Ranger and Shepherd Menken played trusty Tonto.

The Wrather Corporation found out the hard way that even a legend can bomb at the box office, with its remake of *The Legend of the Lone Ranger* in 1981. The movie starred Klinton Spillsbury, an unknown actor, as the Lone Ranger, and Michael Horse as Tonto. Even before the film was released, Hollywood was rife with rumors that Spilsbury refused to wear the requisite mask and that all his dialogue had to be dubbed in after the shooting. These problems were compounded by a court suit seeking to prevent Clayton Moore from wearing the mask in personal appearances in the role of the character with which he had become inextricably linked. The litigation was successful, and Moore had to wear sunglasses.

Fans may not have been daunted by all the publicity surrounding the film, but they were outraged that this modern version of the hero not only was unmasked, violating the cardinal rule of previous Lone Rangers, but also had a romantic interest, which although thwarted, showed that the character was capable of loving more than justice and his horse. However, the real Lone Ranger is safe in the past of radio where his "silver" can never be tarnished.

Despite various scriptwriters' creative attempts to alter the hero and spice up the tried-but-true plot of a good guy triumphing over evil and injustice, there were several consistencies in the shows as they progressed from radio to television and then to movies.

The horse always was called Silver, a name that did not originate from one of the radio show's early sponsors, Silvercup Bread, as popularly assumed. The programs always began with theme music from Rossini's William Tell Overture, with an introduction that most fans knew by heart, "A fiery horse with the speed of light, a cloud of dust and a hearty Hi-Yo Silver — The Lone Ranger. Return with us now to those thrilling days of yesteryear"...next the commercial and ..."From out of the past come the thundering hoofs of the great horse, Silver — The Lone Ranger rides again!" Near the end of every show, a bewildered character saved by the hero would ask, "Who was that masked man?" as the Lone Ranger and Tonto vanished into the horizon.

It remains to be seen if the Masked Rider of the Plains can survive another 50 years. But even if he follows the well-worn path to oblivion, one thing is certain — he will live on, not only in the form of now valuable radio-related premiums, memorabilia, and collectibles, but also in the dream of generations of fans who grew up believing that there is a little bit of the Lone Ranger in all of us.

Who was that masked man anyway? He was our ideal and our dream, and we have never been content to put him away forever. We cannot forget who he was, and who we were then, when we heard that immortal cry from our trusty Philco radio: "Hi-Yo, Silver, Aw-a-a-y!"

Rare advertisement for the Lone Ranger serial in 1938. Anything related to this serial is in demand and expensive.

Lone Ranger Fact Sheet

Radio: First broadcast on January 30, 1933, over station WXYZ in Detroit, Michigan. By 1952, the radio audience was estimated at over 12 million families. Last broadcast on September 4, 1954. Total of 3,000 half-hour episodes broadcast. Starred George Seaton, Earl Graser, Brace Beemer, and John Todd.

Movies/Serials: *The Lone Ranger* a Republic serial released in 1938, 15 chapters, starring Lee Powell and Chief Thundercloud. *The Lone Ranger Rides Again,* 15 chapters. Released in 1939 and produced by Republic, starring Bob Livingston and Chief Thundercloud.

Television: First telecast on September 15, 1949. 221 half-hour episodes produced with 39 in full color. By 1952, television audience estimated at five million. Final season was September 1961.

Feature Movies: *The Lone Ranger*, a full-color picture distributed by Warner Brothers in 1956. *The Lone Ranger and The Lost City of Gold*, a full-color picture by United Artists in 1958. Both starred Clayton Moore and Jay Silverheels, *The Legend of the Lone Ranger*, Wrather Corporation in 1981, starring Klinton Spilsbury and Michael Horse.

Cartoon: First telecast in 1966, CBS network on Saturday morning with estimated audience of 3.5 million each week in summer and 7 million in the winter. Twenty-six half-hour programs, starring the voices of Michael Rye and Sheperd Menken.

The LONE RANGER
EPISODE 1
"HEIGH-YO, SILVER!"
HEIGH-YO, SILVER!
NOW WE'RE ON THE SCREEN!
REPUBLIC PICTURES
The LONE RANGER
THE LONE RANGER
NOW ON THE SCREEN!
Your Phantom Favorites of Radio brought to Pulsing Life in a Smashing, Crashing Motion Picture Serial.
The LONE RANGER
A Republic SERIAL IN 15 EPISODES
THE LONE RANGER
SILVER
TONTO

Typical movie promotional items for the serial *The Lone Ranger*, sells for $75.00 – 750.00.

NOW ON THE SCREEN!
Your Phantom Favorites of Radio brought to Pulsing Life in a Smashing, Crashing Motion Picture Serial.
Republic Pictures Presents the Motion Picture Version of
The LONE RANGER
with
THE LONE RANGER
A Man of Mystery
SILVER
BY SILVER CHIEF
TONTO
Chief Thunder-Cloud
CHAPTER TITLE
A Republic SERIAL IN 15 EPISODES
THE CREDITS
Associate Producer ....SOL C. SIEGEL
Supervised by ....Robert Beche
Directed by..William Witney—John English
Original Screen Play by....Barry Shipman, George Worthing Yates, Franklyn Adreon, Ronald Davidson, Lois Eby
Based on the Radio Serial "The Lone Ranger"
Created by Station WXYZ Detroit and written by..................Fran Striker
Production Manager ....Al Wilsor
Unit Manager ....Mack D'Agostin
Photographed by ....William Nobl
Film Editors..Helene Turner—Edward Tc
Musical Director ....Alberto Color
RCA VICTOR "HIGH FIDELITY" SOUND SYSTEM
A REPUBLIC FIFTEEN EPISODE SE
THE CAST
The Lone Ranger....A MAN OF MYSTERY
Silver ....SILVER CHIEF
Tonto ....CHIEF THUNDER-CLOUD
Joan Blanchard ....LYNN ROBERTS
Bob Stuart ....HAL TALIAFERRO
Bert Rogers ....HERMAN BRIX
Allen King ....LEE POWELL
Dick Forrest ....LANE CHANDLER
Jim Clark ....GEORGE LETZ
Jeffries ....Stanley Andrews
Blanchard ....George Cleveland
Father McKim ....William Farnum
Kester ....John Merton
Sammy ....Sammy McKim
Felton ....Tom London
Drake ....Ted Adams
Major Brennan ....Allan Cavan
Captain Rance ....Edmund Cobb
Taggart ....Raphael Bennett
Snead ....Maston Williams
Regan ....Jack Rockwell
Haskins ....Carl Stockdale
Lincoln ....Frank McGlynn, Sr.

CHAPTER 1 – "HEIGH-YO, SILVER!"

1 Col. Ad Slug or Mat No. 15

Jeffries, a ruthless killer of the post Civil War period, massacres a band of Texas Rangers. One man survives the slaughter, and with Tonto, an Indian friend, sets out to avenge the death of his comrades. The Lone Ranger, the massacre survivor, is joined by four ranchers. This group of men sets up headquarters in an old stockade. When Jeffries learns Blanchard, a Federal officer, is coming to Texas for an investigation, he has a spy plant dynamite at the stockade entrance so that the outlaw troops can get inside. The blast is set off just as the Lone Ranger rides through the gates.

CHAPTER 2 – "THUNDERING EARTH"

EPISODE 2

1 Col. Ad Slug or Mat No. 16

The Lone Ranger miraculously escapes injury and helps drive off the outlaws. He captures Kester, a henchman of Jeffries, and outlaw troopers and ties them on their horses, sending them back to town with a note to Blanchard. Blanchard gets the note and faces Jeffries with it, telling him that he is going to assert his authority and free the Ranchers. Jeffries, meantime, learns of Lincoln's assassination, and realizing that this ends to some extent, Blanchard's power, drives the ranchers into a gorge where he has planted dynamite. The Lone Ranger get there just as the fuse is lighted. The explosion knocks him unconscious.

CHAPTER 3 – "THE PITFALL"

1 Col. Ad Slug or Mat No. 17

Due to the efforts of Tonto the wagon-train escapes the landslide. Blanchard and Joan, his daughter, are captured by Kester and the troopers. Jeffries informs them of the assasination of Lincoln, and forces Blanchard to hand over what power he has. Jeffries sends out men to trap the Ranger. Joan escapes to warn him, but he has meanwhile avoided the pit-fall arranged for him. He sees Joan ridnig toward the pit. He rides to intercept her, but they both fall in.

CHAPTER 4 – "AGENT OF TREACHERY"

1 Col. Ad Slug
or Mat No. 18

The Lone Ranger and Joan, unhurt, get out of the pit. Jeffries sends for Taggart, a criminal noted for his viciousness. The outlaw troopers stage a fake kidnaping of Taggart. The Rangers, falling into the trap, save him, and Taggart tells them he has a grudge against Jeffries. The Lone Ranger meets Taggart at a cabin rendezvous which Jeffries' men surround. They capture Taggart dressed in the Ranger's clothes. The Ranger covers them from behind. One trooper hurls a rock sending the Ranger staggering as the men crowd toward him.

CHAPTER 5 – "THE STEAMING CAULDRON"

1 Col. Ad Slug
or Mat No. 19

Tonto and Silver come up just in time to let the Ranger, dressed in outlaw clothes, mount and escape. Joan writes a note to Father McKim asking for help and drops it into Taggart's room, where dressed in Ranger's clothes, he is waiting to see Jeffries. Taggart substitutes a note telling the Rangers to rescue the father at an old mill, the place where Jeffries keeps his supply of powder. Taggart and the Lone Ranger battle in a cave. The Ranger falls into a geyser hole. The steaming geyser is about to boil up over the Ranger with scalding mud.

CHAPTER 6 – "RED MAN'S COURAGE"

1 Col. Ad Slug
or Mat No. 20

The Ranger escapes from the steam fissure. The Ranger discovers that his friend, Clark, has died. Jeffries sends out men to shoot some Indians, who are friends of the Ranger, and leave silver bullets near the bodies. The revenge-seeking Indians sneak up and capture Tonto. Tonto is being tied to a stake with burning brush around him as the Lone Ranger rides into the scene on Silver, who trips over a fallen tree and the Ranger falls, unconscious, in the midst of the savages.

CHAPTER 7 – "WHEELS OF DISASTER"

1 Col. Ad Slug
or Mat No. 21

The Ranger recovers in time to save himself and Tonto, and convinces the chief he was not responsible for shooting the Indians. The Four Rangers ride to capture the powder which Jeffries is removing. They capture the first wagon-load of powder on its way back to Jeffries' headquarters. Jeffries sends for the rest, but puts Joan Blanchard on the wagon seat beside the driver, thinking no attempt would be made on the wagon, for fear of hurting her. The Ranger manages to get into the back of the wagon. The wagon overturns, exploding the powder and blowing up the wagon.

CHAPTER 8 – "FATAL TREASURE"

1 Col. Ad Slug
or Mat No. 22

The Ranger is safe at the side of the road. Jeffries plans to substitute confederate money for silver, which he has collected as government taxes, but a federal man discovers the horde of silver, defeating Jeffries plan. Jeffries hits on a plan to steal the silver but the Ranger and Tonto take the silver from him. A close chase causes them to abandon the silver. They drop it in a well. The next day four rangers disguised as peon water-carriers go to the well and load burros with kegs of water, which kegs contain the silver. Two rangers stay in the well while the others depart. The guards discover the men in the well. A cannon is fired into the well collapsing it.

CHAPTER 9 – "THE MISSING SPUR"

1 Col. Ad Slug
or Mat No. 23

The two rangers escape through a lateral passage. The outlaw troopers find the Rangers and a free for all battle develops. A federal cavalry troop halts the slaughter. Kester, the troopers and four rangers are taken as prisoners to Fort Bently and questioned by Major Brennan. The Ranger rides to the silver train and delivers it intact to Fort Bently. During a struggle the Ranger loses one of his spurs. Kester attempts to prove the Lone Ranger's identity through it. With the Major, he goes to the guard-house where they find one of the Rangers minus a spur.

PHOTO-MONTAGE OF STARS AND PLAYERS

3-Col. Photo-Montage Cut or Mat No. 45

CHAPTER 10 – "FLAMING FURY"

The LONE RanGER
EPISODE
10
"FLAMING FURY"

1 Col. Ad Slug or Mat No. 24

Each ranger has removed a spur from his boot. Kester leaves in a rage. The following morning the prisoners have escaped. Jeffries takes Joan and forces her to consent to marrying him. Joan sends messages to the Ranger by means of carrier pigeons. Father McKim and the Ranger rush to Joan and stop the ceremony. The Ranger proceeds to give Jeffries a sound thrashing. Troopers rush to Jeffries aid and force the Ranger to flee. The Ranger joins Tonto and the two take refuge in a small storehouse. The house catches fire. The two men are trapped by burning walls.

CHAPTER 11 – "THE SILVER BULLET"

The LONE RanGER
EPISODE
11
"THE SILVER BULLET"

1 Col. Ad Slug or Mat No. 25

The Ranger and Tonto discover a trap-door in the basement and make their escape. The two men ride to a nearby ranch owned by Joe Cannon. Cannon's grandson, Sam, who is gathering evidence against Jeffries, aids the Ranger and Tonto. Jeffries and his gang succeed in recovering the silver and take it to a saloon. The Ranger, through the aid of Tonto, tracks the gang to the saloon. Jeffries' outlaws discover the Ranger and a terrific fight ensues. While the Ranger is defending his life, a gun muzzle is seen poking through a window behind his back.

ALL NEW STORY
THE LONE RANGER
Republic SERIAL IN 15 THRILLING CHAPTERS
ALL NEW ACTION
A Republic SERIAL IN 15 THRILLING CHAPTERS

NOW ON THE SCREEN!
Your Phantom Favorites of Radio brought to Pulsing Life in a Smashing, Crashing Motion Picture Serial.
The LONE RANGER
A Republic SERIAL IN 15 EPISODES
with
THE LONE RANGER
A Man of Mystery
SILVER
BY SILVER CHIEF
TONTO
Chief Thunder-Cloud

794-R-8

The five Lone Ranger suspects that kept audiences guessing as to which one was the masked rider. Shown left to right...Lee Powell, George Letz, Herman Brix, Lane Chandler, and Hal Taliaferro.

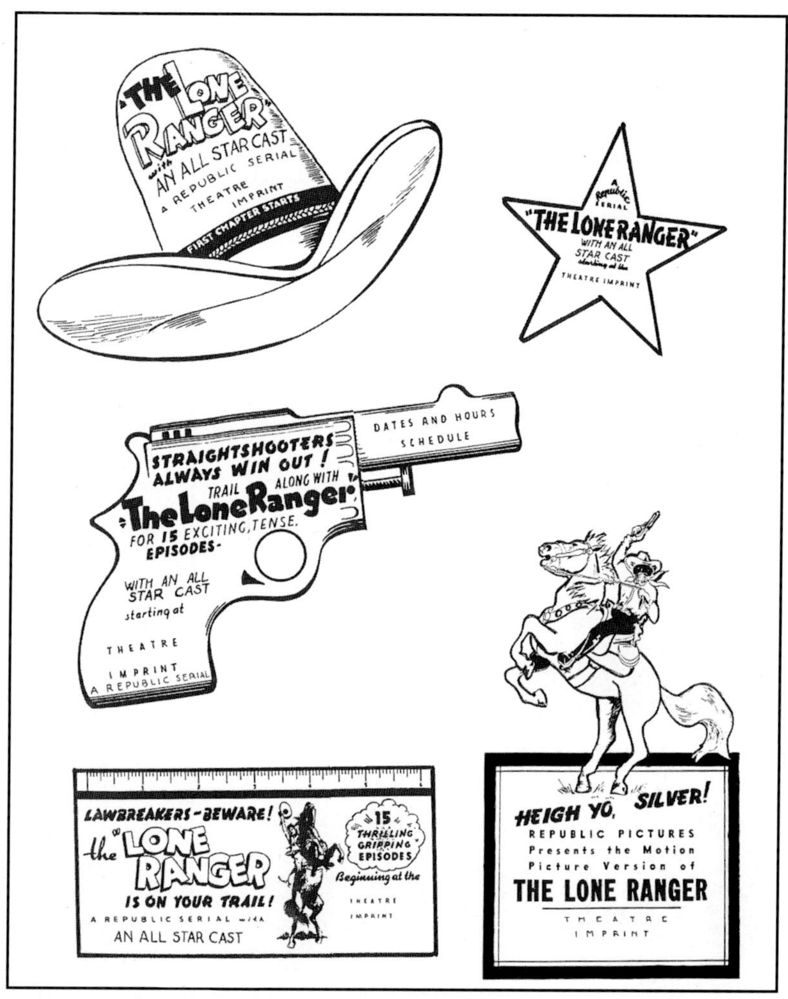

Lone Ranger movie theatre giveaways from 1938 – 1940 are very rare and command top dollar. Prices vary from $35.00 – 225.00.

Lee Powell at left proves to be the Lone Ranger in the final chapter. (Scene is from Chapter 14 of the serial.)

CHAPTER 12 – "ESCAPE"

EPISODE 12

1 Col. Ad Slug
or Mat No. 26

The gun which is pointing at the Ranger's back is that of Tonto's. Together they go to a cave where they succeed in driving off the enemy. Back in Pecos, Joan finds an old picture of Jeffries which identifies the man as a former outlaw with a price on his head. Jeffries learns of this and lays plans to do away with the girl. The Ranger rides to her rescue. He gets to the girl before Jeffries arrive and the two depart from the scene just as Jeffries arrives. Jeffries is in hot pursuit when the coach in which the two are escaping plunges over a cliff.

CHAPTER 13 – "THE FATAL PLUNGE"

EPISODE 13

1 Col. Ad Slug
or Mat No. 27

The Ranger and Joan escape unhurt as the coach plunges down the cliff and make their way to the same cave where Tonto and the Ranger had previously hidden. They bring with them Felton, whom they have captured. Felton escapes by dipping his rawhide-bound hands in a bucket of water which Sammy has left near him. Felton climbs to a ledge high in the cave and holds the rangers at bay, threatening to shoot if they move. Unnoticed, Dick Forrest climbs to the ledge and grapples with Felton. They both fall from the high ledge.

CHAPTER 14 – "MESSENGER OF DOOM"

EPISODE 14

1 Col. Ad Slug
or Mat No. 28

The Ranger who fell over the cliff has a badly wrenched back and is made as comfortable as possible in the cave by Joan. Carrier pigeons are released for help. Jeffries and his men intercept some of the pigeons, however, and learn where the Ranger and Joan are hiding. At the same time the other Rangers get the same message and everyone starts for the cave. The Rangers get there first. A terrific battle ensues and the barrage of shooting brings down the entire cavern roof.

CHAPTER 15 – "THE LAST OF THE RANGERS"

EPISODE 15

1 Col. Ad Slug
or Mat No. 29

The crash results in injuries fatal to Dick Forrest, while the others escape without hurt. Jeffries and his entire gang surround the cave. Rogers and King, two of the Rangers, break through and ride for help. Just as Jeffries' men have smoked the Blanchards, Sammy and Tonto out of the cave, the Lone Ranger arrives with help. The villains are routed and the Lone Ranger and Jeffries fall over a precipice seemingly locked in a death grip. As the state of Texas pays homage to the valiant Rangers who gave their lives freeing it from lawlessness, the Ranger's cry rings out and he comes into view—alive. The Ranger reveals his identity and rides off to new fields.

Lee Powell and Chief Thundercloud ready for action.

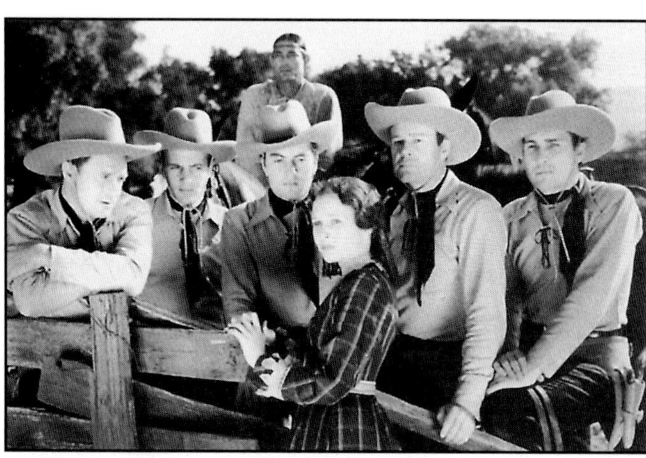

Hal Taliaferro, Herman Brix, George Letz, Chief Thunderclound, Lynn Roberts, Lane Chandler, and Lee Powell in 1938's Lone Ranger serial.

The famous unmasking scene in chapter fifteen of the Lone Ranger, Lee Powell proves to all that he is the Lone Ranger.

Robert Livingston unmasked in *The Lone Ranger Rides Again* (Republic 1939).

THE LONE RANGER
Rides Again
A Republic SERIAL IN 15 THRILLING CHAPTERS

CAST

The Lone Ranger......**ROBERT LIVINGSTON**
Bill Andrews ....**ROBERT LIVINGSTON**
Tonto ....**CHIEF THUNDER-CLOUD**
Silver ....**SILVER CHIEF**
Juan Vasquez ....**DUNCAN RENALDO**
Sue ....**JINX FALKEN**
Bart Dolan ....**RALPH DUNN**
Craig Dolan ....**J. FARRELL MacDONALD**
Jed Scott ....**William Gould**
Evans ....**Rex Lease**
Merritt ....**Ted Mapes**
Pa Daniels ....**Henry Otho**
Hardin ....**John Beach**
Thorne ....**Glenn Strange**
Murdock ....**Stanley Blystone**
Hank ....**Edwin Parker**
Colt ....**Al Taylor**
Logan ....**Carlton Young**
Doc Grover ....**Ernie Adams**

CREDITS

Associate Producer—**Robert Beche**

Directed by **William Witney, John English**

Original screen play by **Franklyn Adreon, Ron Davidson, Sol Shor, Barry Shipman**

Based on the Radio Serial, "The Lone Ranger" by **Frank Striker**

Production Manager—**Al Wilson**

Unit Manager—**Mack D'Agostino**

Photographed by **William Nobles** and **Edg**

Film Editors—**Helene Turner, Edward**

Musical Director—**William Lava**

Recorded by **RCA Victor "High Fideli Sound System**

A REPUBLIC PICTURE

Lone Ranger Rides Again **shows Bob Livingston with mask and many times without it as the lobby cards above show.**

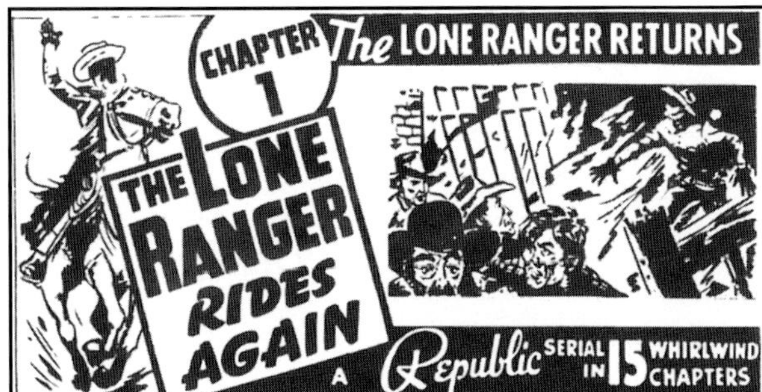

Chapter One—The Lone Ranger Returns

Craig Dolan, a powerful cattleman, makes desperate attempts to rid the San Ramon valley of innocent settlers. Jed Scott, leader of a wagon-train, engages Bill Andrews, a newcomer, to aid in defeating Dolan's henchmen. An imposter acting as the Lone Ranger is seriously wounded in the fight, and Andrews reveals himself as the REAL Lone Ranger, whose disguise was taken by the wounded man, a member of Dolan's gang. The imposter is responsible for the murder of Juan Vasquez' brother, but Dolan frames an innocent man, Jed Scott, by saying he's the murderer. Scott is taken to jail, and an infuriated mob attempts to burn the building. The Lone Ranger intervenes and is trapped as the jail collapses.

Lobby card from the second serial, *The Lone Ranger Rides Again.*

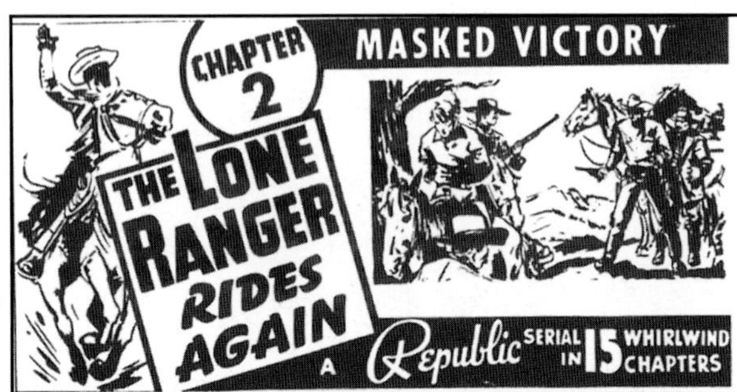

Chapter Two—Masked Victory

Juan Vasquez and the Lone Ranger pull Scott from the burning building. The Dolan interests convince the settlers that one of their number, Doc Grover, was murdered by Scott. They press Scott's conviction but the Lone Ranger insists that Grover is still alive, and safe in the custody of Tonto, the Indian. The settlers demand proof, and the Lone Ranger takes them to the spot where Grover is hidden, to learn later that he has been kidnapped by Murdock and Hardin, Dolan's henchmen. Bart and Slade, two hostile cowmen, prepare to lynch Scott when the Lone Ranger produces the supposedly dead Grover and accuses Slade of crookedness. Slade shoots the Lone Ranger, and he slumps to the ground.

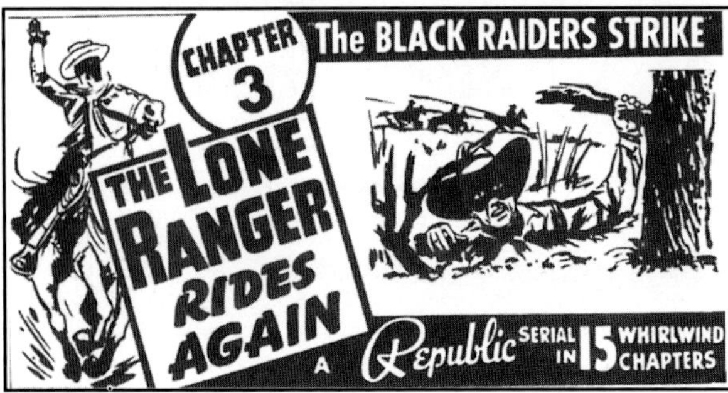

Chapter Three—The Black Raiders Strike

Slade's bullet strikes a bag of silver the Ranger wears under his shirt. He is stunned but uninjured. Scott is cleared of the murder charge and the settlers start homesteading, plagued constantly by the Black Raiders, whom the masked man suspects of being Dolan henchmen. The Lone Ranger hears that the Raiders are going to attack the Daniels' homestead, Vasquez, working closely with him, learns that one of the Raiders rides a horse with a broken shoe. This man, Bart Dolan, trades horses with his sister Sue and thus, she is suspected of complicity. The Lone Ranger defends the Daniels' homestead from attack, and in his subsequent escape is trapped in quicksand.

Chapter Four—The Cavern of Doom

The Lone Ranger escapes death when he is rescued from the quicksand by Tonto. Sue Dolan, who is suspicious of her brother Bart's behavior, accuses him of being in league with the Black Raider gang, and follows him. Bart, aware of his sister's plan, arranges to have his Raider friends capture him in a fake attack, and thus get her off the track. She believing her brother is really in danger, asks Tonto and the Lone Ranger to aid him. A pitched battle in the cave follows. The Lone Ranger and Tonto are driven back, as a fuse is lighted on a keg of powder. Unable to help themselves they are in danger of death as the chapter ends.

Chapter Five—Agents of Deceit

The Ranger's horse, Silver, pushes the powder keg out of the cave, and saves his master and Tonto. Sue is made prisoner with her brother Bart. Their captors are the Raiders (actually in league with Bart). The Ranger rescues them, and their uncle, Craig Dolan, feigning gratitude, agrees to call off the war on the homesteaders. However, the Ranger learns that Bart is plotting to destroy the wagon loads of much needed seed, recently purchased by the settlers. They plan to send a burning wagon down among the seed wagons, but the Lone Ranger alters its path. He saves the seed but endangers his own life when the blazing vehicle overturns before reaching its destination.

Chapter Six—The Trap

The Ranger leaps clear of the burning wagon. A stagecoach is robbed bringing Government forms on which the settlers are to file land claims. The Lone Ranger suspects the Raiders of the theft, and Tonto recovers the forms, which are returned to the land office. The settlers file their claims. The Dolans plot to destroy the claim records, and the Lone Ranger hastens to remove them to a safe place. Tonto and Vasquez learn that the villains have rigged a device, which will instantly kill anyone tampering with the land-office safe. The Lone Ranger unwittingly enters the land-office before Tonto and Vasquez can stop him. He is about to turn the combination.

Lone Ranger Rides Again **paper collectibles (1939), $125.00 – 150.00.**

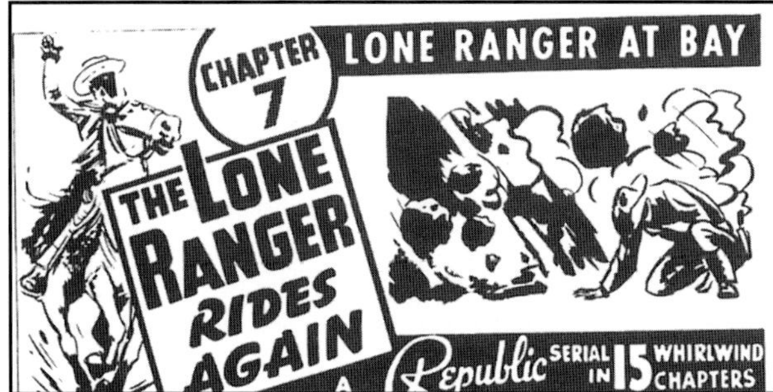

Chapter Seven—Lone Ranger at Bay

Raiders appear on the scene and stop the bullets intended for the Lone Ranger. A gun fight ensues, and the Ranger escapes with the claim-records. In his haste, he leaves a number of silver bullets behind, which implicate him in the murder of one of the Raiders who interfered. The Dolans insist that the Sheriff ride after the Ranger, and recover the claims. Bart sees to it that a few Raiders are included in the deputies that accompany the sheriff. These men are ordered to shoot the Ranger on sight. The Lone Ranger leaves the claims in the safekeeping of Tonto and Vasquez, saving himself from the pursuing cut-throats by precipitating a landslide.

Lobby card from the second serial, *The Lone Ranger Rides Again.*

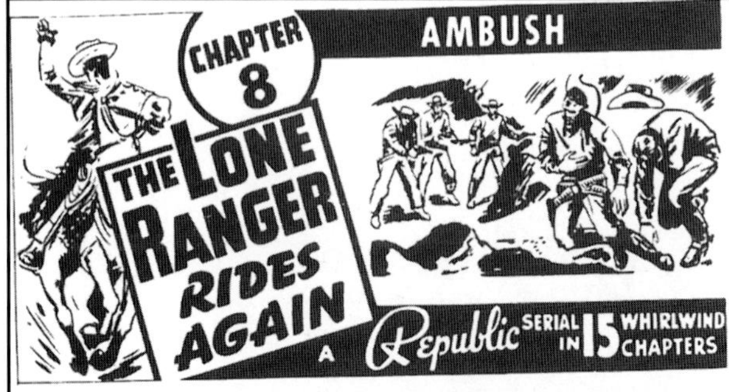

Chapter Eight—Ambush

The Lone Ranger, after great difficulty, succeeds in escaping the landslide. The sheriff, however, is killed. The sheriff's post is now open, and the settlers decide to run Pa Daniels as his successor. The Dolan clan, not satisfied with the candidate, are determined to fight the election. They kidnap Daniels' son, Danny. Pa Daniels pursues, and is also kidnapped. Sue Dolan invokes the aid of the Lone Ranger, who overcomes the Raiders and frees the captives. The other Raiders lie in ambush outside the kidnap cave, and when the Ranger and his friends appear, they are met by a deadly blast of gunfire.

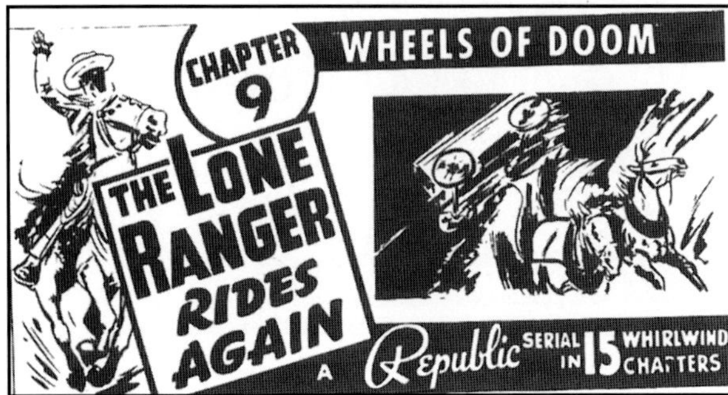

Chapter Nine—Wheels of Doom

The Lone Ranger and Daniels leave the cave together. The Ranger escapes, but Daniels is seriously wounded by the outlaws' gunfire. The settlers now decide to run Scott for Sheriff in Daniels' place. The Dolan clan try desperately to waylay Scott, but are unsuccessful in their efforts. Realizing that it is virtually impossible to stop Scott, they decide to steal the ballot boxes and eventually do away with them. The Lone Ranger overtakes the wagon on which the ballot boxes are being transported and a furious battle with the driver ensues. Suddenly, the horses break loose and run away. The wagon topples over the cliff.

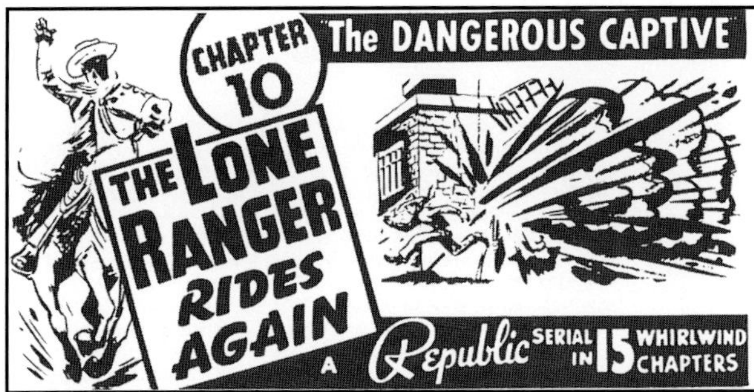

Chapter Ten—The Dangerous Captive

The Lone Ranger jumps from the runaway wagon just before it plunges over the cliff. He recovers the ballot box and returns it safely. Scott is elected sheriff and appoints Andrews (the Lone Ranger), Vasquez, Evans and Powers as his deputies. The Dolan clan, resenting the "nestors" in the sheriff's office, determine to kill them off. The Raiders steal a herd of Dolan's cattle and then set an ambush for the deputies, who go after the rustlers. The Lone Ranger scents trouble and evades this ambush, capturing the Raider leader. Bart Dolan, fearing that the latter will confess, dynamites the jail.

Chapter Eleven—Death Below

Andrews ropes the powder box, and the occupants of the jail are saved. Martin Gibson, newly appointed land claim registrar, is now on his way to the town. The Lone Ranger, fearing the registrar might meet foul play, rides out to insure the man's safety. He learns that the Dolan clan have already approached the registrar and offered him a bribe to falsify reports in favor of the cattlemen. Gibson refuses, and a battle ensues in which Gibson is spirited away. The Lone Ranger and Tonto come to his rescue and help him to escape via a steep bluff. The Ranger, hanging over a cliff, drops as the rope snaps.

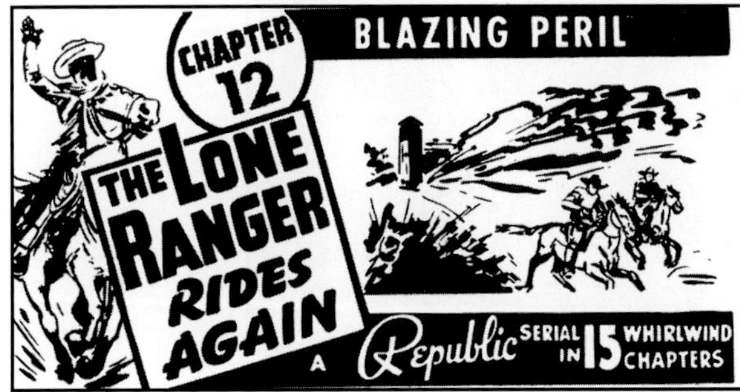

Chapter Twelve—Blazing Peril

The Lone Ranger drops safely on a protruding ledge and makes his way back to Tonto and the registrar. Meanwhile, at Dolan's hacienda, information is received that Gibson has called a meeting of the settlers at Evan's barn. That evening, at the appointed place, the settlers tell Gibson of the trials they have undergone since their arrival. The Raiders, meanwhile, surround the barn with brush soaked in coal-oil. They light the inflammable material, keeping Gibson and the settlers in the barn till it is totally demolished by the intensity of the roaring fire.

Colorful lobby card that helped to bring all the fans back for the second serial.

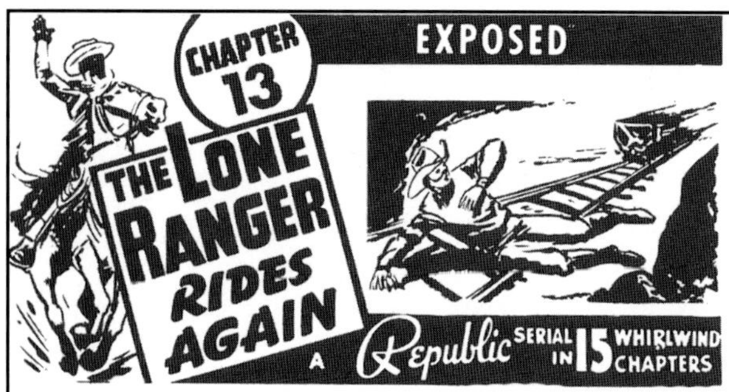

Chapter Thirteen—Exposed

Gibson and the settlers take refuge in the cellar while the building burns over them. They escape and make their way safely to town. Craig Dolan, though an enemy of the "nestors," has done nothing to harm them. The villainy has been done entirely by his nephew, Bart. When Craig confronts him, Bart shoots the elder Dolan, and blames the crime on the Lone Ranger. The masked man proves his innocence and Bart, fearing the Ranger's revenge, attempts to escape. To further his plans, he takes his sister, Sue, as a shield. The Ranger pursues, and a gun battle is the result. A loaded ore car is released, and it rushes toward the Ranger, who is trapped at the foot of a tunnel.

Colorful lobby card that helped to bring all fans back for the second serial.

Chapter Fourteen—Besieged

The Lone Ranger derails the car as it is about to strike him. He and Tonto escape and return to Dolan's. Bart Dolan is desperate and he declares open war on the "nestors." He collects all the outlaws and renegades in the district and sets out to destroy the scattered homesteads. The deputies notify all the homesteaders to find refuge in the fort. Preparations are made to put up a desperate defense, but the ammunition is limited. Andrews volunteers to ride through the enemy lines and get help from the cavalry. He gets clear of the fort, when he is intercepted by a group of Raiders and shot from his horse.

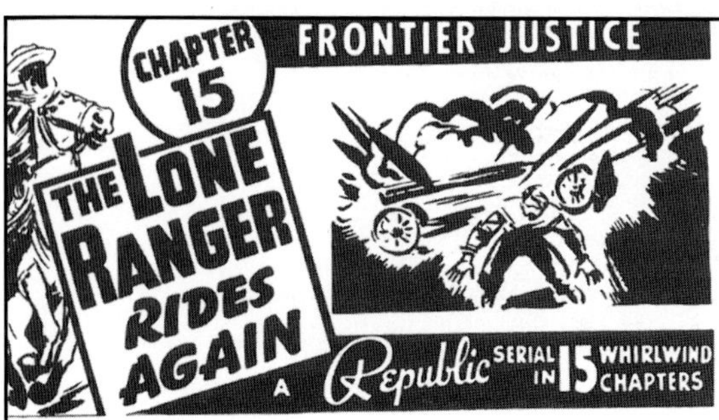

Chapter Fifteen—Frontier Justice

The Lone Ranger falls and he crawls through the brush where Silver is tied. He knows that ambush awaits him, but he evades it and reaches the cavalry. The Raiders, aware of the failure of their plot and fearing the oncoming cavalry, order a wagon-load of explosives rolled down onto the fortress walls. The Ranger, arriving in time, mounts the wagon and brings it to a stop before it crashes. He orders the settlers to the far side of the enclosure. Bert Dolan, investigating the cause of failure, is killed when the explosive finally does its destructive work.

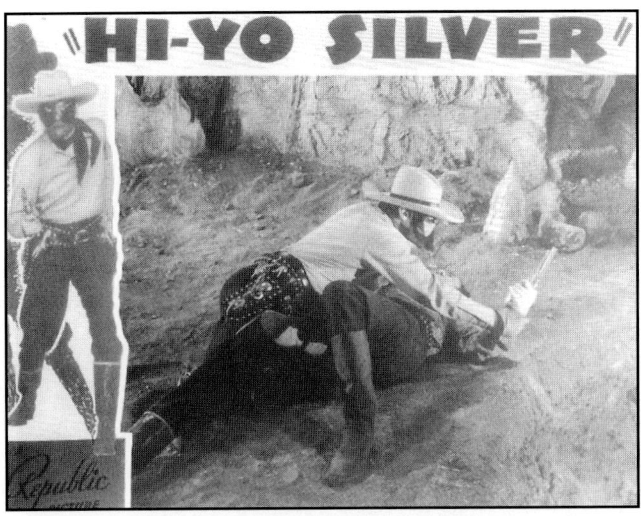

Lobby card from the 1940 feature version of the Lone Ranger serial.

Chief Thundercloud and Lee Powell in the feature version of the 1938 serial.

HY–YO SILVER

LEE POWELL	Allen King
LYNN ROBERTS	Joan Blanchard
CHIEF THUNDERCLOUD	Tonto
HERMAN BRIX	Bert Rogers
STANLEY ANDREWS	Jeffries
GEORGE CLEVELAND	Blanchard
WILLIAM FARNUM	Father McKim
HAL TALIAFERRO	Bob Stuart
LANE CHANDLER	Dick Forrest
GEORGE LETZ	Jim Clark
JOHN MERTON	Kester
SAMMY McKIM	Sammy
TOM LONDON	Felton
RAPHAEL BENNETT	Taggart
MASTON WILLIAMS	Snead
FRANK McGLYNN, SR.	Lincoln

Directors: WILLIAM WITNEY, JOHN ENGLISH
Associate Producer: SOL C. SIEGEL
Story: Based on "The Lone Ranger" radio serial.
Camera: WILLIAM NOBLES
Editors: HELENE TURNER, EDWARD TODD
Musical Score: ALBERTO COLUMBO
Supervisor: ROBERT BECHE
Original Screenplay: BARRY SHIPMAN, GEORGE WORTHINGTON YATES, FRANKLYN ADREON, RONALD DAVIDSON AND LOIS EBY.

HY–YO SILVER was a 69 minute feature version taken from the 1938, 15-chapter serial, THE LONE RANGER. Republic added some new footage featuring Raymond Hatton telling the story to young Dickie Jones. Neither received pressbook nor advertising credit other than publicity mentions and, pure speculation on YESTERDAY'S SATURDAYS part having never seen the feature version, probably didn't appear in the film credits.

And, by not knowing what was used and what was cut from the original serial print, we can't guarantee that all of the listed members of the cast appeared in the feature version,as Republic used a paste-up from the serial for the HI–YO SILVER credits. The serial version had a great many players who may, or may not, have appeared in the feature version in addition to the credited cast, and a partial listing would include: Jack Perrin, Ted Adams, Bud Osborne, Carl Stockdale, Allan Cavan, Jack Rockwell, Edmund Cobb, Jack Ingram, Tex Cooper, Al Taylor, Forbes Murray, Blackie Whiteford.

Lobby card showing Herman Brix, Hal Taliaferro, Chief Thundercloud, and Lee Powell.

Chief Thundercloud and Lee Powell behind the mask.

The Lone Ranger 1-sheet (1956), $85.00 – 250.00.

WARNER BROS.
PRESENT

"The Lone Ranger"

In WARNERCOLOR

THE CAST

The Lone Ranger	Clayton Moore
Tonto	Jay Silverheels
Reece Kilgore	Lyle Bettger
Welcome	Bonita Granville
Ramirez	Perry Lopez
Cassidy	Robert Wilke
Sheriff Kimberly	John Pickard
Lila	Beverly Washburn
Angry Horse	Michael Ansara
Red Hawk	Frank de Kova
The Governor	Charles Meredith
Powder	Mickey Simpson
Goss	Zon Murray
Whitebeard	Lane Chandler

THE CREDITS

Produced by Willis Goldbeck; Directed by Stuart Heisler; Screen Play by Herb Meadow; Based on "The Lone Ranger" Legend; Director of Photography, Edwin DuPar, ASC; Art Director Stanley Fleischer; Film Editor Clarence Kolster, A. C. E.; Sound by M. A. Merrick; Set Decorator G. W. Berntsen; Music by David Buttolph; Makeup Supervisor, Gordon Bau, S.M.A. Assistant Director, Robert Farfan.

A Jack Wrather Production

Assigned by the Governor of the Western territory to investigate the unrest between the settlers and the Indians, The Lone Ranger and Tonto, arrive in time to rescue Peter Ramirez, a cowpuncher, from a band of Indians. On the way back to town Ramirez tells The Lone Ranger that Reece Kilgore, a wealthy rancher, is trying to stir up trouble to prevent the territory from being accepted for statehood.

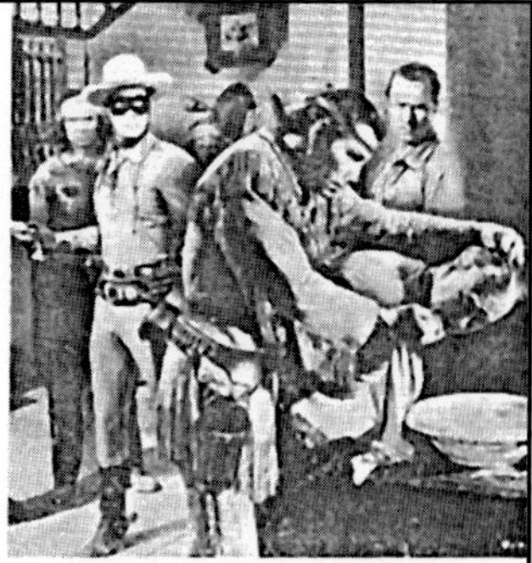

Kilgore has hired a gang of cutthroats to keep the territory in a state of uproar by raiding and killing and blaming it on the Indians. Tonto finds out that the raids are made by Kilgore's men disguised as Indians. Ramirez learns that Kilgore has purchased a large supply of dynamite, but he is killed.The masked rider finds out about the dynamite but, in the meantime, Kilgore has acted. He forces the Sheriff to resign, wires the Governor that war with the Indians is now imminent, and sends his daughter away to safety, but she is captured by Chief Angry Horse's braves.

Hearing of this, The Lone Ranger offers to fight Angry Horse for the safety of the little girl and after a violent struggle, he wins and returns the child to her mother, who accepts the masked man as a friend and tells him that Kilgore and his men are massing with the townspeople to attack the Indians. She also tells that Kilgore has found silver deposits on the Indian's land, providing the motive

The Lone Ranger and Tonto mine the trail leading towards the Indian reservation, creating much confusion on both sides but hurting no one. By this time, the Sheriff has returned with the Cavalry and Kilgore is arrested. Kilgore's wife tells The Lone Ranger her plans for the ranch only to find that he has gone.

Advertising poster still showing artwork of Clayton Moore and Jay Silverheels.

Official Billing

THE LONE RANGER
AND THE LOST CITY OF GOLD

Color By Eastman Color
starring
Clayton Moore as THE LONE RANGER

Jay Silverheels as TONTO
featuring
Douglas Kennedy
Charles Watts
with
Noreen Nash
Lisa Montell
Ralph Moody
Norman Fredric
Directed by Lesley Selander
Produced by Sherman A. Harris
Written by Robert Schaefer and Eric Freiwald
Based upon the Lone Ranger Legend
A JACK WRATHER Production
Released thrue United Artists

The Cast

The Lone Ranger	Clayton Moore
Tonto	Jay Silverheels
Ross Brady	Douglas Kennedy
Oscar Matthison	Charles Watts
Frances Henderson	Noreen Nash
Paviva	Lisa Montell
Padre Vicente Esteban	Ralph Moody
Dr. James Rolfe	Norman Frederic
Tomache	John Miljan
Redbird	Maurice Jara
Travers	Bill Henry
Wilson	Lane Bradford
Caulama	Belle Mitchell

The Story

(Not for Publication)

The Lone Ranger (Clayton Moore) and Tonto (Jay Silverheels) learn that some hooded riders have been murdering Indians near the town of San Doria.

The leader of the raiders, Ross Brady (Douglas Kennedy) and his girl friend, Frances Henderson (Noreen Nash), see a threat to their plot to steal five medallions which when put together reveals the location of an Indian lost city of gold.

Chief Tomache (John Miljan) has given five pieces of the medallion to five of his friends and relatives, three of whom have now been killed. The Lone Ranger takes it upon himself to save the two survivors, a grandson and a nephew. He is too late to save the nephew who is killed by one of Brady's henchmen.

As a result of The Lone Ranger's getting hot on their heels, Brady and Frances have a falling out, and she kills her boyfriend as The Lone Ranger and Tonto come upon them. They take Frances into custody, and the lost city of gold remains with its rightful owners—the Indians.

RUNNING TIME: 80 MINUTES

The Staff

Directed by	Lesley Selander
Produced by	Sherman A. Harris
Written by	Robert Schaefer and Eric Freiwald
Music by	Les Baxter
Song "Hi Yo Silver" by	Lenny Adelson and Les Baxter
Director of Photography	Kenneth Peach, A.S.C.
Film Editor	Robert S. Golden, A.S.E.

The first technicolor feature movie of the Lone Ranger was as popular in 1956 as the early serials. Movie fans were pleased that Clayton Moore and Jay Silverheels continued their successful television roles as the Lone Ranger and Tonto. When watching this movie, it is hard to believe that Jack Wrather produced this successful screen adaption and also the 1981 *Legend of the Lone Ranger* that was totally unacceptable to audiences and fans of the characters.

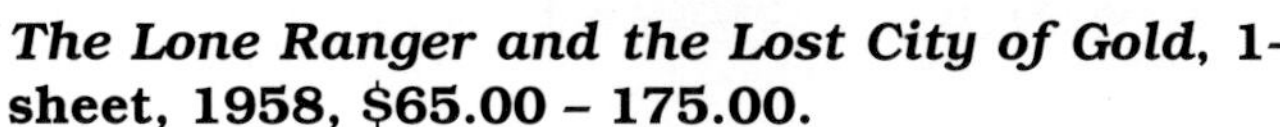

The Lone Ranger and the Lost City of Gold, **1-sheet, 1958, $65.00 – 175.00.**

1958, one sheet for the *Lone Ranger and the Lost City of Gold*, $65.00 – 125.00.

LORD GRADE and JACK WRATHER

Present

A MARTIN STARGER PRODUCTION

"THE LEGEND OF THE LONE RANGER"

THE CAST

The Lone Ranger	KLINTON SPILSBURY
Tonto	MICHAEL HORSE
Cavendish	CHRISTOPHER LLOYD
Sheriff Wiatt	MATT CLARK
Amy Striker	JUANIN CLAY
President Grant	JASON ROBARDS
Dan Reid	JOHN BENNETT PERRY
Collins	DAVID HAYWARD
Lucas Striker	JOHN HART
Wild Bill Hickok	RICHARD FARNSWORTH
General Custer	LINCOLN TATE
Buffalo Bill Cody	TED FLICKER
Young John Reid	MARC GILPIN
Young Tonto	PATRICK MONTOYA
General Rodriguez	DAVID BENNETT
German Passenger	RICK TRAEGER
The Gambler	JAMES BOWMAN
Chinese Passenger	KIT WONG
Waystation Agent	DANIEL NUNEZ
Stagecoach Driver	R.L. TOLBERT
Shotgun	CLAY BOSS
First Chief	JOSE REY TOLEDO
Second Chief	MAX CISNEROS
Mr. Reid	TED WHITE
Mrs. Reid	CHERE BRYSON
Waiter	JAMES LEE CRITE

The Legend of the Lone Ranger is based on stories and characters created by George W. Trendle and Fran Striker

Produced by	WALTER COBLENZ
Directed by	WILLIAM A. FRAKER
Screenplay by	IVAN GOFF & BEN ROBERTS and MICHAEL KANE and WILLIAM ROBERTS
Adaptation by	JERRY DERLOSHON
Executive Producer	MARTIN STARGER
Director of Photography	LASZLO KOVACS, A.S.C.
Production Designer	ALBERT BRENNER
Edited by	THOMAS STANFORD, A.C.E.
The Story of "The Man In The Mask" Sung by	MERLE HAGGARD
All Lyrics by	DEAN PITCHFORD
Original Music by	JOHN BARRY
Executive in Charge of Production	RICHARD L. O'CONNOR
Production Manager	DICK GALLEGLY
1st Assistant Director	CHARLES OKUN
2nd Assistant Director	JOSEPH A. INGRAFFIA
Casting	MIKE FENTON JANE FEINBERG
Casting Associate	LINDA FRANCIS
Associate Producer	DICK GALLEGLY
Assistant to the Producer	CLAUDETTE DUFFY
Assistant to the Director	STEVEN E. SABLOFF
Art Director	DAVID M. HABER
Set Decorator	PHILLIP ABRAMSON
Prop Master	DENNIS PARRISH
Costume Designer	NOEL TAYLOR
Costume Supervisor	DARRYL LEVINE
Camera Operators	ROBERT STEVENS GARY KIBBE
Assistant Cameramen	JOSEPH E. THIBO JEFFREY GERSHMAN
Additional Photography: Director of Photography	BOBBY BYRNE
Sound Mixer	WILLIAM RANDALL
Script Supervisor	MARIE KENNEY
Production Coordinator	MARTHA YATES
Gaffer	JAMES PLANNETTE
Key Grip	GENE KEARNEY
Post Production Supervisor	JAMES POTTER
Assistant Editors	FLORENCE WILLIAMSON HOWARD HEARD
Dialogue Editor	STAN GILBERT - wallaWorks
Supervising Sound Editor	GORDON ECKER, JR.
Music Editor	CLIFFORD C. KOHLWECK

Special thanks for the cooperation from the Film Commissions of the States of New Mexico, Utah, and Nevada, during the filming of "THE LEGEND OF THE LONE RANGER."

FILMED IN PANAVISION

COLOR BY TECHNICOLOR

Running Time: 98 Minutes

THE UNTOLD STORY OF THE MAN BEHIND THE MASK AND THE LEGEND BEHIND THE MAN.

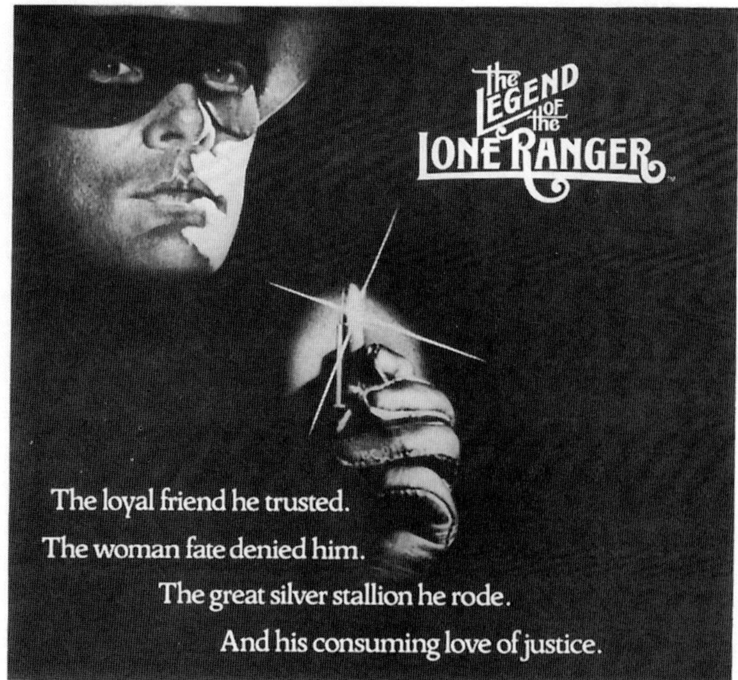

The Legend of the Lone Ranger
The loyal friend he trusted.
The woman fate denied him.
The great silver stallion he rode.
And his consuming love of justice.

LORD GRADE and JACK WRATHER Present A MARTIN STARGER Production "THE LEGEND OF THE LONE RANGER"
Starring KLINTON SPILSBURY MICHAEL HORSE CHRISTOPHER LLOYD and JASON ROBARDS as PRESIDENT ULYSSES S. GRANT
Executive Producer MARTIN STARGER Screenplay by IVAN GOFF & BEN ROBERTS and MICHAEL KANE and WILLIAM ROBERTS
Adaptation by JERRY DERLOSHON Original Music by JOHN BARRY Director of Photography LASZLO KOVACS, A.S.C.
Produced by WALTER COBLENZ Directed by WILLIAM A. FRAKER DISTRIBUTED BY UNIVERSAL PICTURES AND ASSOCIATED FILM DISTRIBUTION CORPORATION

"The Man in the Mask" Sung by MERLE HAGGARD Original Soundtrack Available on MCA Records

PANAVISION® ©ITC/Wrather Productions 1981 ©1981 UNIVERSAL CITY STUDIOS, INC.

PG PARENTAL GUIDANCE SUGGESTED SOME MATERIAL MAY NOT BE SUITABLE FOR CHILDREN

Classic Lone Ranger pose for *Legend of the Lone Ranger.*

The Bulletin Saturday, May 23, 1981

A REVIEW/Legend of the Lone Ranger

A pop hero puts on his mask again

Universal
Klinton Spilsbury

"THE LEGEND OF THE LONE RANGER." Directed by William A. Fraker. Screenplay by Ivan Goff, Ben Roberts, Michael Kane and William Roberts. Rated PG.

BY BOB SOKOLSKY
Bulletin Entertainment Editor

Say, who *is* that masked man?

One thing is certain. He's not the Lone Ranger we remember from earlier films and radio programs.

"The Legend of the Lone Ranger" isn't a movie at all. It's a fallow, shallow imitation that touches slightly upon the theme and never comes remotely close to its spirit.

Part of that is due to casting. It would be difficult for any modern actor to undertake the role of the Lone Ranger. It is darn nigh impossible when that actor is Klinton Spilsbury.

The advance word was that Spilsbury had problems with the part. Even so, he is no worse than anyone else involved in the production, with the possible exceptions of Jason Robards, cast as President Ulysses S. Grant, and the great horse Silver, playing the great horse Silver. The latter, however, probably should not count. He appears to have received a little direction, something not supplied anyone else in the company.

The latest retelling of the vintage story follows traditional lines, telling how the masked man came to be. But until it reaches those lines the entire production appears in danger of being trampled like grass in a stampede.

In what might be the longest preface in screen history, audiences are taken through tangent after tangent and the film is almost an hour long before Spilsbury finally dons his mask and the time-honored overture from "William Tell" blares.

This, unfortunately, is the movie's high point. It lasts approximately 15 seconds and what follows appears to be more afterthought than plot.

The best that might be said is that this remake is no worse than the retellings of "Buck Rogers" and "Flash Gordon."

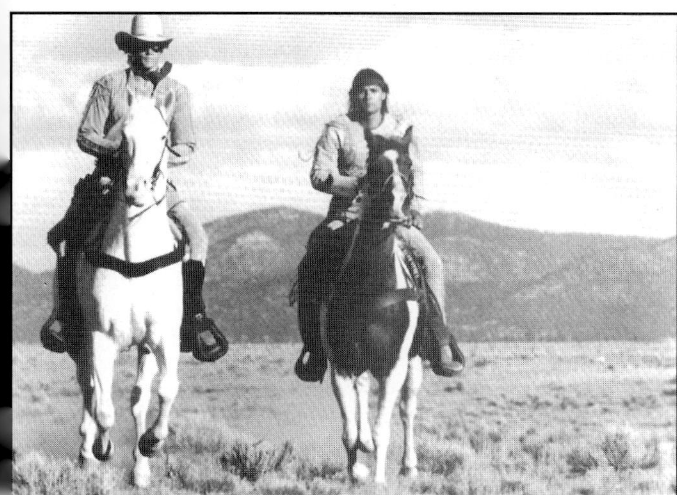

Klinton Spilsbury as the Lone Ranger and Michael Horse as faithful Tonto.

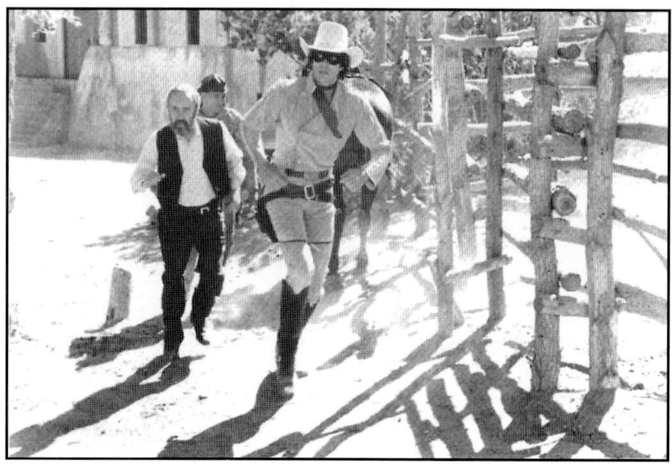

Jason Robards as President Grant is rescued by Spilsbury. Another still from the press kit.

The Lone Ranger characters and theme are used frequently as a base for all types of commercials both television and radio. Some of the more popular concepts were produced by Stan Freeberg for the Jeno's Pizza commercials. Another interesting concept was the "Phone Ranger" approach used by Southern New England Telephone Company. The characters were used for Chrysler's Dodge commercials titled the "Good Guys in the White Hats" concept. That advertising campaign featured the last appearance of Brace Beemer. The theme was tied in with talking to the Lone Ranger by dialing a special number (in one day 3,000 calls were made to Brace Beemer in Detroit).

Some of the other successful campaigns include "The Loan Arranger" concept from First Pennsylvania Bank. Both radio commercials and newspaper ads were utilized. Union Carbide capitalized on a team approach using the Lone Ranger and Tonto as well as Dr. Watson and Sherlock Holmes and Laurel and Hardy. The theme was finding the right partner is just as important in business as in show business.

The Lone Ranger has been used as the center of attention for many, many editorials, editorial cartoons and newspaper articles across the country. He was also featured on screen in the popular Gasoline Alley comic strip. And one individual used the Lone Ranger concept to advertise for the right lady in his life in a personal want ad.

The Lone Ranger and Tonto are "name-dropped" by national personalities on television and radio, in newspapers and magazine features — Johnny Carson, Bill Cosby, Art Buchwald — all relying on the instant identification of viewer and reader to trigger the warmth of recognition.

Today, many people collect and invest in original cartoon art from many famous comic strips that were popular in America from 1910 to the present time. The comic strip is one of the true art forms that is associated only with America. It has been said that comic art is now being associated with the same investment value as fine art. Prices paid vary for comic art depending on the artist and the style of his art work and popularity of the strip.

Over a period of time a lot of the original art work was destroyed by the various syndicates that provided the comic strips to the newspapers. Some of the strips that survived were either saved by the artist or given away by him. Many fans of the strips would write to the artist asking for the original art work or a panel from the comic strip.

There has been in the past several years a great demand of original Lone Ranger comic strip artwork. The prices continue to escalate for early Charles Flanders and Ed Kressy art work. Tom Gill, who drew the Lone Ranger comic books for Dell Publishing Company for over 20 years, is also in demand. Samples of the 1981 – 1982 strip by Russ Heath are also collectible.

Other advertising art work involving the Lone Ranger character is very collectible but very hard to uncover. Prices vary a great deal on original art work and are a nice addition to any collection of Lone Ranger memorabilia.

For old times' sake...Former cast members of the Lone Ranger show re-created a script from its heyday under the careful surveillance of the movie and TV version of the sagebrush hero, Clayton Moore, as part of a record ad campaign for Michigan Dodge dealers.

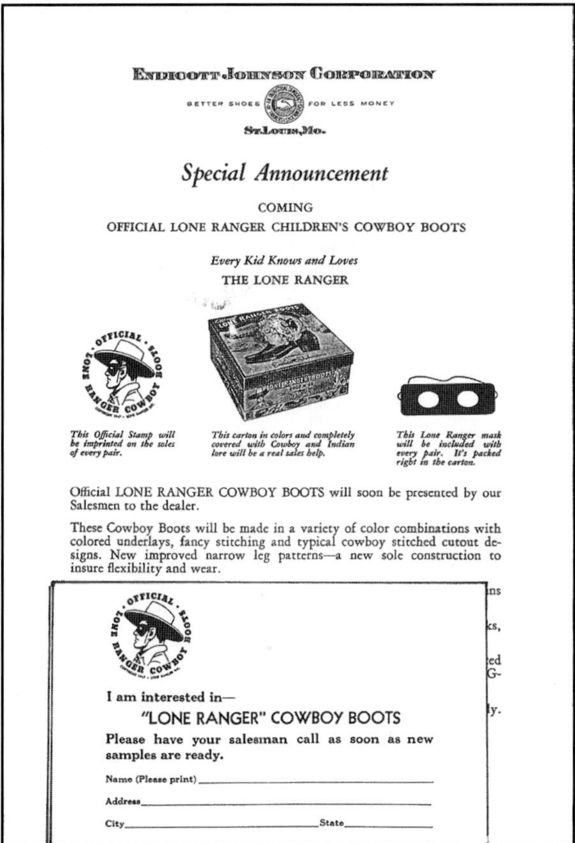

ENDICOTT-JOHNSON CORPORATION

BETTER SHOES FOR LESS MONEY

St. Louis, Mo.

Special Announcement

COMING

OFFICIAL LONE RANGER CHILDREN'S COWBOY BOOTS

Every Kid Knows and Loves

THE LONE RANGER

OFFICIAL · LONE RANGER COWBOY BOOTS

This Official Stamp will be imprinted on the soles of every pair.

This carton in colors and completely covered with Cowboy and Indian lore will be a real sales help.

This Lone Ranger mask will be included with every pair. It's packed right in the carton.

Official LONE RANGER COWBOY BOOTS will soon be presented by our Salesmen to the dealer.

These Cowboy Boots will be made in a variety of color combinations with colored underlays, fancy stitching and typical cowboy stitched cutout designs. New improved narrow leg patterns—a new sole construction to insure flexibility and wear.

OFFICIAL · LONE RANGER COWBOY BOOTS

I am interested in—

"LONE RANGER" COWBOY BOOTS

Please have your salesman call as soon as new samples are ready.

Name (Please print) ____________

Address ____________

City ____________ State ____________

Endicott-Johnson official Lone Ranger cowboy boots, letter, and order card (1947).

Lone Ranger and Tonto advertisement for Kodak computer (1990).

Sample strip used in an issue of *Cracked* magazine utilizing the Lone Ranger and Tonto theme.

Sample of the Gasoline Alley strip showing the Lone Ranger on the movie screen.

Ed Kressy was given the assignment to illustrate the Lone Ranger comic strip in 1938. Although he was not as good as Flanders his cartooning style captured the flavor of the Lone Ranger and Tonto in the early strips of 1938 and part of 1939.

Sample strip by Charles Flanders who drew the strip for King Features Syndicate for 27 years. Flanders early work was outstanding, completely capturing the visual image of the radio character. Unfortunately, his later work lacked the flavor and detail of his earlier strips.

Excellent strip by Gil Kane who was asked to submit several pilot strips for the 1981 version of the Lone Ranger comic strip. Unfortunately, Rus Heath was given the job of illustrating the new comic written by Cary Bates.

Unknown sample of Lone Ranger art work used to illustrate advertising toys in the late fifties.

The Lone Ranger A NEW GENERATION CLASSIC

Sample of the newest version of the Lone Ranger art work used for merchandising the character.

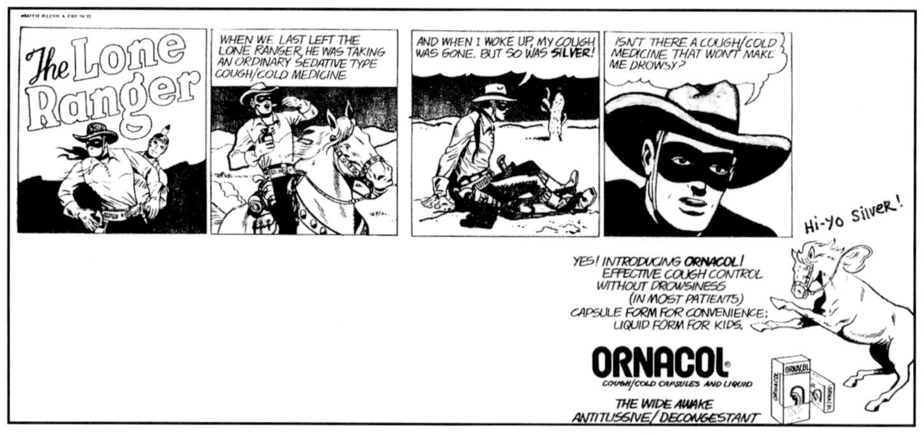

Advertisement for Ornacol a cough control medicine using the Lone Ranger character. This art work was designed for the medicine box designed in late 1965.

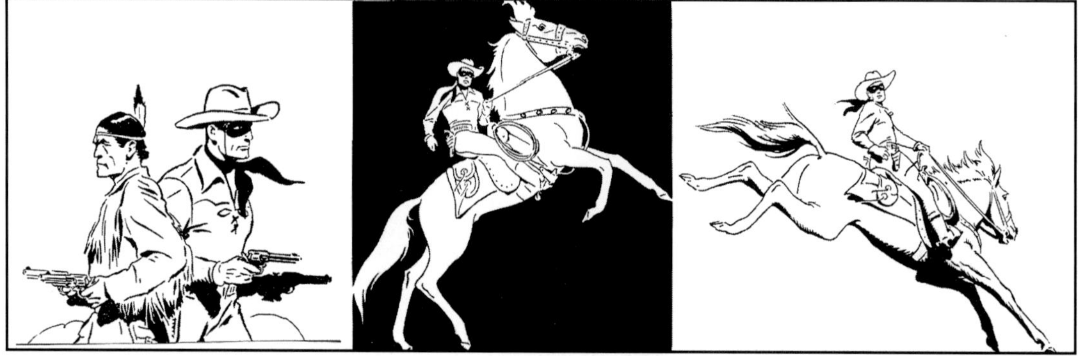

The most prolific of the Lone Ranger artists, Henry Vallely, drew the majority of the Lone Ranger Big Little Books, coloring books, comic books, and feature books in the late 1930s and early 1940s.

Sample cartoon from *Far Side* using Lone Ranger idea. Sample ad campaign for Dodge Dealers.

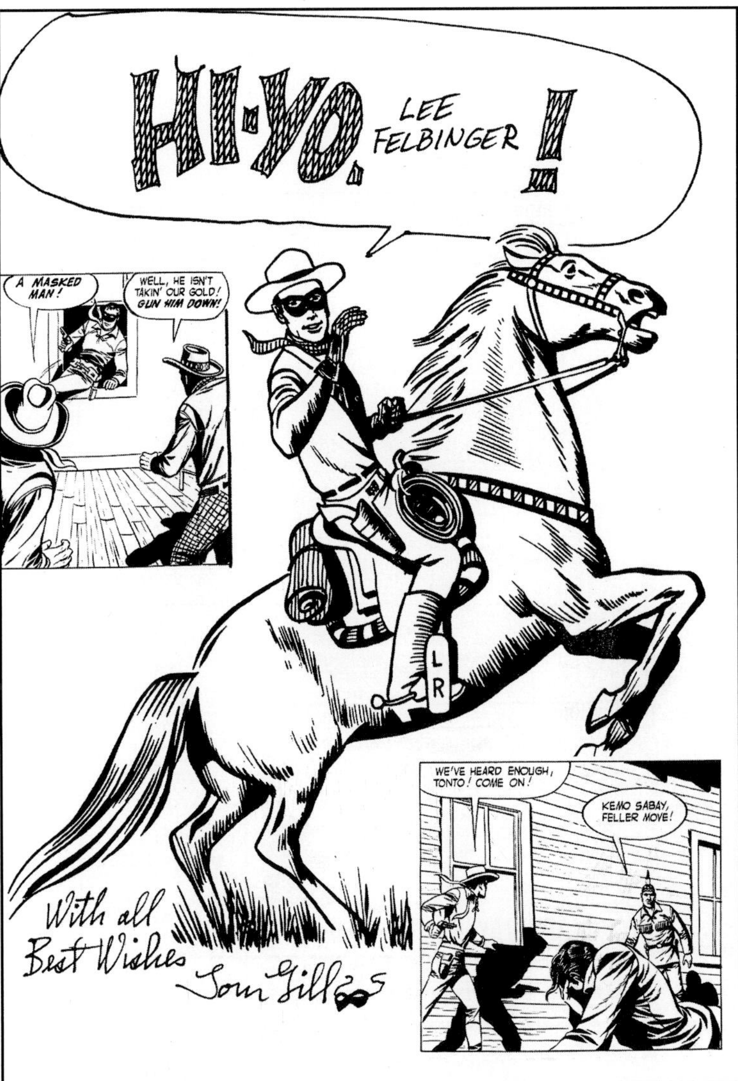

Samples of the work of Tom Gill, the artist who drew the Lone Ranger comic books.

silver rules

Lone Ranger: a square-shooter

By Bob Greene

In this amoral age there remains one true hero, one force for good. He is, of course, the Lone Ranger, and if you disagree, keep away from this space from now on.

I unashamededly admit that I love the Lone Ranger.

You may think that the Lone Ranger became a good guy merely by luck. Not true at all. The reason the Lone Ranger was so good is that his creators, very specifically, set out to make sure everything he did advanced his goodness.

When the original Lone Ranger radio show went on the air, the creators wrote a list of guidelines for Lone Ranger scriptwriters — a list (called "The Lone Ranger's Success Formula") that carried over to the Lone Ranger television show, which even today is viewed in reruns by millions of decent Americans.

I have obtained a copy of the Lone Ranger guidelines. They are more than the key to a successful radio and television show. They can make your life better. They're better than any self-help program pushed by some tootie-frootie doctor promoting his book on a talk show. Here they are. Memorize them.

- Patriotism — Motivated by love of country, and originally a strong desire to help the pioneers who settled in the West, the Lone Ranger teaches a brand of patriotism that consists of more than flag-waving and answering the call of war.

When interpreted from the scripts, it is learned that patriotism means service to the community; voting; aiding in community development of schools and churches; and an obligation to maintain a home in which good citizens may be reared. It further means a respect for law and order and calls for a preservation of our heritage, specifically the rights of freedom of speech and religion.

- Fairness — The Lone Ranger advocates the American Tradition, which gives each man the right to choose his work and to profit in proportion to his effort. He registers disapproval of men who take unfair advantage, those who step beyond the bounds of fair play, and those who attack from behind. He constantly disapproves of bullets.
- Tolerance — If the Lone Ranger accepts the Indian, Tonto, as his closest companion, it becomes obvious to children that great men have no racial or religious prejudice. Nowhere in the stories are any minority groups referred to in a derogatory manner.
- Sympathy — The Lone Ranger chooses the side of the oppressed — the underdog — the little man in need of help, and is a specific example of a man who can be strong, yet tender — a man who can fight hard, yet show his mercy and compassion.
- Sex, Gore, and Brutality — The sanctity of the home is protected, and all love interests are kept wholesome. The circumstances behind the creation of the masked lawman make it necessary never to write a love interest for him into the program, but romance is introduced into the lives of his associates — romance free of triangles, faithlessness, and lurid sex.

Lone Ranger Don'ts:

1. The Lone Ranger is never seen without his mask or a disguise.
2. With emphasis on logic, the Lone Ranger is never captured or held for any length of time by lawmen, avoiding his being unmasked.
3. At all times, the Lone Ranger uses perfect grammar and precise speech completely devoid of slang and colloquial phrases.
4. When he has to use guns, the Lone Ranger never shoots to kill, but rather only to disarm his opponent as painlessly as possible.
5. Logically, too, the Lone Ranger never wins against hopeless odds; i.e., he is never seen escaping from a barrage of bullets merely by riding into the horizon.
6. Even though the Lone Ranger offers his aid to individuals or small groups, the ultimate objective of his story is to imply that their benefit is only a by-product of a greater achievement — the development of the West or our country. His adversaries are usually groups whose power is such that large areas are at stake.
7. All adversaries are Americans to avoid criticism from minority groups.
8. Names of unsympathetic characters are carefully chosen, avoiding the use of two names as much as possible to avoid even further vicarious association. More often than not a single nickname is selected.
9. The Lone Ranger does not drink or smoke, and saloon scenes are usually interpreted as cafes, with waiters and food instead of bartenders and liquor.

Quote from J. Edgar Hoover — "The Lone Ranger is one of the greatest forces for good in the country."

Additional editorial cartoon and article by columnist Bob Greene about the Lone Ranger Silver Rules.

Advertising Age, July 26, 1976

Hoping the public may still believe in heroes, Philadelphia's First Pennsylvania Bank has been using the Lone Ranger and Tonto, dubbed the "Loan Arranger and Pronto," in its newspaper and radio advertising. Polaroid Pronto SX-70 cameras were given to those qualifying for personal loans of more than $2,500.

The Lone Ranger rides again in ads for Pa. bank loans

PHILADELPHIA—The masked man who has been showing up lately at branches of the First Pennsylvania Bank here is not a robber. He is actually a member of the bank's senior management impersonating the "loan arranger."

It's all part of an advertising campaign, including newspapers and radio, which the bank has been running to push its direct installment loans. Anyone who received a direct personal loan of more than $2,500 through last week, was presented with a Polaroid Pronto SX-70 camera, carrying case and tripod adapter by the bank.

Hence, the "Loan Arranger and Pronto" theme. Spiro & Associates created the campaign. #

Lone Ranger and Tonto

Barnum and Bailey have joined the Carbide team. So have Laurel and Hardy, Holmes and Watson, and the Lone Ranger and Tonto.

These famous entrepreneurial, comedy, detective and wild west teams are all part of an enterprising print advertising program by the Solvents and Intermediates Division (S&I) to bring home the point: "Finding the right partner is just as important in your business as in show business."

Sample Lone Ranger ad campaigns.

Auditions for the Lone Ranger's horse

Hi Ho SILVER
SPRING SALE

YOU RIDE AWAY With the savings NOW at McKNIGHT RD. DODGE

In order to maintain our #1 position in sales this month, every new and used car has been cut to the bone to save you money and get us volume (300 Cars Must Be Sold This Month)
MON. TUES. WED. ONLY — DON'T BE LEFT OUT

You'll never save more - Come in now

LET'S BOTH BE WINNERS

STOCK #3-1317 New 1973 Dodge Swinger Spcl. Tourqueflite trans., radio, p. steering, dlx. wheel covers, etc., etc.
SALE PRICE $2649.00

SALE PRICE $3399.00

STOCK 2-0078 New 1972 Dodge Colt. Automatic, Radio, White Walls, ect.
SALE PRICE $2389.00

1973 Dodge Coronet Custom 4-dr. V8, auto., p.s., p.b., Air, v. roof, pkg. LOADED. Extended warranty. List $4099.00.
SALE PRICE $3199.00

SALE PRICE $3698.00

SALE PRICE $4399.00

DODGE
SILVER BULLET
SPECIALS

'71 PLYMOUTH
340 Duster, power steering, 4 speed, sharp!
$2295

'70 PLYMOUTH
Fury I, police car.
$695

'69 OPEL GT
2 door coupe, auto. trans., radio & heater.
$1550

'68 DODGE
Coronet, 2 door hardtop, cylinder, radio & heater.
$695

'68 PLYMOUTH
Barracuda, 2 door hardtop, p. steering, auto., 6 cylinder.
$1295

'66 DODGE
Polara, 2 door hardtop.
$595

'65 JEEP
½ ton pickup, 4 wheel drive, 4 speed trans., with plow.
$395

'72 FORD
Club wagon, 12 pass., auto. trans., p. steering, V8, heavy duty package, rust proof, 9000 original miles.
$3695

Happiness Is Dependable Transportation From BURGUNDER MOTORS

BURGUNDER DODGE
RTS. 50 AND 519
BRIDGEVILLE
563-7112 221-9500

A FIREY HORSE, A CLOUD OF DUST & A HEARTY "HI-YO SILVER . . . AWAY" (The Lone Stranger Rides Again) the masked man is back in town and looking for his female Kemo-Sabay. If you are (25-35) 5'10"+ sincere, honest, personable, down to earth, energetic, intelligent, mature, humorous, with a touch of craziness, Reply with Bio/Photo to PO Box 2072, Ventnor, NJ 08406.

Additional samples of Lone Ranger advertising and cartoons. This idea was very clever...I wonder if he ever got his female Tonto?

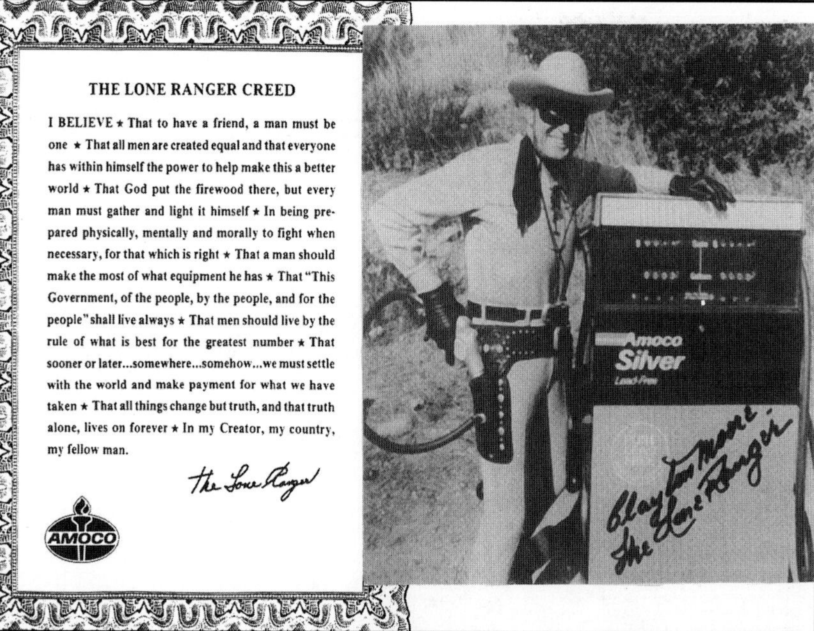

THE LONE RANGER CREED

I BELIEVE ★ That to have a friend, a man must be one ★ That all men are created equal and that everyone has within himself the power to help make this a better world ★ That God put the firewood there, but every man must gather and light it himself ★ In being prepared physically, mentally and morally to fight when necessary, for that which is right ★ That a man should make the most of what equipment he has ★ That "This Government, of the people, by the people, and for the people" shall live always ★ That men should live by the rule of what is best for the greatest number ★ That sooner or later...somewhere...somehow...we must settle with the world and make payment for what we have taken ★ That all things change but truth, and that truth alone, lives on forever ★ In my Creator, my country, my fellow man.

The Lone Ranger

AMOCO

Amoco giveaway items featuring the Lone Ranger including a photo of Clayton Moore and a copy of the Lone Ranger Creed.

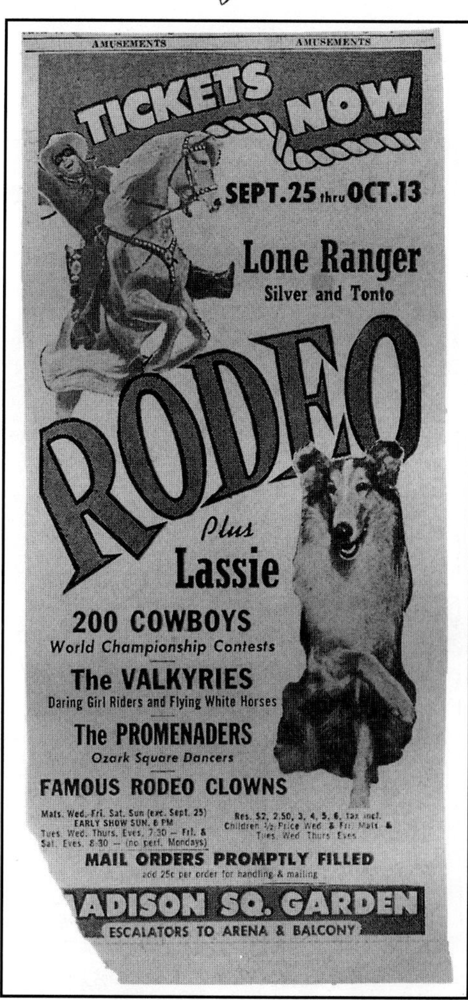

Madison Square Garden advertisement promoting the Lone Ranger and Lassie. Most people were aware that both the Lone Ranger and Lassie were owned by the Jack Wrather Corporation.

***Life* magazine ad for ABC featuring the Lone Ranger program (1947).**

WE'RE THE TEAM YOU CAN COUNT ON.

In the old West, enlisting the help of this team gave you a sense of security and assured you of success. If you're a public fund, you, too, have to round up the right combination of people to handle your complex needs.

With more than $75 billion of public fund assets under custody and relationships ranging from the biggest cities and states to smaller towns and municipalities, we're today's dependable team with the never-miss-the-mark service you can rely on.

We're in 39 states (and the District of Columbia, too). We have a 90-country network, and 26 of our 34 securities settlement locations worldwide are Citibank branches. No one else can match that. When it comes to custody and delivering information on international portfolios, being the local bank with the global reach is important.

Our relationship management approach and the ways we help earn extra income through such programs as Securities Lending and Dividend Reinvestment get high marks from our clients, too. So much so, that 100% of our clients required to review Master Custodians last year signed back with us.

Give us a call. We'll earn your trust.

CITIBANK

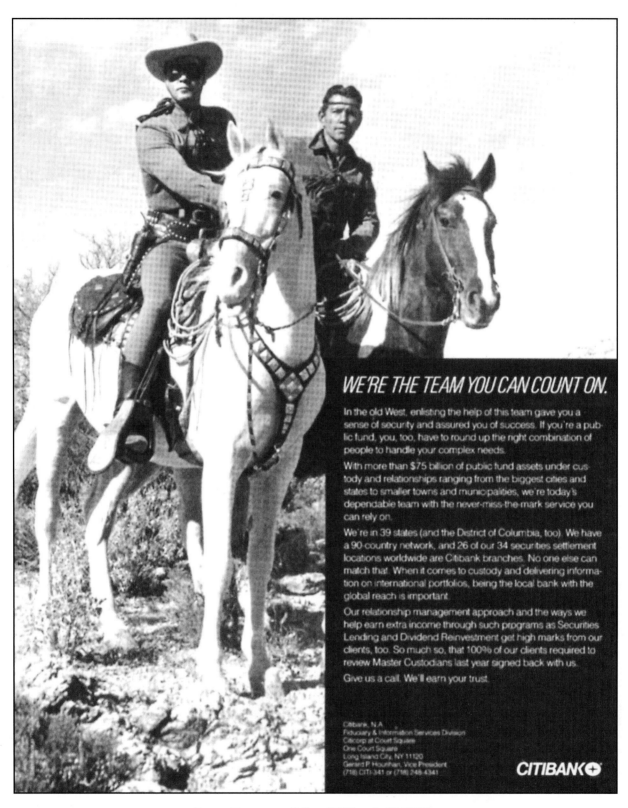

Lone Ranger ad for Citibank (1989).

The last, and most recent, campaign using Clayton Moore as the Lone Ranger was the AMOCO campaign in 1988. In addition to newspaper ads, large posters were displayed by local gas stations. This material is also very collectible to fans of the masked rider.

This was a good indication of how popular the Lone Ranger character was back in the early 1940s. This full page ad appeared in *Good Housekeeping* magazine, a very collectible item. Note the Lone Ranger pilot radio in small drawing.

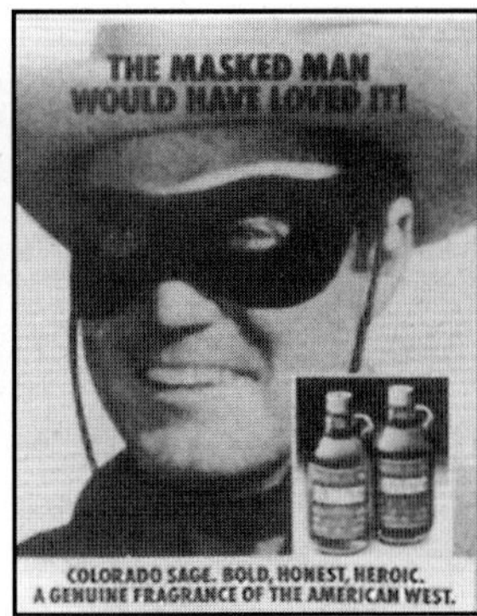

Samples of local advertising, using the Lone Ranger theme, are all very collectible and sought after by fans of the Lone Ranger.

Advertisement

Franchise Marvel: A Brand-New Idea That's 40 Years Old

"Hi-yo Silver® . . . Away!"

The Lone Ranger rides again. This time in a saga unparalleled in the restaurant franchise industry.

The dazzling new red, white and blue Lone Ranger family, fast-food restaurants, soon to rise across America, are the latest in a phenomenal parlay of successes for world-famed industrialist, hotel man and restaurateur, Jack Wrather.

And he's had several. Muzak, the "Grand-Daddy" in franchising which was founded in 1934, numbers 220 worldwide. His Disneyland Hotel has grown from 90 to nearly 1,000 rooms since 1955. The Wrather-owned "Lassie" series is the longest-running filmed half-hour in TV history. And then there's the huge hotel with restaurant and convention facilities aboard the liner "Queen Mary," to be jointly operated with Sky Chefs (a subsidiary of American Airlines), slated to open this year in its new Long Beach (Calif.) berth.

Wrather knows how to capture crowds. And keep them coming. The new Lone Ranger operation proves it. Headed by Ralph Lanphar, former president of Shakey's and previously a key figure in the McDonald's success story, The Lone Ranger Franchise System, Inc. is armed with an arsenal of sure-fire promotions.

They include 221 Lone Ranger TV shows, two full-length color films, 26 color cartoons, 52 radio shows, records, comic books, and 48 exclusive Lone Ranger products. And there's the masked rider himself to attend press-covered grand openings. The Lone Ranger licensee can be provided with television and radio commercials, among other advertising material.

The Lone Ranger "image" is a winner, reports Ralph Lanphar. "We devoted one year and commited over $1,000,000 to perfect the franchise package. Research solidly confirmed the Lone Ranger's nationwide appeal to kids, adults—everyone." Noting that over 70% of Lone Ranger restaurant trade consists of young families with children, Lanphar adds: "The Lone Ranger concept of food and merchandising draws them.

For nearly 40 years the symbol of adventure, excitement and fair play to millions, the powerful Lone Ranger legend is cleverly relived in every phase of the new Lone Ranger restaurants. The sparkling Old West interiors seat 80 to 100 diners, and cater to brisk take-out trade, as well. The Lone Ranger legend in photos decorates the walls. Lamps wear nostalgic white hats and black masks.

And the 16-item menu is all-American. Hamburgers and western-style fried chicken lead the lineup. Also the Sheriff's Steak Sandwich, plus Saddlebag meals to go. The latter are packed in handsome reusable containers, simulating rich hand-tooled leather.

The big crowd-pleaser (kids love it!) is the Lone Ranger "Quick Draw Drink Bar." Here, the customer buys a cup of ice for the price of a soft-drink, then treats himself to as many "fill-ups" as desired. "Each cup," says Lanphar, "can be filled up to eight times and still be profitable to the licensee."

Today, The Lone Ranger Franchise System, Inc. is marketing national and overseas licenses for individual owner-operators or multiple unit buyers. Required is a minimum $35,000 investment and $5,000 capital reserve. Perhaps, the most convincing reason to own a Lone Ranger restaurant can be found in the first year's income projections which accompany the descriptive color brochure mailed to interested people. The potential return, alone, is enough to set this opportunity apart from others.

With 16 new Lone Ranger restaurants scheduled to open in the Los Angeles market alone this year and another dozen in the planning, a 40-year-old idea is scoring a brand-new impact. Wrather successfully.

We interrupt these franchise ads to bring you an unfair advantage.

All restaurant franchises are not created equal. Not by a long shot. This isn't just one more of the many. We have developed a fast-food, "eat-in or take-out" system with advantages you won't find elsewhere.

We made sure by spending over a year and committing over $1,000,000 to perfect our package. Nothing has been left to chance!

A built-in reputation. The Lone Ranger. It's one of the best known names in America. Based on 40 years of hero worship in TV, radio, comics, records. It means instant popularity for our licensees.

Ride with Wrather. Behind this legend is the successful Wrather Corporation. The Disneyland Hotel and its family restaurants, serving 95,000 meals a month. Muzak, the pioneer of franchising. The Queen Mary ocean liner hotel and restaurants (joint venture with Sky Chefs Inc., a subsidiary of American Airlines) projecting 3,000,000 visitors the first year. The internationally known Lassie television series.

The winning team. We have the experts in every facet from real estate to operations to finance. Each has an impressive track record. Like President Ralph Lanphar, former head of Shakey's Pizza, key executive with McDonald's.

Our full program contains imaginative new promotions to attract traffic. And the most effective merchandising. Pity the poor competitor!

You supply the ambition. We'll provide the training and methods. Exclusive area and foreign licenses available for individual and group purchases...one or multiple units. Minimum investment is $35,000 and $5,000 working reserve. The Lone Ranger Franchise System, Inc., Disneyland Hotel, Plaza Bldg., Suite 1, Anaheim, California 92802. Phone: (714) 778-3400.

And here's the word from our sponsor:

FREE!
Full facts in full color brochure
For additional information: mail this coupon or call Mr. John Barry, VP, (714) 778-3400
The Lone Ranger Franchise System, Inc.
Disneyland Hotel, Plaza Building, Suite 1, Anaheim, Calif. 92802

NAME
ADDRESS
CITY STATE ZIP
PHONE E370

Want t
For more informati
opportunities advertis
postpaid inquiry ca
ESQUIRE's I-R-I-S Serv

ESQUIRE: MARCH 1969

Typical ad for the Lone Ranger Restaurants, appearing in many publications in 1969. A total of 16 Lone Ranger Restaurants were scheduled to open in Los Angeles that same year. There are many items from the early restaurants that are highly collectible today.

Advertisement for 3M using the Lone Ranger idea in a clever approach that sold a lot of products.

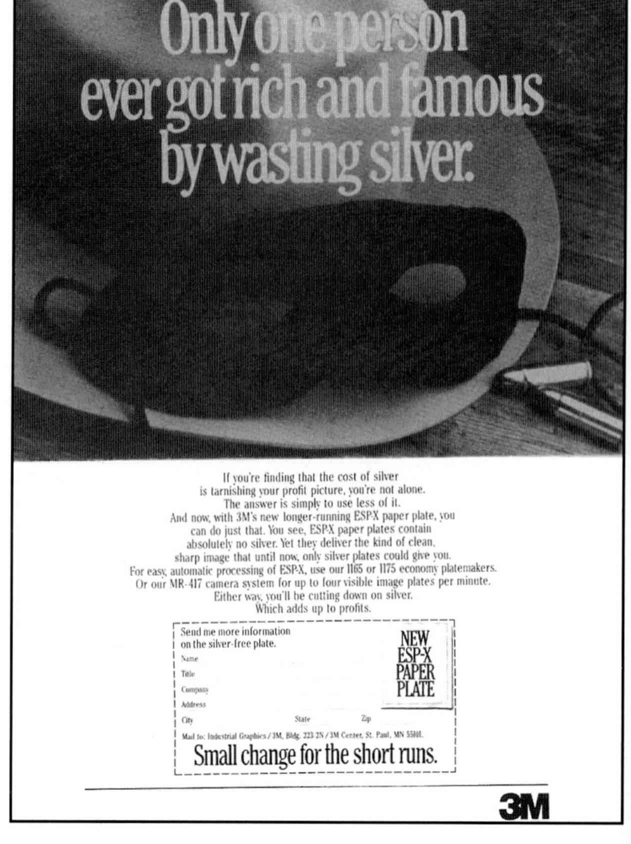

16-A Wednesday, May 8, 1985 The Philadelphia Inquirer

'Lone Rangers'

Veterans rescue 18 from a burning building

United Press International

NEW YORK — Eight Vietnam veterans returning from a memorial service rescued 18 people, including eight children, from a burning Queens building early yesterday, then left without waiting for an official "thank you."

Fire Department officials said they were looking for the former soldiers to express their gratitude for help in evacuating the three-story building.

The veterans were identified as Bill Warner, Patrick Regan, Billy Pavano, Jack DeFrancis, Doug Paterson, Bill Giovanniello, Bill Hubell and Doug Carlson.

The department identified the eight through fire marshals' reports and the media, and it was recommending them for consideration for civilian commendations.

"There were no civilian injuries due to the actions of these Vietnam veterans. They got all the people out," said Lt. Jim Powell, a Fire Department spokesman.

Six firefighters were injured battling the two-alarm blaze, which was being investigated as suspicious. Three were treated and released; the others were treated and put on medical leave.

The veterans, who said they were members of the Queens Vietnam Veterans Outreach Center, were returning from the unveiling of a Manhattan memorial to veterans of the war when they noticed the fire about 2 a.m.

The blaze began in first-floor stairwell and spread throughout the building in minutes.

"They alerted the tenants and evacuated them down a front fire escape, which was necessary because the main escape route in the interior of the building was blocked by fire," Powell said. "The only way to get people out was the fire escape."

"These guys came out of the night, did what they had to do and they left the scene — like Lone Rangers," said firefighter Joe Ward, an assistant battalion chief on the scene. "They didn't hang around for glory."

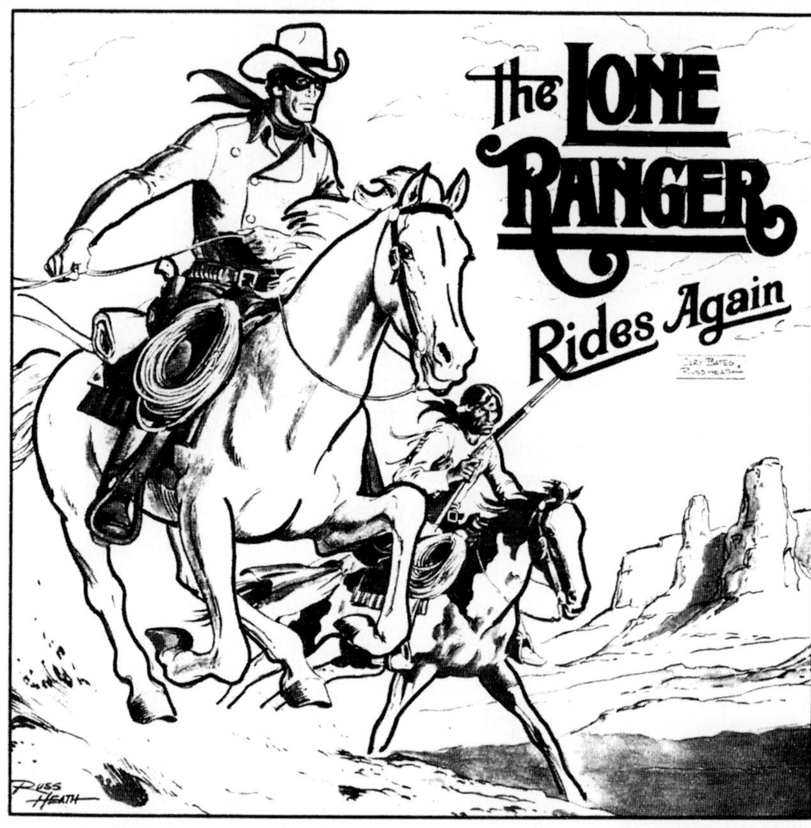

Starting September 13, newspaper readers around the world will thrill once again to the strains of a hearty "Hi-yo, Silver, awaaaay!" as the masked man gallops to the defense of law and order on the frontier. Brand-new adventures, written by Cary Bates and magnificently illustrated by Russ Heath. Daily and Sunday in half-, third- and quarter-standard and half- and full-tabloid.

Special Features
SYNDICATION SALES CORP.
200 Park Avenue, New York, NY 10166
Eastern Sales (212) 972-1070. Telex: 640-198. For sales west of the Mississippi, and in the Latin American and the Caribbean area, contact Paul Finch, Vice President, West Coast Division, 6420 Wilshire Blvd. (Suite 1100), Los Angeles, CA 90048. (213) 852-1579. Telex: 194-941.

Advertisement for the new Lone Ranger comic strip with sample of Russ Heath's version of the masked rider.

The Original Good Guy in the White Hat

The Lone Ranger galloped through performance after performance of radio heroism on Detroit's WXYZ. He was a favorite of both children and adults. His dramatic "Hi-Yo Silver" echoed through living rooms all over the world.

Who could ever forget those tense moments of excitement when "the thundering hooves of the great horse, Silver" were heard on the plains, via the air waves, bearing the Masked Rider intent upon rescue, wearing his virtue like a banner, with his Indian friend, Tonto, at his side.

When the Lone Ranger was first broadcast, the identity of the sonorous voiced hero was a closely guarded secret. Then, at a children's circus given by the Detroit Department of Parks and Recreation, Brace Beemer made the first personal appearance as the Lone Ranger.

A huge crowd of youngsters and their parents cheered wildly as the masked man rode his snow-white horse across the Belle Isle field. The children deserted their seats to run to him and follow him into the arena, like children following the Pied Piper!

A new hero was born that day, and from that moment until the day of his death, Brace Beemer, was also besieged by a devoted public. Today, long after his death on March 1, 1965, at the age of 62, Beemer's memory remains firmly entrenched in the hearts and imaginations of those who followed his exploits as the Masked Rider of the Plains.

Placing Brace Beemer in the role of the Lone Ranger was perfect casting. He was a tall man, measuring 6'3" and loved the outdoors. An expert rider and crack shot, Beemer was a "man's man"; his appeal stemmed from his rugged charm and virile appearance. During his earlier years in the role, he made personal Lone Ranger appearances in black regalia. As the months passed by and popularity increased, Beemer allowed the Lone Ranger to don a set of elaborate pastels. One favorite was a light gray hue. Soon Beemer found that the Lone Ranger was continually in demand. He made personal appearance tours and appeared at rodeos, circuses, and benefits. He posed for countless photographic sessions for newspaper and magazine layouts. He traveled extensively for promotional purposes.

He became an honorary "blood brother" in several Indian tribes, was made an honorary member of the Legion of Frontiersmen of Canada, and was deputized in Texas. Among his close friends were former vice president Alben Barkley and J. Edgar Hoover, who admired Beemer's skill on the pistol range (he once racked up a perfect score on the FBI range).

Brace Beemer was born in Illinois. His family moved to Indiana when Brace was very young. At the age of 14, Brace enlisted in the U.S. Army, where he was awarded a Purple Heart for wounds received in action. Following his youthful stint in the service, he began singing on a radio station in Indianapolis. When he was offered a position at WXYZ in Detroit, he eagerly made the move.

Before becoming the Lone Ranger, Beemer appeared as one of the Wandering Vagabonds and also read poetry on a program, titled "The Night Shall Be Filled With Music."

Beemer married songstress Leta Wales in Toledo, soon after coming to Oxford Township in 1942, and purchased a 300-acre estate, called Paint Creek Acres. Here he, his wife, and their four children, J.D., Richard, Robert, and Barbara, lived among a bevy of dogs and horses. All became expert riders, as Paint Creek Acres maintained a stable of 30 horses. One of those horses was called Silver's Pride.

Although Trendle, Campbell, and Meurer, owners of WXYZ and the Lone Ranger series, owned a horse named Silver, Beemer preferred to appear with Silver's Pride, an Albino-Arabian stallion, since Brace had personally spent many hours with his horse and could ride him with ease, despite the vast crowds he encountered in the audiences. Following Beemer's death, Silver's Pride was cared for by Leta Beemer, and the horse died at the age of 27 years.

The Lone Ranger, as portrayed by Brace Beemer, was indeed a legend of our times, a legend that will live on in the memories of those who recall radio's golden years when "the thundering hooves of the great horse, Silver" swept out the western air waves from the small studios of WXYZ, to capture a nation's heart.

"Say, who was that masked man?" It was Brace Beemer, of course.

Photos of Brace showing him dressed in his World War I uniform, at the age of 10 years (far right), and loading a field cannon. Brace was a member of the 150th Field Artillery, Battery E, Rainbow Division under MacArthur, and the youngest soldier to be wounded in World War I.

In 1934, a series of eight photographs were taken of Brace Beemer and John Todd as the Lone Ranger and Tonto for possible use as publicity photos or early premium giveaways. The horse was rented and, if you check carefully, the bridle used on Silver is English, not Western. The outfit Brace is wearing is similar to the early painting that was used as a premium and for publicity. These photos were probably given to the artist as a guide for that painting, which he stylized to tie in with the vivid image the radio show created of the Lone Ranger and Silver.

Photo 7, 3, and 4...The 4th photo was used as a color tinted photo for the back of the Big Little Book, *The Lone Ranger and His Horse Silver* (1935).

Photo 5...Showing John Todd, Silver, and Brace Beemer.

Photo 6...Showing Silver and Brace Beemer.

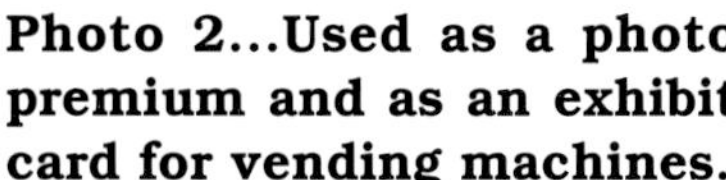

Photo 2...Used as a photo premium and as an exhibit card for vending machines.

Photo 1 was chosen as the key photo for all publicty purposes showing both Tonto and the Lone Ranger on the great horse, Silver. Several years later, Tonto was given his own horse.

OFFICE OF THE DIRECTOR

Federal Bureau of Investigation
United States Department of Justice
Washington 25, D. C.

February 26, 1946

Mr. Brace Beemer
1344 West Drahner Road
Oxford, Michigan

Dear Mr. Beemer:

I did want to write and personally express my own appreciation and the gratitude of my co-workers in the Federal Bureau of Investigation for your enthusiastic support and cooperation during World War II. The Lone Ranger is a symbol of Americanism and I know that in his various lectures and tours he has made definite contributions in the field of crime prevention and the repression of juvenile criminality.

It is a privilege to have your confidence and I hope that whenever you are in Washington you will stop in at FBI Headquarters and visit your many friends.

With best wishes and kind regards,

Sincerely yours,

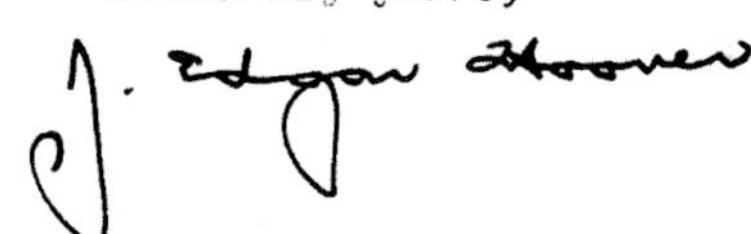

J. Edgar Hoover

Letter from J. Edgar Hoover thanking Brace for his support and cooperation during the war years.

LONE RANGER — Brace Beemer, who will carry on the tradition of "The Lone Ranger." He is no stranger to the role, since he was the original portrayer more than nine years ago. Although he retired from radio work, Beemer retained his job as narrator on the Ranger's programs all through the years. He is married, has three boys and one girl, and lives on a farm near Rochester, Mich., where he raises saddle and thoroughbred horses. He is 38.

Boston Paper Sent
by Louise Clifford

Newspaper article stating that Brace will carry on the tradition of the Lone Ranger after Earl Grazer's death (1941).

Brace Beemer and Silver (Hero) make the first appearance at a circus on Belle Island in Detroit (ca. 1933).

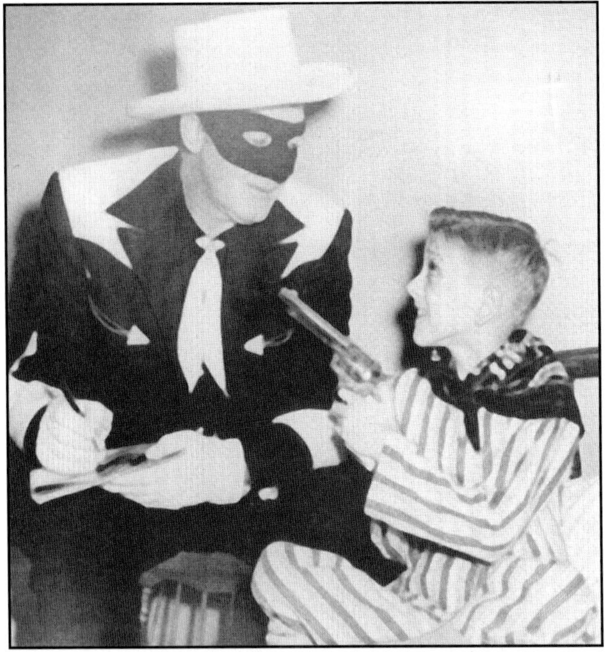

Brace Beemer autographs for bedridden young cowboy (wearing Lone Ranger bandanna) during one of his many hospital visits.

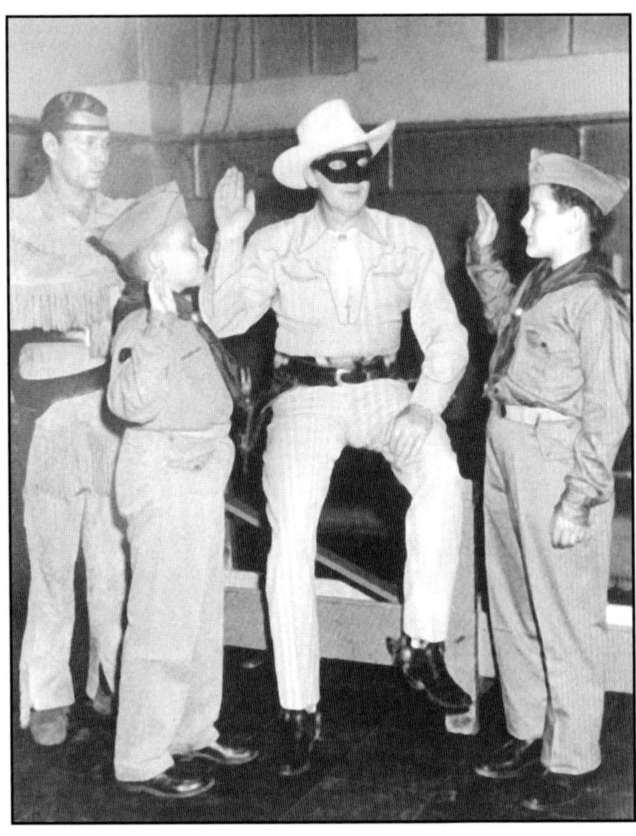

Brace Beemer swears in new Boy Scout "Deputies" (note Lone Ranger Deputy badge on boy at right), as television's Tonto (Jay Silverheels) looks on during a visit to New York.

The programs from Lone Ranger personal appearances are highly collectible. Shown here are programs from Chicago's Olympia Circus in 1943 (the first personal appearance outside of Detroit) and a later program from 1950.

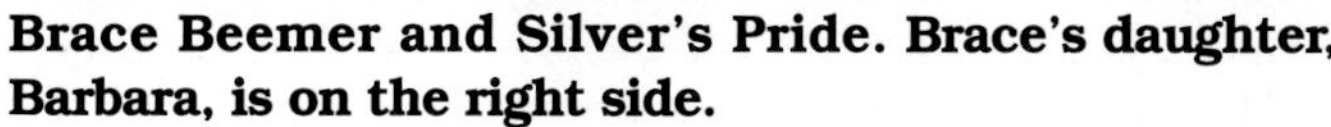
Brace Beemer and Silver's Pride. Brace's daughter, Barbara, is on the right side.

Brace Beemer shows his expertise at duck decoy making to his daughter, Barbara (center) and friend in the family kitchen.

On many occasions Brace had both Trendle's Silver and Brace's own horse Silver's Pride, which he preferred to use on a great many personal appearances.

Brace Beemer was made a frontiersman of Canada, quite an honor. The photo above was taken at the same time.

Brace shaking hands with a group of devoted Lone Ranger deputies at a circus appearance in 1944.

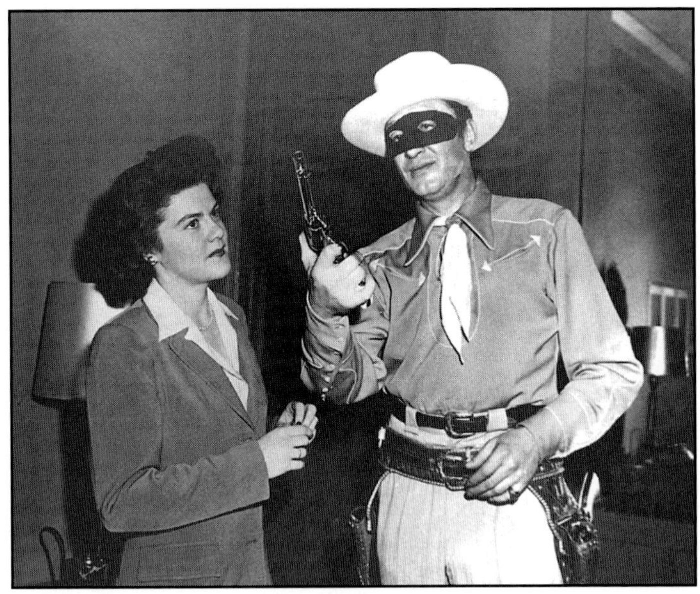

During a personal appearance Brace displays one of his famous six-shooter to a interested young lady.

At the Olympia circus appearance Brace Beemer and Silver take time out to meet the Quiz Kids — Joel Kupperman and Ruth Duskin (ca. 1943).

Very rare photo of two cowboy greats at Madison Square Garden, New York. Needless to say the fans loved seeing both Roy Rogers and the Lone Ranger together.

Mr. and Mrs. Jack Wrather, owners of the Lone Ranger program receive an award along with Brace Beemer in Washington, D.C.

Photo taken in the Beemers' family room. The girl near the fireplace is Brace's daughter, Barbara, with two friends. The dog with Barbara was Blondie, Brace's best pal when after pheasants. The other dog was Lady, Mrs. Beemer's pride and joy.

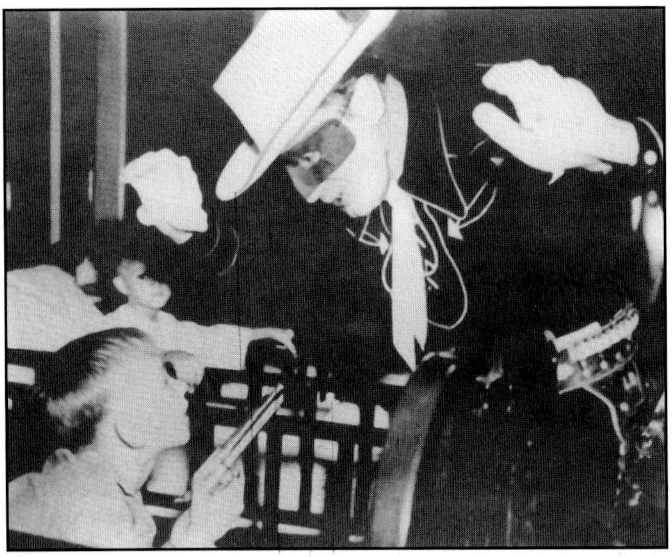

Brace would always visit the local children's hospital and visit with his fans to cheer them on to recovery.

Brace Beemer distributing silver bullets to three Lone Ranger fans. (These are highly prized by collectors today!)

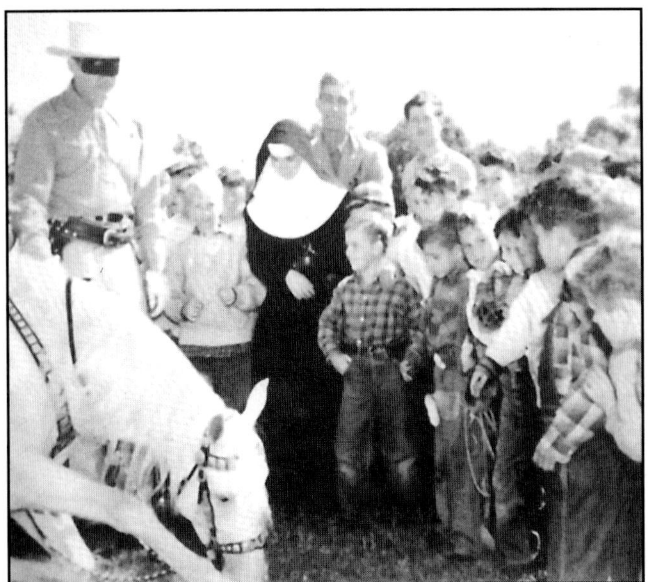

Brace Beemer was always fond of kids and would go out of his way to accomodate them while making personal appearances.

When it came to signing autographs, Brace was always willing, as the photo above shows, Brace surrounded by his fans, with pen in hand.

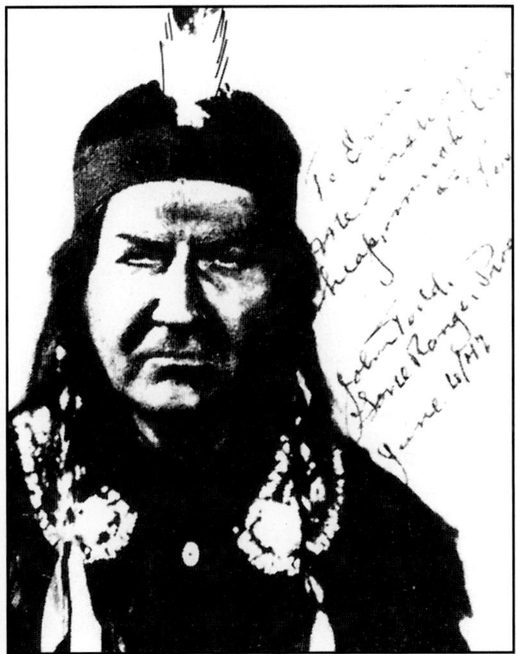

John Todd, a former Shakespearian actor, was in his sixties when he started the role of Tonto and was well into his eighties when he performed in the last live Lone Ranger broadcast.

Photo of Brace Beemer as a guest of J. Edgar Hoover on the rifle range of the F.B.I. (Brace was one of a few to score a perfect round).

Brace and Silver, even in retirement they projected a strong, dynamic, image together.

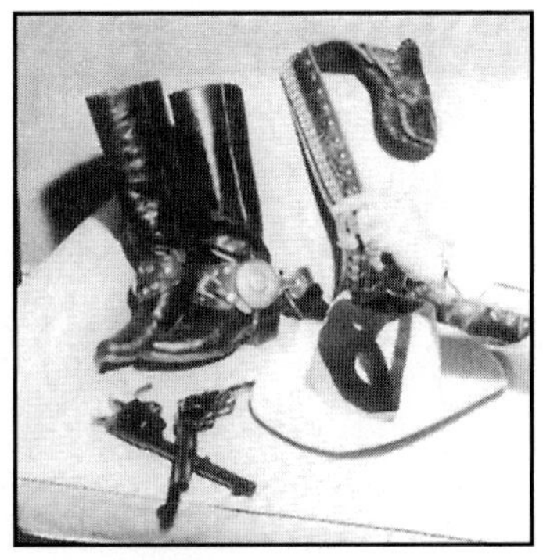

Lone Ranger memorabilia, boots, guns and holsters, hat, mask, and a supply of silver bullets, were loaned to the Burton Historical Collection, Detroit, Michigan, by Mrs. Beemer (also included were all the original photographs used in this book).

JOHN EDGAR HOOVER
DIRECTOR

Federal Bureau of Investigation
United States Department of Justice
Washington, D. C.

November 17, 1944

Mr. Brace Beemer
"The Lone Ranger"
King-Trendle Broadcasting Corporation
17th Floor, Stroh Building
Detroit, Michigan

Dear Mr. Beemer:

I want to thank you so much for your very fine letter of November 13th. It was really a privilege, as well as a pleasure, for me to have the opportunity of meeting you when you were in Washington. I do hope sometime that you will be back so that we will be able to visit together again and for a longer period.

It is indeed grand to have your approbation and confidence. You, yourself, are doing a fine piece of work. Maybe you are too close to your daily task to realize what a constructive piec of building you are doing with the youth of this country. It shows what can be done with a radio program when it is built upon constructive and clean and wholesome lines. We need so many more with the same trend to cope with the younger generation, which basically is clean and sound, but gets out of hand because of adult delinquency rather than juvenile delinquency.

With every good wish, I am

Sincerely,

J. Edgar Hoover

Letter to Brace Beemer from J. Edgar Hoover, Director of Federal Bureau of Investigation, thanking him for his visit to Washington D.C. in 1944.

After Brace retired from the Lone Ranger program, he was always rembered by his fans. Here Brace reads several fan letters on his Oxford, Michigan, farm.

Here Brace is welcomed into the tribe as an honorary chief by the Tribal Council.

Three adoring Indian girls meet their favorite radio hero of the early 40s, Brace Beemer.

Lone Ranger (Brace Beemer) and Silver, a radio legend America took to its heart.

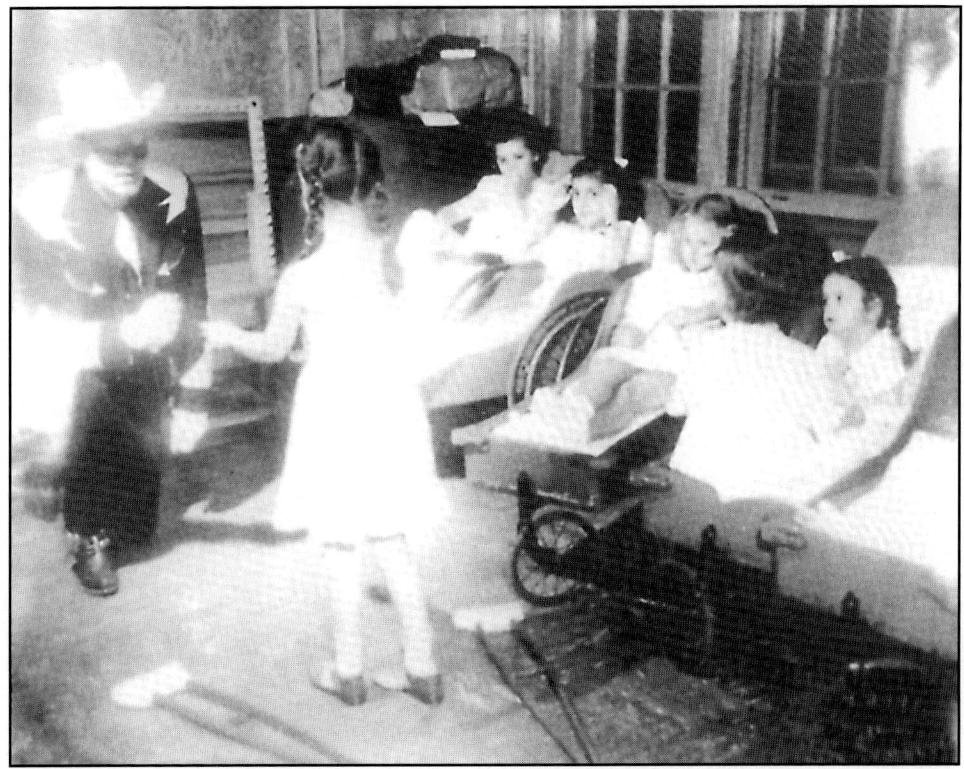

A total believing little girl steps forward for a silver bullet from her hero. (Note old wooden wheelchairs. Early 1930s.)

This photo was taken in South Dakota on a hunting trip by Remington Fire Arms photographers who were following taking pictures. Brace, due to his Lone Ranger contract, had to were a mask.

When the first regularly scheduled broadcast of the Lone Ranger was heard on January 30, 1933, an actor named Jack Deeds played the title role for the first six broadcasts. He was replaced by a young actor, George Stenius (later famous as George Seaton, movie producer). He continued the role for the next three months.

Brace Beemer was then station manager. When Stenius quit the role, Beemer was selected. After playing the role for a few months, Beemer quit to open his own advertising agency. The next actor to play the part was Earl W. Graser. He continued in the role of the Lone Ranger until his untimely death in an automobile accident on April 8, 1941.

Graser had developed an easy-going naturalness that was a strong identification with the listening audience. The producers were baffled as to how they were going to replace him. The next few episodes had a plot to explain his absence. This plot centered around Tonto, and had the Lone Ranger critically wounded and unconscious, silent, except for some heavy breathing.

Finally, the masked man grew stronger and able to speak a few words. The new voice was quite similar to the one heard before, but was deeper, richer, and sterner. Brace Beemer had returned to the role that he was destined to become so closely attached to in the future years. He continued to be the Lone Ranger until the last live broadcast, on Sept. 3, 1954.

As for radio's Tonto, the same actor was heard in every episode. A former Shakespearian actor, John Todd was over 60 years old when he took the part.

In the 1938 serial, the part of the Lone Ranger was played by Lee Powell. Tonto was played by a real-life Indian, Chief Thundercloud.

"The Lone Ranger Rides Again," the 1939 second serial, had a change in actors. This time, Bob Livingston was credited as the Ranger. Chief Thundercloud was once again Tonto.

The Lone Ranger and Tonto reached the television screen in 1948, with Clayton Moore as the masked man and Jay Silverheels as Tonto. After one year, Moore was replaced by actor, John Hart. After one full season, Hart was replaced by Clayton Moore, who continued in the part for the remainder of the TV series.

Once Clayton Moore returned to the role, he would remain in it up until it ended in 1961. Needless to say, he was a top-notch actor and could handle all the action sequences, as well.

In 1956, a big screen technicolor Lone Ranger movie was produced by Warner Brothers. Clayton Moore and Jay Silverheels, a real-life Mohawk Indian, were chosen to portray the two legendary characters.

A second feature-length film, starring the same pair, was released in 1958. It was titled, *The Lone Ranger and the Lost City of Gold.*

Last, but not least, a TV cartoon series was developed in 1970 and shown on Saturday. The voices of the actors were Michael Rye (Lone Ranger) and Shepard Menken (trusty Tonto).

A long-awaited new movie version was introduced in 1981 titled *The Legend of the Lone Ranger,* and was produced by the Wrather Corporation. Klinton Spilsbury was the new Lone Ranger and Michael Horse was cast as Tonto.

However, Beemer on radio and Moore on TV are the actors most identified with the Lone Ranger character. Both were excellent and were responsible for creating and developing the role that audiences have loved and enjoyed for many years.

Lone Ranger Safety Club.

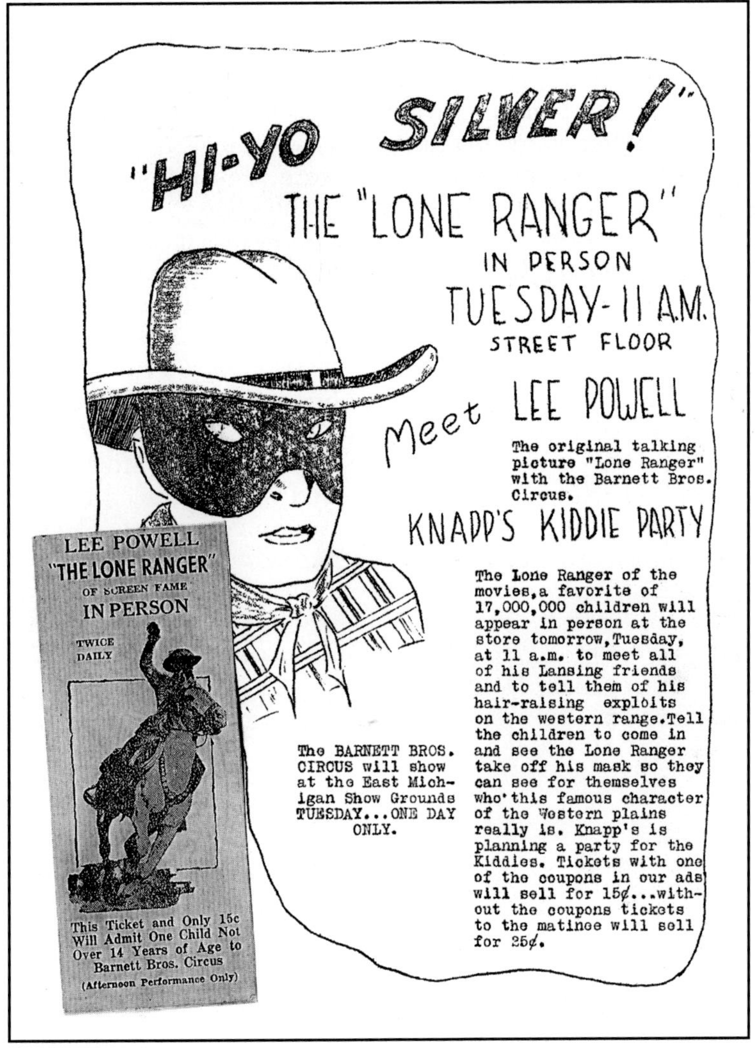

Early advertisement for Barnett Brothers Circus featuring serial Ranger Lee Powell.

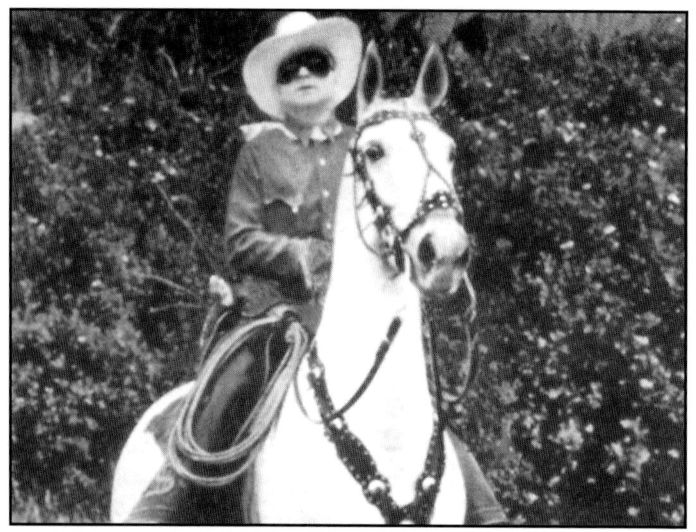

Earl Graser, popular radio Lone Ranger.

Here's Lee Powell, as the Lone Ranger, with sidekick Tonto, as played by Chief Thundercloud (Victor Daniels).

John Todd and Brace Beemer, radio's Tonto and the Lone Ranger.

That's Bob Livingston, in 1939, in the second popular serial about the masked rider.

All of the above actors wore the Lone Ranger mask at one time in the popular 1938 serial *The Lone Ranger*. Shown left to right are Lane Chandler, Lee Powell, Herman Brix, George Letz, and Hal Talarferro.

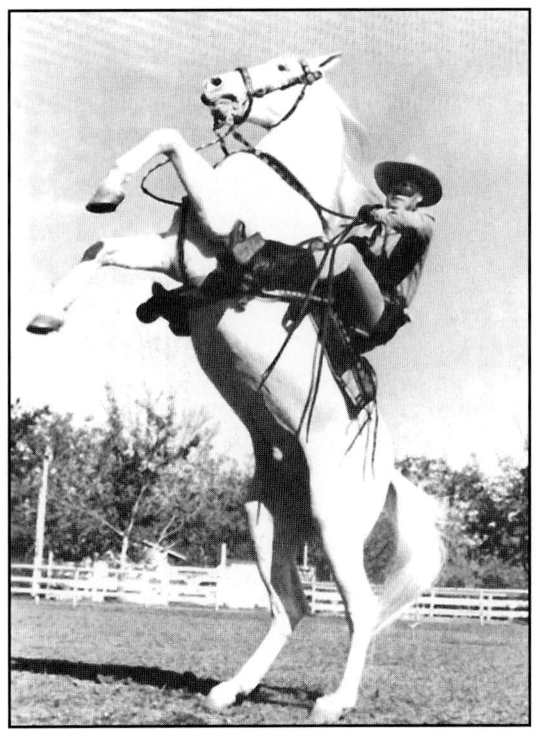

Clayton Moore as the television and movie hero.

Michael Horse and Klinton Spilsbury as the new Tonto and Lone Ranger.

Although he only played the Lone Ranger for one season, John Hart was suited for the part visually, and impressed George W. Trendle. But for some reason, Hart just could not handle the action and acting that the role demanded. He was replaced after 52 epicodes by Clayton Moore, the man that he had replaced a year earlier. However, it is interesting that George W. Trendle always preferred the Hart shows and his interpretations of the Lone Ranger character as being closer to the original radio image of the Lone Ranger character.

Brace Beemer – Most famous of radio rangers.

Earl Graser – He was killed in an auto accident.

George Seaton – First Lone Ranger.

John Hart – He was glad his stint in the role was over.

Clayton Moore – He's the current masked man.

A Word from Our Sponsor

Today, in the advertising community, partnerships between client and agency traditionally are not long-term relationships. It is only on rare occasions that you hear of a company that has used the same spokesperson for their advertising messages over many years.

This has not been the case with the Lone Ranger character. The radio and television shows primarily had two strong sponsorships that lasted for the entire run of the show. These two sponsors were pleased and proud of their association with the Lone Ranger for many, many years. Both sponsors started early in the radio days and continued to the last days of the successful television years.

Although there were, over the years, other sponsors at various times, the two key sponsors closely associated with the fine American virtues of the Lone Ranger program were General Mills and American Bakeries.

Every kid waited to hear deep-voiced announcer, Fred Foy, state just before the middle commercial break..."And now a word from our sponsor." If you were a Lone Ranger Deputy or a Safety Scout, you knew that this message just might mean another Lone Ranger premium would soon be available for one thin dime and a box top from Cheerios or a wrapper from Merita Bread. There was always a frantic hunt for a sharp pencil and a piece of paper. Once you had the information and that all important address, you only had to convince your parents of making that key purchase at the grocery store so that you could tape your dime in with the box top or wrapper and mail it immediately. And then the long wait (three to six weeks) for that special brown box containing the newest and best Lone Ranger premium. Every day after school, you would hopefully ask, "Did I get any mail today?" Then one day, you would come home and there, sitting on the dining room table was that special premium package, with your name on it, that never disappointed young Lone Ranger deputies.

General Mills new breakfast cereal, Cheerios, the famous ready-to-eat cereal developed in the early 1940s, was originally called "Cheerioats." Three years after its introduction, Cheerioats became Cheerios, a name that has proven to be worthy of the product's popularity over the long years. To advertise the new Cheerios, General Mills was smart enough to employ one of the most successful radio serial heroes, The Lone Ranger.

General Mills' sponsorship of the Lone Ranger radio program began on the ABC network on May 4, 1941. When the program was picked up by the NBC network, on May 30, 1955, General Mills was still the sponsor and they continued in that role right up until the show's cancellation on May 25, 1956.

The television show was also sponsored by General Mills, with the first show viewed by the American public on September 15, 1949, and the last show at the end of the 1961 season.

The major products sponsored by the masked rider's program over the years were Kix (approximate dates 1941 – 1948); Cheerios (1944 – 1958); and the final years included Wheaties and Trix (1958 – 1961).

The most successful radio premium promotion was the Lone Ranger Frontier Town. In addition to the premium offer of four special map sections of Frontier Town along with the total of 72 models, special models were also printed on the back of Cheerios packages. Each of the special sections was offered for 10¢ and a Cheerios box top. However, not every kid was fortunate enough to get four dimes and four box tops from his parents to get the entire town. I remember very clearly that a box of Cheerios cost 18¢, quite expensive for a dry cereal in 1948! Most kids decided on the section of the map that included the Lone Ranger's secret hideout, since that section was heavily promoted, and if they could only get the money for one section, that was the most important section to have. This is a big factor in why this complete premium is so expensive and hard to locate today. Also, there were additional models on the back of Cheerios packages that were needed to complete your Frontier Town.

However, the Frontier Town promotions continued for one year, with each local program taking place in the town so that the listeners could follow the action with their sections of Frontier Town. Then a special announcement was made that a special anniversary show of the Lone Ranger would be broadcast from Cheyenne, Wyoming, which interestingly enough, was renamed Frontier Town. The show was broadcast from the center of town on June 30, 1948, with the original cast dressed for the special show. A one hour ABC special news report was also broadcast that day, officially named Cheyenne — the

Lone Ranger Frontier Town. Guests included the president of ABC, president of General Mills, the Governor of Wyoming and Mayor of Cheyenne, and, of course, Brace Beemer. To my knowledge, this was the only news special ever created to honor a radio show.

General Mills held an auction of over 1,000 radio premiums, including many popular Lone Ranger premiums. This auction was held on July 29, 1984, with a special catalog, selling for $5.00, listing the items available. All proceeds from the auction were given to the Como Zoological Society in Minnesota. The bid items were considered by many to be overpriced, but this was expected since all purchases would be tax deductible. I was pleased to personally obtain several choice items for my collection, and also had the pleasure of working with representatives of General Mills on the catalog and providing assistance on some of the materials. The auction was quite successful and attendance was exceptional, creating a lot of additional interest in the Lone Ranger, Green Hornet, and Jack Armstrong premiums and the old radio shows themselves.

"Hi-Yo, Silver – The Lone Ranger" first rang throughout the southland in September 1938. That now famous introduction opened an important chapter for American Bakeries' Merita Bread and has proven over the years to be one of the most successful ventures in the annals of modern advertising.

When Merita brought the Lone Ranger, with his stirring radio adventures, to the South for the first time in 1938, the broadcasts were presented three times a week over 28 stations. As a result of the popularity of the radio programs, the number of stations continued to grow until in 1951, a total of 77 stations were broadcasting the show through the American Broadcasting Company network.

Another dramatic chapter in Merita's Lone Ranger story opened in October of 1949, when American Bakeries began a weekly half-hour television broadcast of the Lone Ranger over the TV stations of the ABC Network. By doing this, they became a true pioneer in this spectacular new medium (the first company to sponsor a network television program). Merita's telecasts began over stations in Atlanta, Birmingham, Jacksonville, Miami, and New Orleans. Later, stations in Charlotte and Greensboro, and others, were added to the network. Over the years, Merita's Lone Ranger broadcasts have consistently ranked among the top in popularity in TV, just as they have for many years in radio. Along with the masked rider's programs, Merita also has sponsored the Lone Ranger's Safety Club for many years.

An article that appeared in a company publication from 1951 stated, "When the Lone Ranger's first cry of Hi-Yo Silver rang through Meritaland, its impetus was felt by everyone. For 13 sales-packed years, Merita has ridden with the Lone Ranger for greater sales and good will, but in April 1951, the Miami Plant realized to the fullest extent the power of the man with the black mask. When the famed Lone Ranger made a personal appearance in Miami's great Orange Bowl, the town rocked with the echo of the masked rider's cry. It was one of the greatest experiences any company could enjoy!"

Another quote from the same article, "An eventful day was the 1938 Sales Meeting, when the Lone Ranger program was introduced as part of Merita's advertising. The wearing of the ten gallon hat, the bandanna, and the spirit the salesmen had in introducing this advertising had all the kids and many grownups yelling Hi-Yo Silver over the whole territory. It would be impossible to measure the value of the Lone Ranger in our sales success over the past 13 years."

American Bakeries, like General Mills, knew how to promote and merchandise the Lone Ranger. The Lone Ranger Safety Club offered a multitude of premiums for members of the club. The Merita premiums — paper cutouts, tin signs, badges, masks, silver bullets, letters offering the premiums — are sought after by collectors across the country.

The entire Merita family is proud of its long, happy, and prosperous association with the Lone Ranger in his capacity as public ambassador of good will. They enthusiastically echo the sentiments of the announcer at the Madison Square Garden Rodeo (where Lone Ranger and Silver were the featured attractions on September 26, 1951) who hailed the masked rider as he rode triumphantly from the great arena at the end of each performance, with the words, "Goodbye, Lone Ranger and Tonto. May you ride the airways forever!"

The author's daughter, Jennifer, talking Clayton Moore into autographing a copy of her father's first book.

WYOMING

EXECUTIVE DEPARTMENT

LESTER C. HUNT
GOVERNOR
CHEYENNE, WYOMING

June 30, 1948

Lone Ranger:

Because you personify friendliness - justice and fair play.

Because you have instilled in millions of young Americans the philosophy of the Golden Rule, and for your great contribution to American boys and girls for making America a better place to live, I take great pleasure in behalf of my State to honor you and I do so by designating you officially a co-captain of the Wyoming Highway Courtesy Patrol, and your co-captain, Bradley will present you with, and place on your breast the official badge of your office.

Lester Hunt
Governor

Letter from Governor Lester C. Hunt officially designating the Lone Ranger (Brace Beemer) a co-captain of the Wyoming Highway Courtesy Patrol on June 30, 1948, during the Frontier Town Celebration.

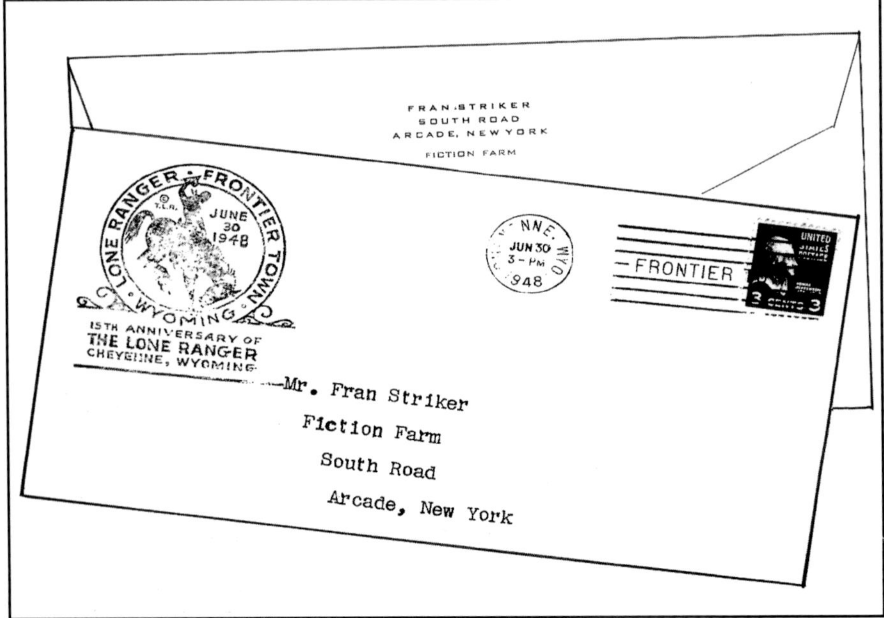

Special Frontier Town postmark envelope that Fran Striker had sent to his home in Arcade, New York (from the author's collection).

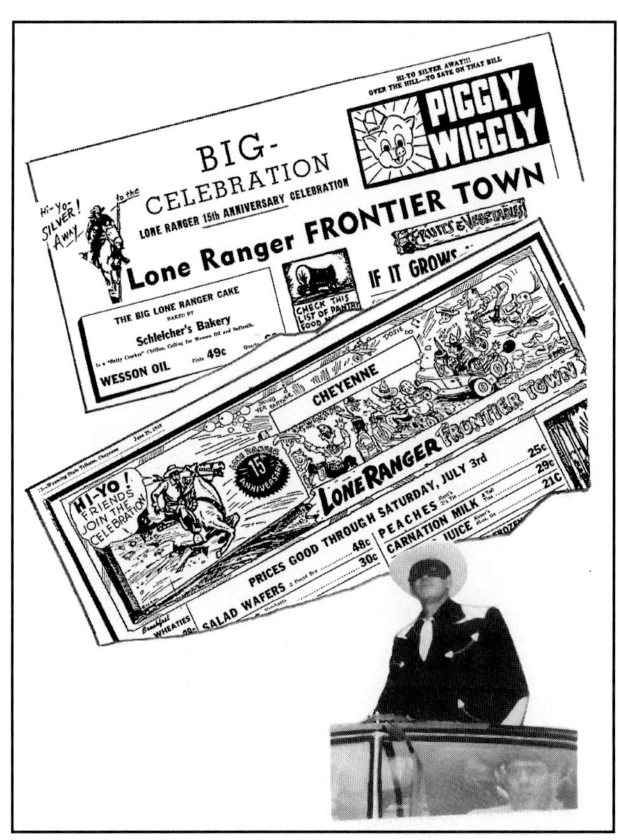

**Copies of local newspaper advertising the Lone Ranger Frontier Town promotion.
Brace Beemer leading the special parade activities prior to performing the Lone Ranger broadcast.**

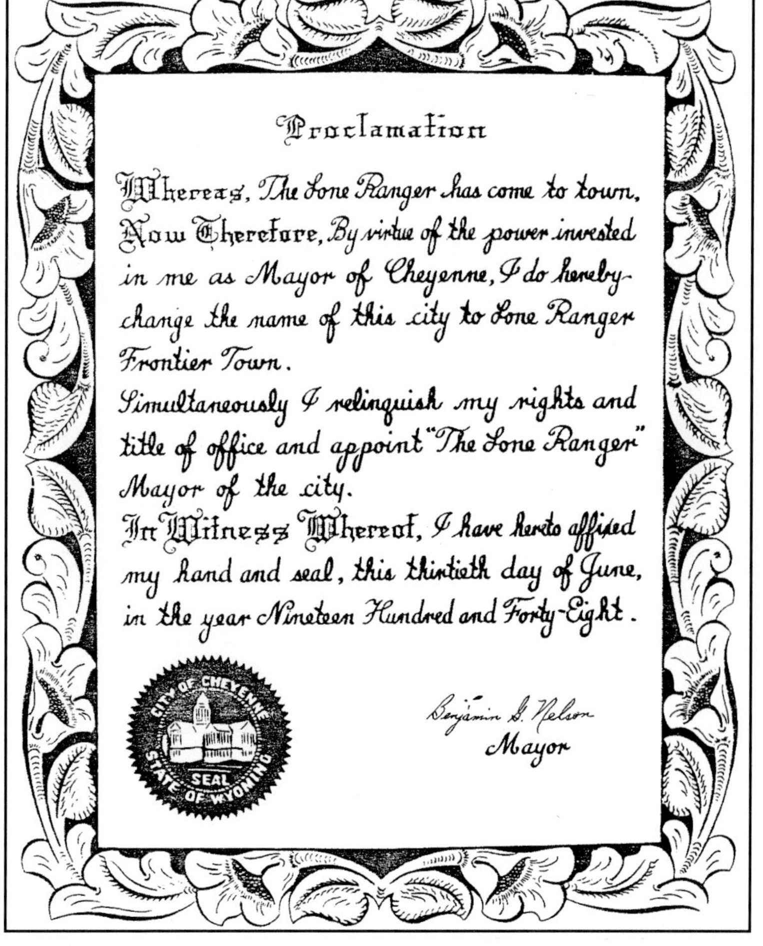

Proclamation

Whereas, The Lone Ranger has come to town,
Now Therefore, By virtue of the power invested in me as Mayor of Cheyenne, I do hereby change the name of this city to Lone Ranger Frontier Town.
Simultaneously I relinquish my rights and title of office and appoint "The Lone Ranger" Mayor of the city.
In Witness Whereof, I have hereto affixed my hand and seal, this thirtieth day of June, in the year Nineteen Hundred and Forty-Eight.

CITY OF CHEYENNE SEAL STATE OF WYOMING

Benjamin G. Nelson
Mayor

Copy of the special proclamation naming the City of Cheyenne the official Lone Ranger Frontier Town signed by Mayor Benjamin G. Nelson.

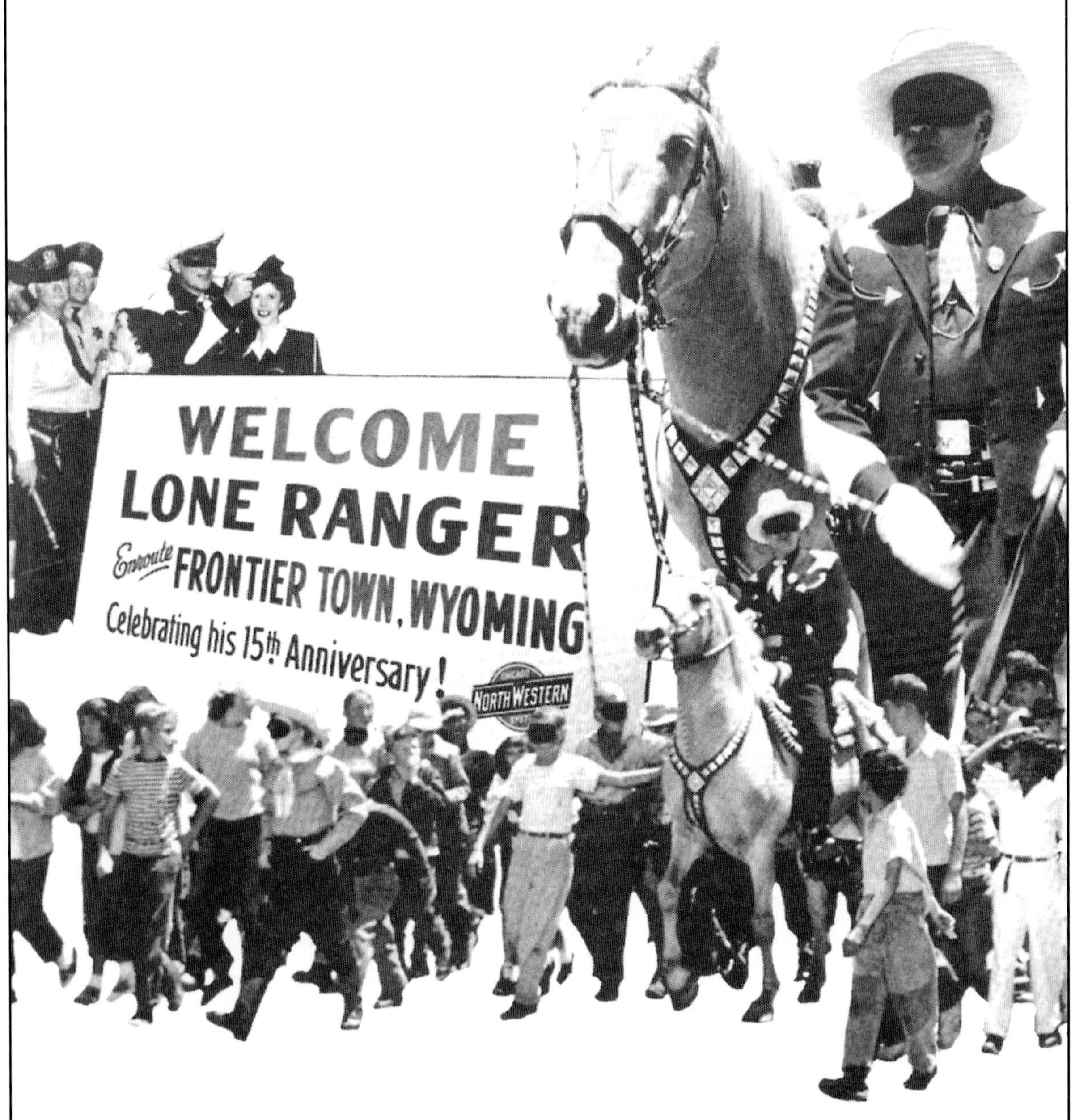

Entire town turns out to celebrate The Lone Ranger's fifteenth year on radio . . . Oldsters, parents, children laugh and cry at sight of hero.

On June 30th last, citizens of Cheyenne, Wyo., awoke to find themselves in *Lone Ranger Frontier Town.* City fathers had so designated it for that day to honor radio's top hero, celebrating his fifteenth year on the air by visiting town. Streets were decorated with bunting, store interiors and fronts were changed to look like old-time general stores, entire population turned out to greet Lone Ranger, whose fight against juvenile delinquency adds to reputation as strong character who can do no wrong.

Ranger takes cue for broadcast, during which he's proclaimed honorary sheriff and honorary mayor, gets keys to town.

En route, Ranger stopped at Illinois Hospital School for Crippled Children in Chicago, where he met young admirers, told them about Silver, his horse.

Above: Miss Frontier Days (Susan Murray) presents him with immense cake. Left: Children wore black mask which always conceals Ranger's identity.

MOVIE STARS PARADE 69

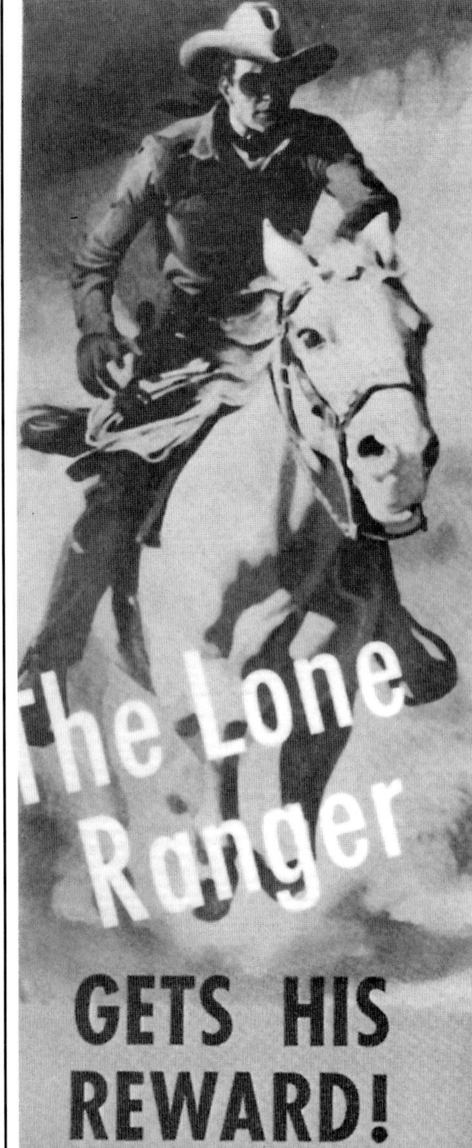

GETS HIS REWARD!

The last day in June of this year was a big day in the lives of a lot of soft drawlin', hard shootin' fellows from New York and down around Cheyenne. That was the day on which Cheyenne, Wyoming, changed its name to "Lone Ranger Frontier Town" in honor of the Lone Ranger's fifteenth anniversary on the air. Beginning at noon, the rest of the day was given over to celebration as the city's 35-thousand inhabitants went "Wild West" in a big way to greet Brace Beemer, who plays the legendary figure on the air, and a bunch of key men from the ABC network and the sponsor's organization, including network president Mark Woods, sponsor L. M. Perrin and agency president H. M. Dancer. The town went all out on the celebration which also marked the ending of a nation-wide contest to aid crippled children which had been conducted through the Lone Ranger show. Lone Ranger Frontier Town, by official proclamation of the Mayor, Honorable Benjamin C. Nelson, even used a special post office cancellation stamp reading "Frontier Town" on all the city's mail. It was all done in real Old West style, except for one little anachronism—The Lone Ranger came to town on a special train at the Union Pacific station — but he quickly changed his mount to "Silver."

56

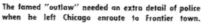

The famed "outlaw" needed an extra detail of police when he left Chicago enroute to Frontier town.

The Lone Ranger hopped a Union Pacific streamliner for the Frontier Town celebration.

The "masked man" thanks Cheyenne's Mayor B. G. Nelson for the naming of Lone Ranger Frontier Town.

The Lone Ranger and Gov. Lester C. Hunt posed beside the birthday cake weighing three hundred pounds.

This mammoth-size postcard, signed by thousands of Wyoming youngsters, was Lone Ranger's gift.

Radio & Television Best — October 1948

The name of Cheyenne was officially changed to the Lone Ranger Frontier Town by official proclamation.

Preparing for the hero's visit were: Miss Frontier Days, Susan Murray, and friend Norma Jean Bell.

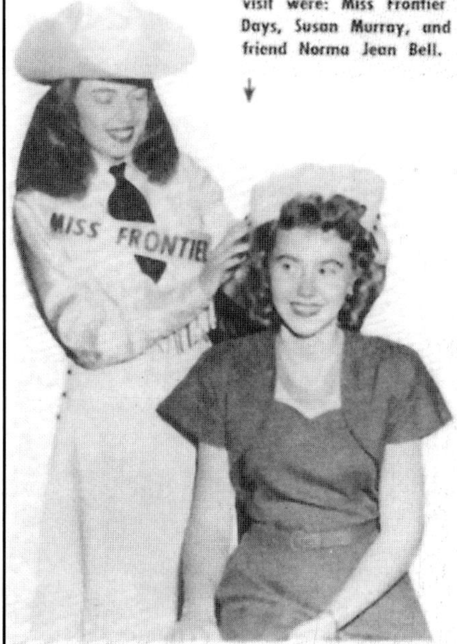

Little Tommy Sykes, representing the National Society for Crippled Children, was the envy of all the kids.

Part of the crowd of 30,000 people in Cheyenne that turned up for the day of old, wild west festivities.

The Lone Ranger was inducted into the Ogallala Sioux Indian tribe by Princess Blue Water. Tonto liked it.

The parade featured a replica of the old time Unio Pacific trains used in old wild west days of Wyomin

The Radio & Television Picture Magazine

Cheerios Frontier Town cereal box is one of the most popular collector boxes. A total of nine boxes were needed to complete the Frontier Town models (1948).

Kix Airbase cereal box, another popular Lone Ranger collector box from 1945.

Dear Comrades:

I'm delighted to know you've joined together to form your own neighborhood Chapter of The Lone Ranger Safety Club.

Here is your Club Charter, with your Chapter Number duly entered and sealed with the official gold seal of the Club. Each of the ten Charter Members of your Chapter should sign his or her name in one of the ten blank spaces. The Charter is not official until all ten have signed.

Now here are some suggestions for conducting your Chapter of The Lone Ranger Safety Club.

First, elect the following officers: Chief Ranger, First and Second Assistant Chief Rangers; Recording Ranger, who keeps the minutes of all meetings; Corresponding Ranger, who writes the club's official letters; Treasurer Ranger, Librarian Ranger; Ranger-at-Arms, Master-of-Ceremonies and Official Scout.

Have a Clubroom -- maybe in a member's home -- where you can hold regular meetings, in secret. Preserve your Charter carefully in the clubroom. Always wear your Lone Ranger Safety Badges at meetings. If any boys or girls in your Chapter do not have badges, my radio programs will tell how to get them, easily and quickly. Discuss safety matters at meetings, when all members should report what they are doing to aid the cause of Safety.

Enter into every Safety movement in your city or neighborhood. Make your Club's influence for Safety felt in every possible way. Ask your teachers to help you organize your school for Safety. I would like to know all about your Chapter. Write and tell me what your Chapter is doing for Safety. Any officer of your Chapter who writes me should sign his or her name and title as a Club officer.

Have your friends join the Safety Club, and enroll them in your Chapter. Every boy and girl in your Chapter must first be a member of The Lone Ranger Safety Club. They can join by asking any grocer for a free card.

I wish the best of everything to your Chapter and all its members. Until my next broadcast,

HI-YO, SILVER!

Lone Ranger

THE LONE RANGER

P. S. Remember, every member should be loyal to MERITA. Each member should ask Mother to be sure to always serve MERITA Bread and MERITA Cakes.

This letter from the Lone Ranger promoting the Safety Club of 1939 was included with the Official Charter for the Club.

LONE RANGER SAFETY CLUB
SPONSORED BY MERITA BREAD AND CAKE

Dear Victory Ranger:

Here is the picture of yours truly riding Silver, that you asked for.

Now, there are other surprises ahead, which the Merita folks and I want you to have as rewards for your loyalty to the Safety Club and its Victory Rules.

The next present we have for you is a handsome picture of my faithful friend Tonto, riding his horse, Scout. It is the same size as the one of Silver and me, and is a companion picture to it. Every boy and girl will surely want to have one of these pictures of Tonto and Scout, printed in attractive colors. You can obtain one, at no cost, by getting three new members to join the Lone Ranger Safety Club.

It is inspiring to know that you, and many thousands of boys and girls, have pledged to help Uncle Sam by following the Victory rules of our club. Certainly it is important to have every boy and girl we know pledged to follow those rules, just like you are doing. That will be a real help to our country.

That's why I will send you a picture of Tonto and Scout if you will get three of your friends to join. Here's all you have to do. It's easy. With this letter I am enclosing three Lone Ranger Safety Club pledge tickets. Show them to three of your friends or schoolmates and ask each of them to fill in his name and complete address. (Ask your friends to print their names and addresses plainly.) Then just write me a short letter, saying "Here are the tickets for three new members. Please send my picture of Tonto." Print your own name and complete address plainly, and don't forget to put the three tickets in with your letter. Send your letter and the tickets to: The Lone Ranger, care of Merita Bread, Atlanta, Ga.

When I send you the picture, I will tell you how to get the next free reward. Meanwhile, I hope you're listening to all my radio programs.

Your friend,

Lone Ranger

THE LONE RANGER

VNF HJOCZM OJ BZO
HZMDOV WMZVY AJM
TJP VGRVTN

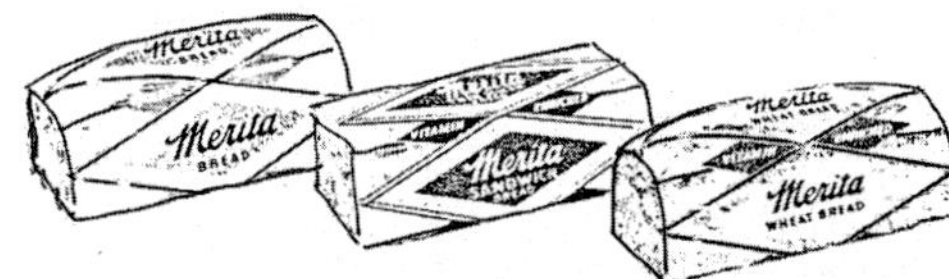

Enjoy Merita's Big Three--- The Bread Winners of America

Copyright, 1943, The Lone Ranger, Inc. (2)

TUNE IN "THE LONE RANGER" THREE TIMES A WEEK OVER A STATION NEAR YOU

Merita bread promotion offering a full-color picture of Tonto and Scout. Valued at $75.00 to $150.00 each. A complete set of both pictures would command even a higher price.

The New

HEADQUARTERS

LONE RANGER SAFETY CLUB

SPONSORED BY MERITA BREAD AND CAKE

Dear Safety Ranger:

Welcome to my new club! I'm happy to enroll you officially as a fully qualified Safety Ranger, and I'll depend on you to help me promote safety. By doing so, you render yourself, your parents and your community a valuable service.

Our club is really new in every way. There are new rules, a brand new Secret Code, and many surprises in store for you as an active member. The new rules are shown on the enclosed Pledge Certificate. Sign it and put it on your wall or mirror, so you can learn the rules by heart and observe them every day. Your Official Membership Card is enclosed, too. Sign it and take good care of it. Don't show it to anyone not a member of the new club (except Mother or Dad) because on the back is my new Secret Code, which members use to exchange messages.

Nearly 400,000 boys and girls joined my original Safety Club, sponsored by the Merita folks, and they've done splendid safety work. Our new rules are even finer than the old ones, because they help prevent accidents not only on the street, but at home and at school, too. Since everything is new, it's important for all members of the original club to join the New Lone Ranger Safety Club. I'll count on you to see that your friends join it.

You'll Surely want all the big surprises which are in store for members of the new club. Here's the first one—the Lone Ranger Mask, like I wear. You can get one free. Just send me the names of three housewives who promise to try Merita Bread. Simply write their names on a postcard and say, "Please send my Lone Ranger Mask." Print your name and complete address plainly, so I'll know where to send the mask. Address the card to The Lone Ranger, care of Merita Bread, Atlanta, Ga. Don't delay. Send for your mask right away.

CYF'E OVN STP Q RVUL FVBYFJYU IVU ESIYFO SCRSOE.

Your friend,

Lone Ranger

THE LONE RANGER

P.S. LOOK! After you send for your mask, I'll tell you how to get other grand gifts, like the Tonto Headdress, the Lone Ranger Lucky Coin, official Safety Club Badge, and a Charter for your own Safety Club.

TUNE IN "THE LONE RANGER" THREE TIMES A WEEK OVER A STATION NEAR YOU

This letter stated over 400,000 boys and girls have joined the Lone Ranger Safety Club and offered the Lone Ranger mask with the Merita logo from 1942.

The New

HEADQUARTERS

LONE RANGER SAFETY CLUB

SPONSORED BY MERITA BREAD AND CAKE

Dear Safety Ranger:

Here's your Lone Ranger Lucky Coin. Isn't it a beauty? Surely you'll want to take good care of it and be sure that you never lose it.

Now don't forget that your loyalty to Merita makes it possible for me not only to bring you my radio programs, but also to carry on the work of the new Lone Ranger Safety Club, and to offer you all these fine free gifts too. Each of these surprises is a reward for your loyalty. So, be sure to enjoy Merita Bread and Cakes at your house always, and tell all your friends that when they eat Merita Products, they help to support the new Lone Ranger Safety Club.

And say, there are still more good things in store for you. Here is a picture of the next one. It's the official Lone Ranger Safety Club Badge... an emblem of honor you'll be proud to wear. Don't fail to send for one. It's a fine star-shaped, gold-colored badge with red and blue lettering which shows you are an official Safety Ranger. And it's easy for you to get one. Just write on a postcard, the words "Please send my Safety Club Badge" and then print your name and complete address plainly, so I'll know where to send the badge. Then, at the bottom of the postcard, write the word "MERITA" in the secret code of our club. Send for yours right away. Mail the postcard to The Lone Ranger, care of Merita Bread, Atlanta, Ga.

UYKYKAYU. KYUQFS AUYSP STP HSLYE KSLY VNU HCNA DVEEQACY.

Your friend,

Lone Ranger

THE LONE RANGER

P.S. Do you want to have your own neighborhood charter of The Lone Ranger Safety Club? After you send for the badge, I'll tell you how to form a club and get the handsome club charter.

TUNE IN "THE LONE RANGER" THREE TIMES A WEEK OVER A STATION NEAR YOU

Letter from Merita offering the free Lone Ranger Safety Club Badge. All you had to do was send for it on a postcard with your name and address so the Lone Ranger would know where to send the badge.

Letter that was sent with Lone Ranger Mask from 1942. The letter offered a Tonto Headdress for getting three housewives to try Merita bread. The value of the mask is $15.00 to $25.00 and the Tonto headdress is of equal value to collectors.

The New

HEADQUARTERS

LONE RANGER SAFETY CLUB

SPONSORED BY MERITA BREAD AND CAKE

Dear Safety Ranger:

Here's your Lone Ranger Mask. The Merita people and I are pleased to send it to you as a reward for being a loyal member of my new club. I hope you'll have a lot of fun with it.

Now, there are still more swell rewards ahead, and I'll tell you about the next one in a minute. First, a few words about our new club rules. I hope you know all ten by heart and that you keep your Pledge Certificate where you can see it every day, so you'll obey the rules always.

Here's another way to help further the cause of safety. Tell all your friends about the new Lone Ranger Safety Club and the many fine surprises for each member. I'm anxious to have everyone who was a member of my original club to join the new one.

Now for news of my next gift for you. It's a swell Indian headdress, like Tonto wears. This picture of it can't begin to show how colorful it is, with its big bright feather. Here's how you can get a genuine Tonto headdress free. Just send me, on a postcard, the names of three housewives who promise to try Merita Cakes. It's easy to get friends or neighbors to try delicious Merita Cakes, specially when you tell them about the New Lone Ranger Safety Club and its fine rules. Write their names on the postcard and say: "Please send my Tonto Headdress." Be sure to print your name and complete address plainly. Do it right away. Send the postcard to: The Lone Ranger, care of Merita Bread, Atlanta, Ga.

TVR, "EV CVTB" NTFQC KO TYGF KYUQFS DUVBUSK.

Your friend,

Lone Ranger

THE LONE RANGER

P.S. Say, after you send for your headdress, I'll tell you how to get other gifts free, like the Lone Ranger Lucky Coin, official Safety Club Badge, and a Safety Club Charter.

TUNE IN "THE LONE RANGER" THREE TIMES A WEEK OVER A STATION NEAR YOU

The New

HEADQUARTERS

LONE RANGER SAFETY CLUB

SPONSORED BY MERITA BREAD AND CAKE

Dear Safety Ranger:

It's a real pleasure to send you your Tonto Headdress and I look forward to sending you the other rewards for your loyalty that the Merita Bakers want you to enjoy.

Now, I know you want to help me get more members, because the more boys and girls we have in our new club, the more accidents we can prevent. Also, I'm sure you want your friends to belong, so you can exchange messages in my new Secret Code and work together for Safety. So Merita has a gift you'll want to get right away.

This gift is a beautiful, bright, shining silvered Lone Ranger Lucky Coin. One side shows our club emblem, and the other shows Silver's Lucky Horseshoe. It's a good luck token you'll want to treasure always. Here's how to get it free. With this letter are three safety club cards. Get three of your friends to fill out the cards so they can join the club. Then, put the filled-out cards in an envelope with a slip of paper showing your name and complete address printed plainly, and the words, "Please send my Lucky Coin." Address the envelope to The Lone Ranger, care of Merita Bread, Atlanta, Ga.

SEL KVFJYU FV AY ENUY FJY AUYSP OVN YSF QE KYUQFS.

Your friend,

Lone Ranger

THE LONE RANGER

P.S. More surprises ahead! After you send for the coin, I'll tell you how to get a free official Safety Club badge and a handsome charter for your own safety club.

TUNE IN "THE LONE RANGER" THREE TIMES A WEEK OVER A STATION NEAR YOU

The year 1942 was jam packed with special offers for Lone Ranger Safety Rangers. This letter was sent with the Tonto headdress and offered the free Lone Ranger Lucky Coin for getting three friends to join the Club.

LONE RANGER SAFETY CLUB

SPONSORED BY MERITA BREAD AND CAKE

Dear Victory Ranger:

Here is your official badge of membership in the Lone Ranger Safety Club. Take good care of it, because it will remind you and other folks of the Victory rules of the club, which you promised to follow. It shows you are doing your part to help Uncle Sam.

Now, wouldn't you like to have your own neighborhood chapter of the Lone Ranger Safety Club, right in your block, your school or your neighborhood? Wouldn't you like to have your friends band together with you as members? Just think of all the things you can do, for Victory, working together as a chapter of our club!

Working together, you can round up lots of scrap metal to turn in. You can have club activities that will be a real help to your community's safety drive. And what's more, you can have loads of fun, with picnics, hikes, sporting events, parades and other club activities.

The Merita folks and I believe you would enjoy having a Lone Ranger Club among your friends, and we know it's a fine way for you to get together and help protect your country's safety. So we have reserved for you a handsome charter for your club. You can obtain it absolutely free. Here's all you need to do. It's easy as ABC. Just write one word for me in your secret Victory code of the Lone Ranger Safety Club. Here's the word: Merita. The code is on the back of the official membership card I sent you, and it won't take but a minute to write that one word in the code, on a penny postcard. Then say: "Please send me a club charter," and be sure to print your name and complete address plainly. Mail the card to: The Lone Ranger, care of Merita Bread, Atlanta, Ga.

CHARTER

I'll be looking for a card from you, so that I can send your charter quickly. Meanwhile, listen to all my Merita radio programs.

Your friend,

DO CZGKN OCZ GJIZ MVIBZM OJ
WMDIB PN CDN MVYDJ KMJBMVHN VIY
CDN NVAZOT XGPW RCZI RZ WPT
HZMDOV WMZVY VIY XVFZN

Lone Ranger

THE LONE RANGER

Enjoy Merita's Big Three--- The Bread Winners of America

Copyright, 1943 The Lone Ranger, Inc.

(4)

TUNE IN "THE LONE RANGER" THREE TIMES A WEEK OVER A STATION NEAR YOU

A 1943 Merita letter that was sent with Lone Ranger Safety Club Badge. The letter offered the Club Charter Certificate free to members. Value today $35.00 to $95.00.

HEADQUARTERS

c/o MERITA BREAD
BOX 2180, ATLANTA 1, GA.

LONE RANGER SAFETY CLUB

SPONSORED BY MERITA BREAD AND CAKE

Dear Safety Ranger:

Welcome into the Lone Ranger Safety Club! I'm proud to have you working with me for safety and good citizenship.

Your Pledge Certificate is enclosed. Put it on your wall or mirror. It will remind you to observe its ten rules every day. Besides rules for safety, it has rules that will help you and your fellow members to be good citizens. They encourage respect for other people's property, fair play and good habits, service to our country and obedience to our parents.

Also enclosed is your Official Membership Card. On the back of it is the Secret Code of our club, which members use to exchange messages.

Now, let me tell you about a big surprise the Merita folks have for you as a reward for your loyalty to the Safety Club. My faithful friend, Tonto, has drawn an interesting map of the great Western Land where our adventures take place. There's a copy of it ready and waiting for you, free.

I can't begin to say how much you will enjoy Tonto's map. It shows the trails we ride . . . and dozens of the places where you've heard us track down outlaws. It shows where various Indian tribes live. It's more than 17 by 22 inches in size, printed in many colors. You'll want it on the wall of your room, and you can have lots of fun following our future radio adventures on this big, colorful, exciting map.

Here's how to get your map, free. Just ask three housewives to try delicious Merita, next time they buy bread. Write their names on a postcard and say: "Please send your map". Then, be sure to print your own name and complete address plainly. Send the postcard to: TONTO, CARE OF MERITA BREAD, BOX 2180, ATLANTA 1, GEORGIA.

Tonto will send you your map. When he does, you'll learn about more grand rewards you can obtain free. Meanwhile, be sure to listen to all our radio programs, for more news about the Safety Club.

Your friend

YUJH BJON NENAH MJH

Lone Ranger

THE LONE RANGER

Enjoy Merita's Big Three . . . Favorites of Active Boys and Girls

Another Merita Bread promotional letter offering Tonto's map. These promotional letters are also hard to find and have a value to collectors of $35.00 to $75.00 each.

LONE RANGER SAFETY CLUB
SPONSORED BY MERITA BREAD AND CAKE

Dear Victory Ranger:

I'm proud that you want to work with me to help Uncle Sam for Victory. I shall count on you to do all you can to help back up our country's fighting men.

With this letter is your Victory Pledge Certificate. Sign it and put it up in your room where it will remind you every day to help Uncle Sam by following its ten rules. Five of them give you ways you can take part in the war effort. The other five are safety rules, which are now more important than ever, because every accident we have in America helps our country's enemies.

I also enclose your official membership card. On the back of it is my Secret Victory Code, which members use to exchange messages.

While they last, I have a number of fine presents that the Merita people and I want you to have, as rewards for your loyalty to our Safety Club and its Victory Pledge. I'll tell you about the first one now, and after you send for it, I'll tell you about the other surprises you can get free.

Many of my young friends have written to ask for a picture of me riding my horse, Silver. So the Merita folks have had a picture made that shows Silver leaping forward, with all his powerful muscles bulging, to carry me away on the trail to adventure. It has been reproduced in beautiful colors, and is suitable for framing. Here is how you can obtain it, free.

Just send me the names of three housewives who say they will try delicious Merita Bread. Write their names on a postcard and say, "Please send the picture of you and Silver." Be sure to print your own name and complete address plainly. Send the postcard to: The Lone Ranger, care of Merita Bread, Atlanta, Ga.

When I send you the picture, I will tell you about other gifts you can obtain free, and how you may get them. And meanwhile, listen to all my radio programs, for announcements about the ways you can work with me for Victory and for Safety.

Your friend,

Lone Ranger

THE LONE RANGER

ZIEJT QDOVHDI-ZIMDXCZY
HZMDOV WMZVY ZQZMT YVT.

Enjoy Merita's Big Three--- The Bread Winners of America

Copyright, 1941, The Lone Ranger, Inc. (1)

TUNE IN "THE LONE RANGER" THREE TIMES A WEEK OVER A STATION NEAR YOU

Merita promotional letter promoting the Lone Ranger Victory Pledge Certificate from 1941. During the war years many premiums tied-in with the Victory Club and how members could help the Lone Ranger and Uncle Sam.

April 1951

Merita

FAMILY MAGAZINE

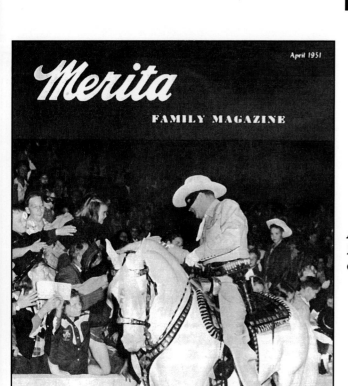

A cover from American Bakeries *Merita Family Magazine* from April 1951 with Brace Beemer on the cover.

As a Victory Ranger I Solemnly Promise to Obey My Victory Pledge to

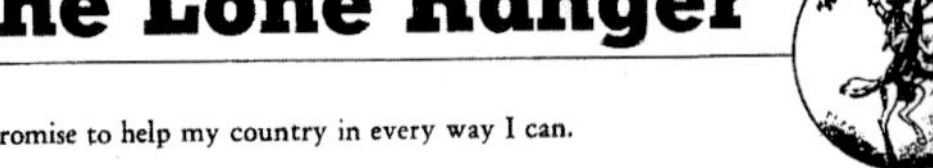

The Lone Ranger

1. I promise to help my country in every way I can.

2. I promise not to play in the street or cross against traffic lights.

3. I promise not to hitch-hike or to hang on behind autos.

4. I promise to cooperate with school traffic patrols and to help other children avoid danger.

5. I promise not to ride my bike on the sidewalk or the wrong side of the street and not to make turns without signalling.

6. I promise not to leave toys or other objects where someone might fall over them.

7. I promise to be careful climbing ladders and to guard my family against the dangers of falls.

8. I promise to guard against burns or cuts around my home.

9. I promise to promote safety always—at home, at school and on the street —and to encourage others to join this safety movement.

10. I promise to obey parents or guardians always.

[It is the duty of every Victory Ranger to memorize and observe these rules at all times.]

SIGNED Richard Lloyd Muse

MEMBER, THE LONE RANGER SAFETY CLUB

This Safety Club, designed to guard boys and girls from accidents and to help them work with Uncle Sam, for Victory, is sponsored by Merita Bread and Cakes.

(1A)

Lone Ranger Safety Club Victory Pledge Certificate from 1945 shortly before the end of world War II. This would be valued between $35.00 to $50.00 in good condition.

HEADQUARTERS
c/o MERITA BAKERS
BOX 2180, ATLANTA 1, GA.

LONE RANGER SAFETY CLUB
SPONSORED BY MERITA BREAD AND CAKE

"Tai, Kemo Sabe"

That Indian for "Greetings faithful friend". Tonto greet you with every good wish.

Here your Lone Ranger Safety Club pencil-sharpener bullet. Merita people send it with their good wishes. See how it shine with gleaming silver color. See how well it sharpen pencils too.

Best of all, it is token showing you help Lone Ranger in his Safety Club, just like his own silver bullets show him Lone Ranger.

Tonto not write too good, but me got more good news. Merita folks got more fine things for you. They want you have these things free, because you good member of Safety Club.

LOOK, FRIEND! Next thing Merita folks want give you is beautiful picture. Me sure you want um to put on wall your room. Picture show Lone Ranger, Dan Reid and Tonto around campfire. It show our horses too -- Silver, Scout and Victor. Picture printed in many bright colors.

Here how you get your picture free. In this letter you find two Safety Club blanks. These blanks to use for boys or girls to sign, to join up in Club. You get um two friends to fill out blanks, so they can join Club and be member like you. Ask um print plainly, and show full address.

After two friends fill out blanks, you send um filled-out blanks to Lone Ranger, care of Merita. With blanks, send your name and address and ask for your picture of Lone Ranger, Dan Reid and Tonto.

When Lone Ranger send you picture, he tell you how get Official Lone Ranger Safety Club Badge free. And that not all. There more fine free things after that.

Be sure get um two new members, and send for your picture right off.

AWLJ DLQP LWHLJD

Your friend,

TONTO

TONTO

ENJOY TENDER-BLENDED MERITA BREAD, THE FAVORITE OF ACTIVE BOYS AND GIRLS

FILL IN COUPON, CUT ON DOTTED LINES AND MAIL TO THE LONE RANGER (or send him same information by card or letter). BE SURE TO PRINT YOUR NAME AND COMPLETE ADDRESS PLAINLY.

LONE RANGER, c/o MERITA BAKERS, BOX 2180, ATLANTA 1, GA.

I enclose two club membership blanks, each signed by a friend who wants to join the Club, and showing their names and complete addresses. Please make my two friends members, and send me my free picture of you and Tonto and Dan Reid around the campfire.

My name: ________

My address: ________ (Street)

________ (City) ________ (State)

(2)

Copyright, 1949 The Lone Ranger, Inc.

TUNE IN "THE LONE RANGER" THREE TIMES EACH WEEK

Tonto promotional letter offering the Silver Bullet Pencil Sharpener. This letter dated 1949 was sent with the Tonto and Dan Reid photo promotion.

Lone Ranger Merita Bread pictures (1943), $75.00 – 150.00 each.

Early premium cards for stations WGN and WXYZ that were sponsored by Silvercup bread, $75.00 – 125.00 each.

Lone Ranger Merita bread color pictures from 1943. Valued between $75.00 –150.00 each.

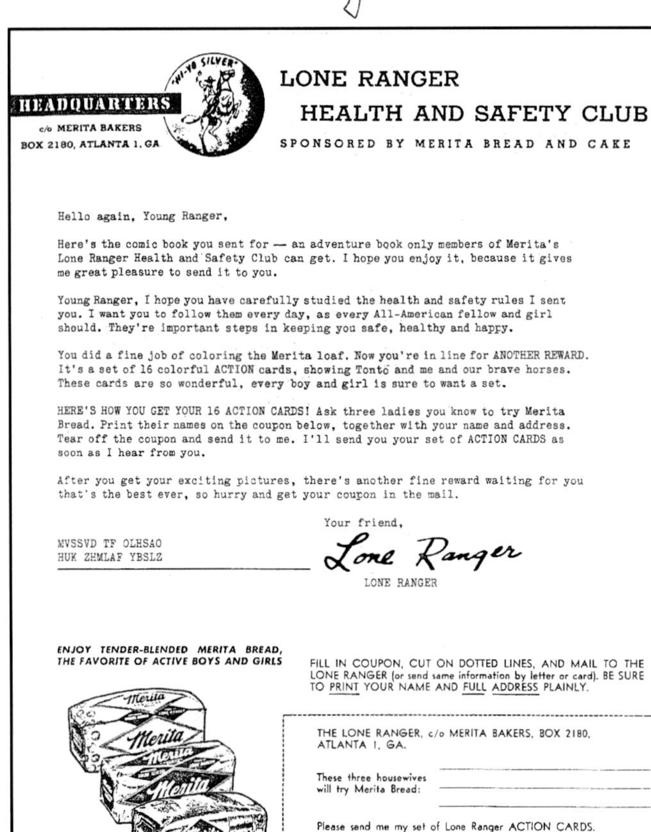

HEADQUARTERS
c/o MERITA BAKERS
BOX 2180, ATLANTA 1, GA

"HI-YO SILVER"

LONE RANGER
HEALTH AND SAFETY CLUB
SPONSORED BY MERITA BREAD AND CAKE

Hello again, Young Ranger,

Here's the comic book you sent for — an adventure book only members of Merita's Lone Ranger Health and Safety Club can get. I hope you enjoy it, because it gives me great pleasure to send it to you.

Young Ranger, I hope you have carefully studied the health and safety rules I sent you. I want you to follow them every day, as every All-American fellow and girl should. They're important steps in keeping you safe, healthy and happy.

You did a fine job of coloring the Merita loaf. Now you're in line for ANOTHER REWARD. It's a set of 16 colorful ACTION cards, showing Tonto and me and our brave horses. These cards are so wonderful, every boy and girl is sure to want a set.

HERE'S HOW YOU GET YOUR 16 ACTION CARDS! Ask three ladies you know to try Merita Bread. Print their names on the coupon below, together with your name and address. Tear off the coupon and send it to me. I'll send you your set of ACTION CARDS as soon as I hear from you.

After you get your exciting pictures, there's another fine reward waiting for you that's the best ever, so hurry and get your coupon in the mail.

Your friend,

MVSSVD TF OLHSAO
HUK ZHMLAF YBSLZ

Lone Ranger
LONE RANGER

ENJOY TENDER-BLENDED MERITA BREAD, THE FAVORITE OF ACTIVE BOYS AND GIRLS

FILL IN COUPON, CUT ON DOTTED LINES, AND MAIL TO THE LONE RANGER (or send same information by letter or card). BE SURE TO PRINT YOUR NAME AND FULL ADDRESS PLAINLY.

THE LONE RANGER, c/o MERITA BAKERS, BOX 2180, ATLANTA 1, GA.

These three housewives will try Merita Bread: ______

Please send me my set of Lone Ranger ACTION CARDS.

My name: ______

My address: ______ (Street)

______ (City) ______ (State)

(2)

© 1954 TLR, Inc.

TUNE IN THE LONE RANGER THREE TIMES EACH WEEK

The Lone Ranger Health and Safety Club letter from 1954 offering the 16 action cards of the Lone Ranger. Cards are valued at $50.00 to $75.00 for the complete set.

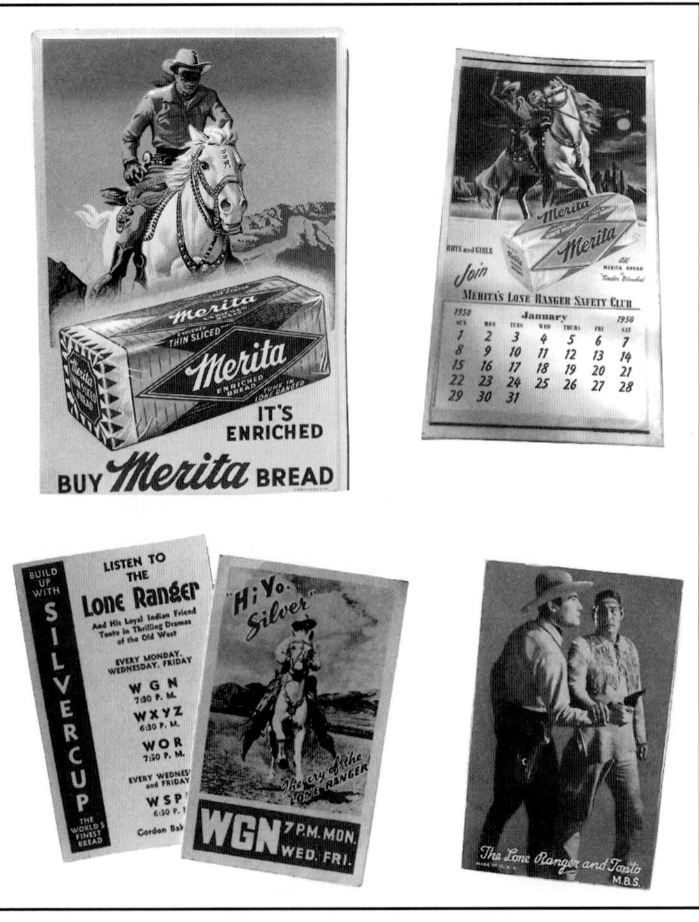

By the late thirties the Lone Ranger radio show was heavily promoted with many bread company premiums, calendars, and exhibit cards. All are very collectible today and command prices from $25.00 – 850.00.

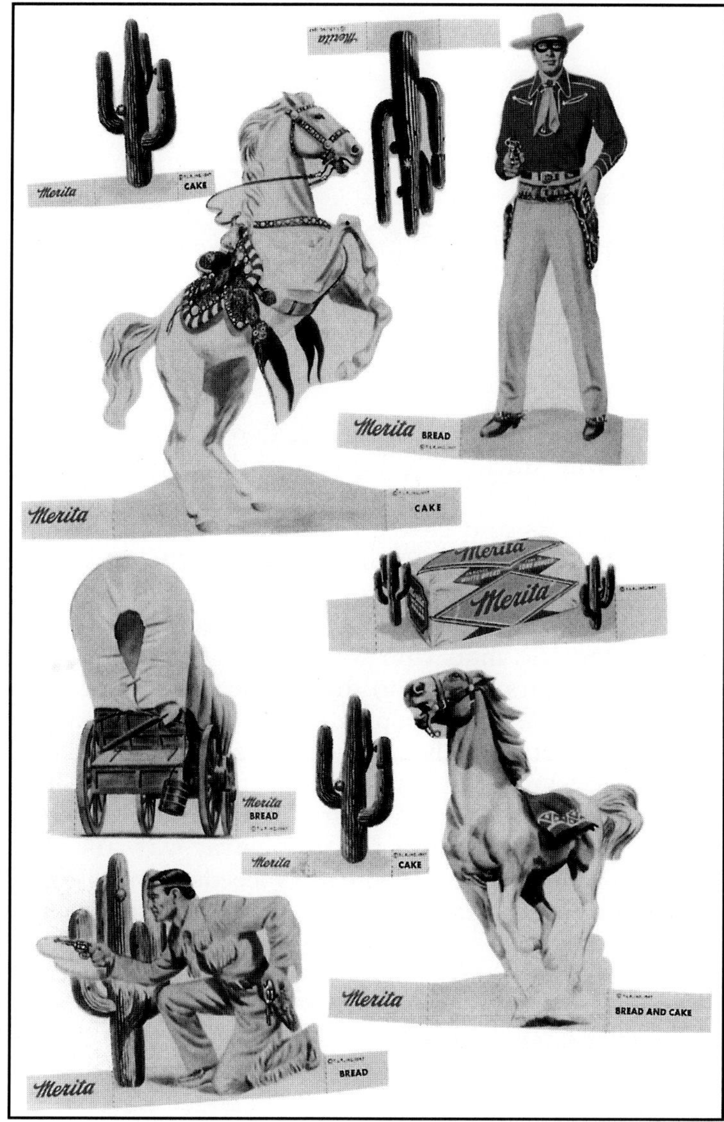

Merita Bread cut-out set premium from 1948. Today commands prices of $150.00 - 350.00 for a complete set.

Promotion letter from Merita Bread offering the free Lone Ranger cutouts for getting three mothers to try Merita. The cutouts are one of the rare premium items and have a value of $85.00 to $350.00.

HEADQUARTERS
c/o MERITA BREAD
BOX 2180, ATLANTA 1, GA.

LONE RANGER SAFETY CLUB
SPONSORED BY MERITA BREAD AND CAKE

Dear Safety Ranger:

Welcome to the Lone Ranger Safety Club. I'm proud to have you as a member.

Enclosed are your Official Membership Card, with our Secret Code on the back, and your Pledge Certificate. Put the Certificate on your wall or mirror where you'll see it daily as a reminder to follow the club rules for safety, good citizenship and fair play.

Nothing's more important than preventing accidents, so you'll get lots of satisfaction working for safety. You'll have fun and excitement too as a member. And there are some grand FREE GIFTS for you as rewards for your loyalty to the Safety Club and to its sponsors, the Merita folks.

JUST LOOK! Here's the news about the first gift! It's a thrilling 10-piece Lone Ranger Cutout Set, printed in vivid, glowing colors on sturdy cardboard. There are cutouts of Tonto and me with guns ready. You'll see our horses, Silver and Scout, in stirring action. The beauty of Silver's hand-tooled saddle and silver-studded harness will amaze you! There are cutouts too of a picturesque covered wagon, the old corral fence, genuine Western scenery.

Now, these cutouts are not sold anywhere. If they were, they'd cost a lot. BUT, the Merita folks have one waiting for you, free! Here's all you do. Merita wants you to ask three housewives to try Merita Bread. Send their names to Tonto, care of Merita Bakers. Use the coupon below to send the names and ask for your cutout set.

AND THAT'S NOT ALL! More free rewards await you—a fine fabric Lone Ranger Mask and other grand gifts. But first, send for your cutout set. Then we'll tell how to get the other gifts. Don't delay. Send for your cutout set now!

Your friend,

Lone Ranger

THE LONE RANGER

AWPLDP SPWA XP
HZCV QZC DLQPEJ

ENJOY TENDER-BLENDED MERITA BREAD, THE FAVORITE OF ACTIVE BOYS AND GIRLS

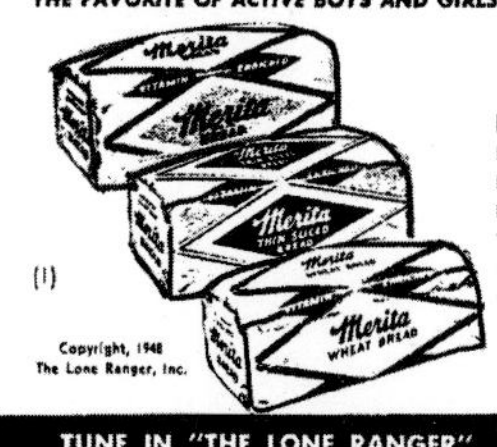

(1)

Copyright, 1948
The Lone Ranger, Inc.

TUNE IN "THE LONE RANGER" THREE TIMES EACH WEEK

FILL IN COUPON, CUT ON DOTTED LINES AND MAIL TO TONTO (or send same information by letter or card). BE SURE TO PRINT YOUR NAME AND FULL ADDRESS PLAINLY.

TONTO, c/o MERITA BAKERS, BOX 2180, ATLANTA 1, GA.

These three housewives will try Merita Bread:

Please send me my Lone Ranger Cutout Set free.

My name: ____________________

My address: ____________________ (Street)

____________________ (City) __________ (State)

The Lone Ranger rode again in Oxford, Michigan, as local residents gathered to pay tribute to their most famous resident and radio's famous Lone Ranger, the late Brace Beemer.

In 1982 the excitement, parties, winter weather, and special events for Super Bowl XVI at the Pontiac Silverdome was contrasted by the quiet memorial to a hometown hero in the tiny, rural village of Oxford, Michigan.

It featured the same kind of attractions as other festivities — concerts and raffles, and other tributes to the local radio hero. And the hometown hero memorialized was Brace Beemer, the legendary radio voice of the Lone Ranger heard for many years over WXYZ radio in Detroit!

Brace Beemer, moved to a farm in Oxford in 1942, and has been hailed as one of the area's greatest and most famous residents. Mr. Beemer passed away in 1965.

However, anyone who visited the Oxford area during Super Bowl week might think the Lone Ranger and Silver were riding again.

White hats, black masks, silver bullets, and colorful signs about the Loner Ranger were everywhere in the village and townships.

Oxford was once known as the gravel capitol of the world, but now residents and the Chamber of Commerce have changed their image. Newly painted signs alert persons entering Oxford that this is where Beemer lived. The colorful signs proudly state "Welcome to Oxford – Home of the radio Lone Ranger."

A nearby water tower for the village has a black mask neatly painted on it to further promote the new image of the township. Every town wants to be famous for something, and Oxford picked someone who was nationally known and admired during radio's golden years.

Officials and citizens dedicated a future site for the Brace Beemer memorial statue in the Centennial Park in downtown Oxford.

Local officials plan to have a life-size statue of Beemer, the man who was radio's Lone Ranger for over 13 years, placed in the middle of the park in the near future. Small copies of the statue of the Lone Ranger astride Silver were also sold as part of the fund-raising activities.

A special Brace Beemer Benefit Ball, featuring Lionel Hampton and his orchestra, was also held during the week's activities. Proceeds from all fund-raising activities were used for the Brace Beemer statue.

Residents also had the opportunity to see the recent movie *Legend of the Lone Ranger* at a local theatre offering tickets at 1930s prices.

Lone Ranger memorabilia on sale included original radio broadcasts, lucite embedded silver bullet paperweights, 50th anniversary solid silver coins, silver bullet pencils, masks, special newspaper supplements, dedication programs, balloons, plastic clips of silver bullets, white hats, and books about the Lone Ranger (including the author's).

From a collective viewpoint the Oxford Lone Ranger memorabilia items are already in demand and prices vary according to availability and supply. The Remington-like statues of the Ranger on a rearing Silver are in great demand and command the highest price of all the items made available during the 1982 local tribute to the masked rider.

This photo was one of the last taken of Brace astride Silver's Pride.

Brace Beemer

Brace Beemer became the radio voice of The Lone Ranger and station WXYZ April 9, 1941. Prior to that he made whatever personal appearances were required.

It is Brace Beemer's voice most people remember as the "daring and resourceful masked rider of the plains" who galloped through living rooms three nights a week.

He did over 2,000 broadcasts on 129 radio stations during his 13 years as The Lone Ranger. The show left the air Sept. 4, 1954.

Brace Beemer moved his family to his 300-acre West Drahner Road farm in Oxford in 1942. Besides the family of Leta Wales Beemer, sons Bob, JD and Dick, and daughter Barbara, the great horse Silver came to the farm.

Brace Beemer's contract forbid him to sign his name when he made any of his numerous personal appearances in the United States and Canada. Always he had to wear his mask when in costume, and live the image of The Lone Ranger in public appearances.

His travels took him to Madison Square Gardens, the Rose Bowl, the Bing Crosby show in California, on stage with Tex Ritter and Roy Rogers in Texas, and many children's hospitals across the land.

He performed on the White House lawn for President Roosevelt's grandson, was a personal friend of the late top G-man, J. Edgar Hoover, and was an honorary Indian chief, Texas Ranger, and veteran of WWI, which he entered at age 14. He was wounded in action in the war.

Brace Beemer also went on radio for the National Lutheran Hour, emceed CKLW's 'Detroit Lutherans Present' radio show in 1959, and appeared in the Pontiac historical pageant in 1960.

It was often written, "Brace Beemer is the image of The Lone Ranger". Besides the marvelous speaking voice, he had he-man looks. He was 6'3", 190 pounds, straight and erect, strong and always in command.

He was a hero to millions of people.

J. Edgar Hoover wrote to Brace Beemer . . . "Maybe you are too close to your daily task to realize what a constructive piece of building you are doing with the youth of this country."

Special Lone Ranger page from the Brace Beemer souvenir program, distributed to help with the Lone Ranger statue in Oxford.

Lone Ranger 50th Anniversary solid silver coin (1983), $175.00 - 275.00.

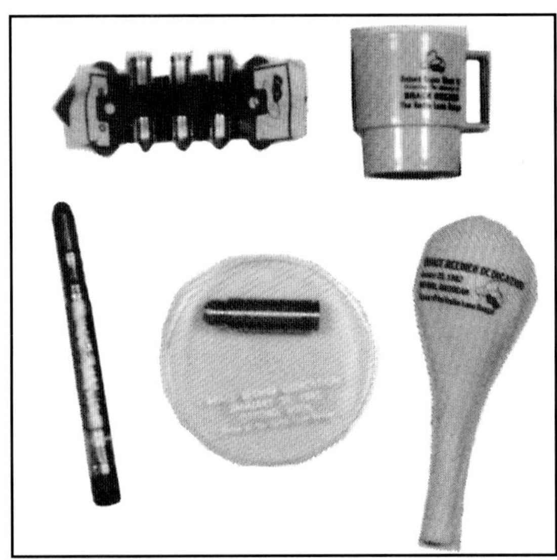

Lone Ranger Silver Bullet Clip, 1982, $35.00 - 65.00.

Lone Ranger Plastic Cup, Oxford Celebration, 1982, $35.00 - 65.00.

Lucite Silver Bullet, Oxford Celebration, 1982, $75.00 - 125.00.

Brace Beemer Pencil, Oxford Celebration, 1982, $25.00 - 50.00.

Lone Ranger Balloon, Oxford Celebration, 1982, $20.00 - 35.00.

8 Wed., Dec. 30, 1981 The Oxford (Mich.) Leader

Brace Beemer

'A Legend in His Own Time'

[*Editor's note: In our research on Brace Beemer, The Lone Ranger of radio, we jotted down several interesting facts. This is the first in a series of this collection.*]

* * *

Each broadcast began with . . .

"Return with us to those thrilling days of yesteryear, from out of the past come the thundering hoofbeats of the great horse, Silver. The Lone Ranger rides again."

* * *

- Throughout the hundreds of clippings in Brace Beemer's scrapbook reporters noted that he "looked the image of The Lone Ranger".
- He stood over 6 ft. 3, weighed 192, and had that tremendous, resonant baritone voice.
- Reporters said, "Brace Beemer is a man's man, an outdoorsman, a horseman, and strong. He lives the image of The Lone Ranger".
- He had auburn hair and grey-blue eyes. The Montreal Herald said, "Hiyo, Silver is more familiar than little Red Riding Hood."
- He was a dispatch rider in the Army under Col. Douglas MacArthur in the Rainbow division in France at age 14 in WWI. He was wounded and has a purple heart, Victory medal, and accolage from President Wilson.
- He was a very close friend to vice president Alben Barkley and J. Edgar Hoover.
- Brace Beemer was deputized as a Texas Ranger, was an honorary chief of many tribes' including the Sioux and Pawnee, and was an honorary Legion Frontiersman in Canada.
- In a South Dakota town of 2200, 67,000 including the governor came to see him at a breakfast-Round Up.
- 7,000 filled the Atlanta's Georgian Terrace Hotel for a War Fund rally.
- The Lone Ranger, Brace Beemer, did over 2,000 radio shows on 129 stations.

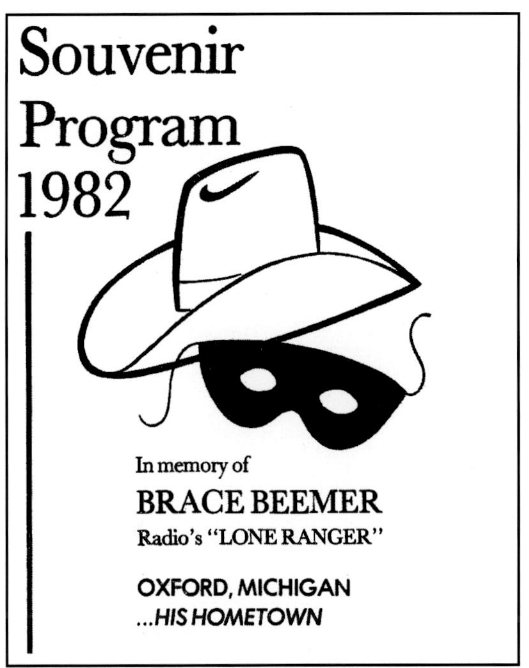

Souvenir
Program
1982
In memory of
BRACE BEEMER
Radio's "LONE RANGER"
OXFORD, MICHIGAN
...HIS HOMETOWN

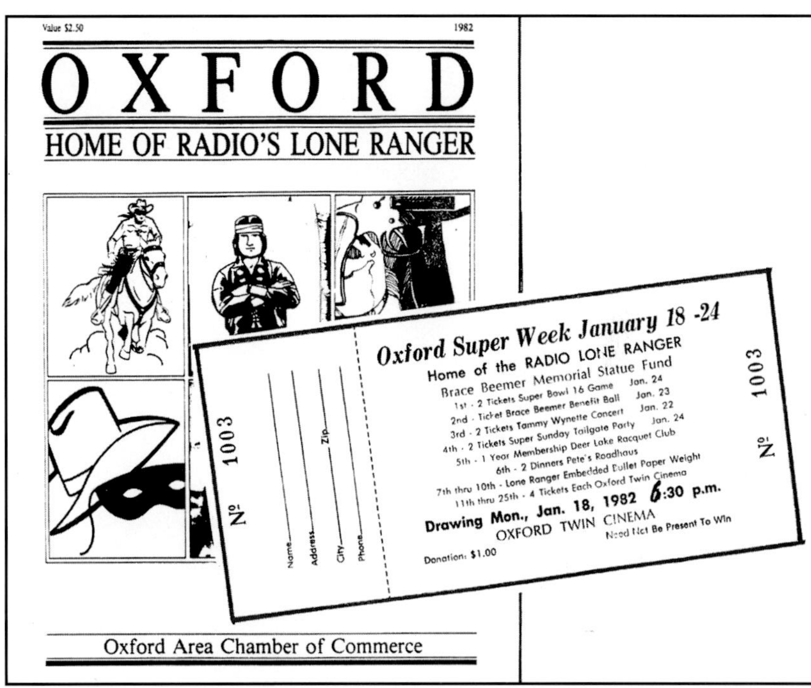

The special souvenir program that was sold during Oxford, Michigan's Super Week during the Superbowl activities in 1982. The program was dedicated to Brace Beemer's memory by his hometown. A very interesting collectible that will escalate in price during the next several years.

Brace Beemer Memorial statue ticket is also a very collectible Lone Ranger item. Also a copy of the Oxford Chamber of Commerce booklet carrying the first use of the new slogan, "Home of the Radio Lone Ranger." This also is a very collectible item that will increase in value.

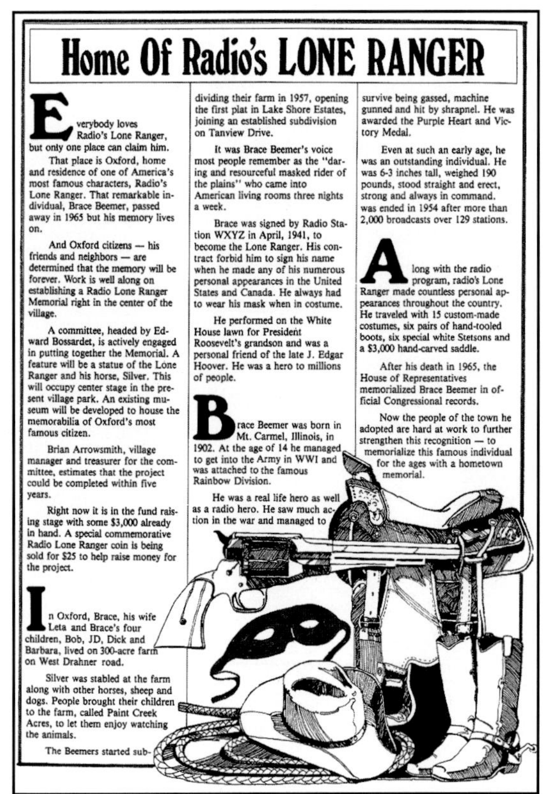

Home Of Radio's LONE RANGER

Everybody loves Radio's Lone Ranger, but only one place can claim him.

That place is Oxford, home and residence of one of America's most famous characters, Radio's Lone Ranger. That remarkable individual, Brace Beemer, passed away in 1965 but his memory lives on.

And Oxford citizens — his friends and neighbors — are determined that the memory will be forever. Work is well along on establishing a Radio Lone Ranger Memorial right in the center of the village.

A committee, headed by Edward Bossardet, is actively engaged in putting together the Memorial. A feature will be a statue of the Lone Ranger and his horse, Silver. This will occupy center stage in the present village park. An existing museum will be developed to house the memorabilia of Oxford's most famous citizen.

Brian Arrowsmith, village manager and treasurer for the committee, estimates that the project could be completed within five years.

Right now it is in the fund raising stage with some $3,000 already in hand. A special commemorative Radio Lone Ranger coin is being sold for $25 to help raise money for the project.

In Oxford, Brace, his wife Leta and Brace's four children, Bob, JD, Dick and Barbara, lived on 300-acre farm on West Drahner road.

Silver was stabled at the farm along with other horses, sheep and dogs. People brought their children to the farm, called Paint Creek Acres, to let them enjoy watching the animals.

The Beemers started subdividing their farm in 1957, opening the first plat in Lake Shore Estates, joining an established subdivision on Tanview Drive.

It was Brace Beemer's voice most people remember as the "daring and resourceful masked rider of the plains" who came into American living rooms three nights a week.

Brace was signed by Radio Station WXYZ in April, 1941, to become the Lone Ranger. His contract forbid him to sign his name when he made any of his numerous personal appearances in the United States and Canada. He always had to wear his mask when in costume.

He performed on the White House lawn for President Roosevelt's grandson and was a personal friend of the late J. Edgar Hoover. He was a hero to millions of people.

Brace Beemer was born in Mt. Carmel, Illinois, in 1902. At the age of 14 he managed to get into the Army in WWI and was attached to the famous Rainbow Division.

He was a real life hero as well as a radio hero. He saw much action in the war and managed to survive being gassed, machine gunned and hit by shrapnel. He was awarded the Purple Heart and Victory Medal.

Even at such an early age, he was an outstanding individual. He was 6-3 inches tall, weighed 190 pounds, stood straight and erect, strong and always in command. was ended in 1954 after more than 2,000 broadcasts over 129 stations.

Along with the radio program, radio's Lone Ranger made countless personal appearances throughout the country. He traveled with 15 custom-made costumes, six pairs of hand-tooled boots, six special white Stetsons and a $3,000 hand-carved saddle.

After his death in 1965, the House of Representatives memorialized Brace Beemer in official Congressional records.

Now the people of the town he adopted are hard at work to further strengthen this recognition — to memorialize this famous individual for the ages with a hometown memorial.

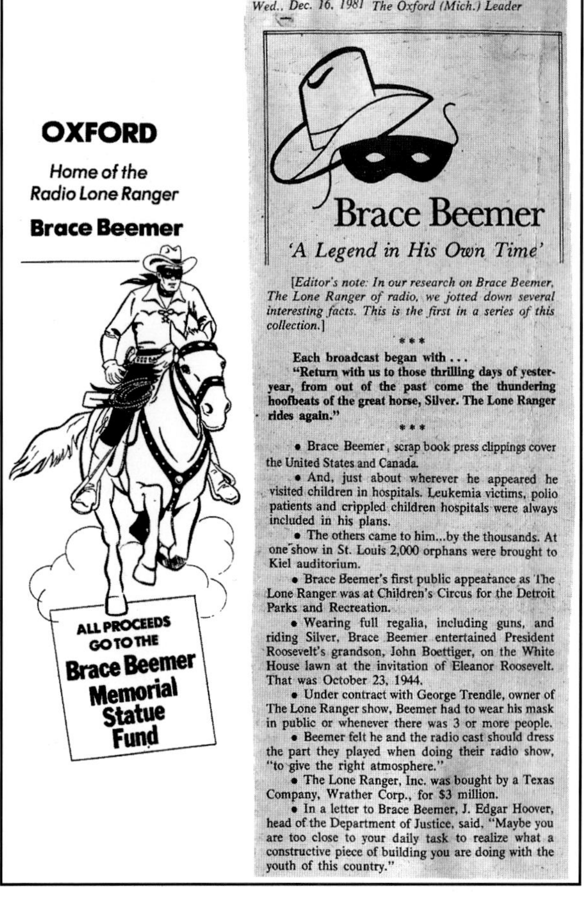

OXFORD
Home of the Radio Lone Ranger
Brace Beemer

ALL PROCEEDS GO TO THE Brace Beemer Memorial Statue Fund

Wed., Dec. 16, 1981 The Oxford (Mich.) Leader

Brace Beemer

'A Legend in His Own Time'

[*Editor's note: In our research on Brace Beemer, The Lone Ranger of radio, we jotted down several interesting facts. This is the first in a series of this collection.*]

***

Each broadcast began with . . .

"Return with us to those thrilling days of yesteryear, from out of the past come the thundering hoofbeats of the great horse, Silver. The Lone Ranger rides again."

***

- Brace Beemer, scrap book press clippings cover the United States and Canada.
- And, just about wherever he appeared he visited children in hospitals. Leukemia victims, polio patients and crippled children hospitals were always included in his plans.
- The others came to him...by the thousands. At one show in St. Louis 2,000 orphans were brought to Kiel auditorium.
- Brace Beemer's first public appearance as The Lone Ranger was at Children's Circus for the Detroit Parks and Recreation.
- Wearing full regalia, including guns, and riding Silver, Brace Beemer entertained President Roosevelt's grandson, John Boettiger, on the White House lawn at the invitation of Eleanor Roosevelt. That was October 23, 1944.
- Under contract with George Trendle, owner of The Lone Ranger show, Beemer had to wear his mask in public or whenever there was 3 or more people.
- Beemer felt he and the radio cast should dress the part they played when doing their radio show, "to give the right atmosphere."
- The Lone Ranger, Inc. was bought by a Texas Company, Wrather Corp., for $3 million.
- In a letter to Brace Beemer, J. Edgar Hoover, head of the Department of Justice, said, "Maybe you are too close to your daily task to realize what a constructive piece of building you are doing with the youth of this country."

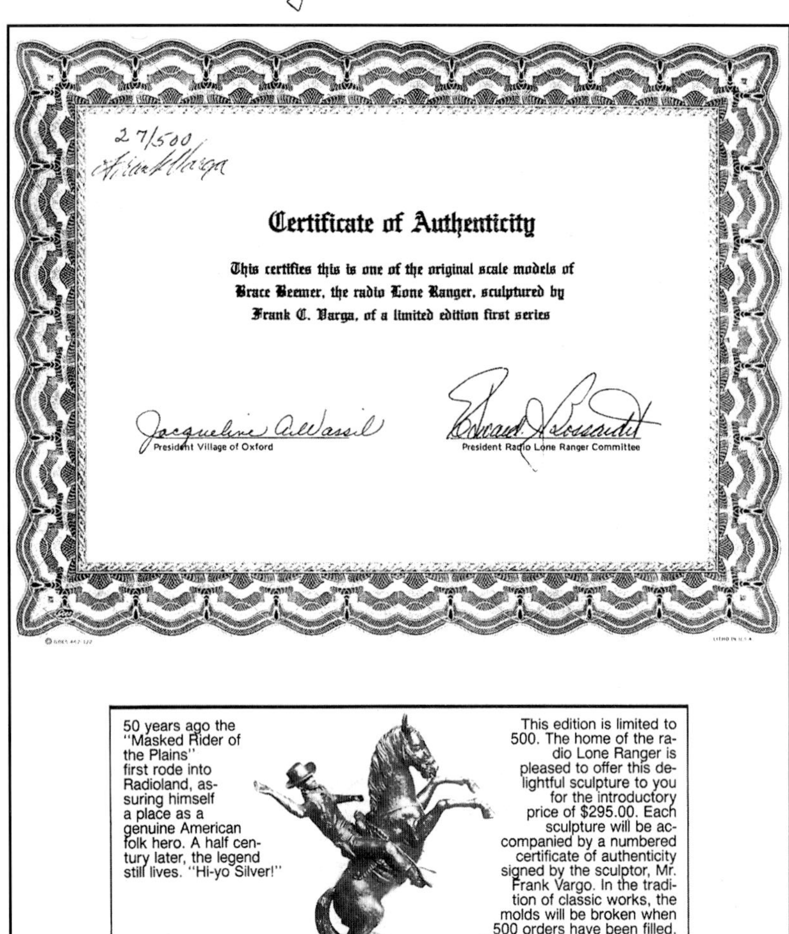

27/500
Frank Varga

Certificate of Authenticity

This certifies this is one of the original scale models of Brace Beemer, the radio Lone Ranger, sculptured by Frank C. Varga, of a limited edition first series

Jacqueline AlWassil
President Village of Oxford

Edward J. Bossardet
President Radio Lone Ranger Committee

50 years ago the "Masked Rider of the Plains" first rode into Radioland, assuring himself a place as a genuine American folk hero. A half century later, the legend still lives. "Hi-yo Silver!"

The Lone Ranger and his horse, Silver. (Brace Beemer)

This edition is limited to 500. The home of the radio Lone Ranger is pleased to offer this delightful sculpture to you for the introductory price of $295.00. Each sculpture will be accompanied by a numbered certificate of authenticity signed by the sculptor, Mr. Frank Vargo. In the tradition of classic works, the molds will be broken when 500 orders have been filled. Orders will be on a first come, first serve basis and numbers issued accordingly.

Brace Beemer
Radio Lone Ranger
Memorial Comm.
P.O. Box 516
Oxford, MI 48051
Att: Mr. Arnold Simmons, V.C.
Please add $2.50 for shipping and handling. MI residents add 4% sales tax.

I have enclosed a check for $ ____
OR CHARGE VISA MASTERCARD
Account # ____ Expiration date ____
Signature ____
Name ____
Street ____
City ____ State ____ Zip ____

C6 The Saginaw NEWS SUNDAY, OCTOBER 2, 1983

Town wants to honor 'Lone Ranger' from radio days

By Booth News Service

OXFORD — Astride his fiery horse, Silver, the Lone Ranger one day will ride into the village park here, where the duo of radio fame will stand watch over the masked man's adopted home town.

That, at least, is the dream of a group of townsfolk who are seeking to raise $60,000 to build a statue to pay homage to this quiet Oakland County village's most famous resident.

It was during Superbowl XVI festivities that local officials decided they were tired of being known as the Gravel Capital of the World, as it was identified on roadside signs at the edges of town.

Today, those signs have been replaced with ones reading "Oxford, Home of Brace Beemer, Radio Lone Ranger."

During the football weekend celebration, plans also were announced to enlarge the village park and begin downtown redevelopment. It was time, all agreed, to get the town moving.

A Lone Ranger Memorial Committee was formed to plan a fund-raising campaign for the statue during 1983, the 50th anniversary of the popular Detroit-originated radio program.

Although the initial Lone Ranger broadcast was aired on WXYZ on Jan. 30, 1933, the fifth and most renowned "voice" was the late Brace Beemer, who made his first full-time radio appearance as the masked man April 9, 1941, a role be played for 17 years.

Prior to that, as the station's general manager and chief announcer, he had filled in as the Lone Ranger on the air.

And, according to his son, Bob, an Oxford resident, businessman and civic leader, "He was the first and only Lone Ranger who ever made personal appearances. None of the others could ride!"

On July 30, 1943, on Belle Isle, his father made the first public appearance as the radio hero, according to Bob Beemer. "The station rented a horse, Hero, from a well-known animal trainer in the Detroit area, Carl Romig, for the event," he recalled.

From 1943 on, Brace Beemer, an expert horseman, rode his own stallion, Silver's Pride — called Pride by the family, Silver by the millions of Lone Ranger fans who grew up to the call "Come on, Silver. Let's go, big fella. Hi-yo, Silver, away!"

Brace Beemer moved his family, and Pride/Silver, from the Detroit area to a 240-acre farm on West Drahner Road in 1943. He died here at age 62 in 1965 after having done more than 2,000 broadcasts before the show left the air Sept. 14, 1954.

His wife, Leta, 82, continues to live in the family home.

"She still walks a minimum of two miles a day, rain or shine, snow or sleet," said Bob Beemer. Throughout his career his father referred to Oxford as his "hometown," he recalled.

Bob Beemer is an admitted Lone Ranger fan. He recalls enjoying the program as an 8-year-old, but not knowing the daring and resourceful masked rider was his father.

"He used a projected voice for the part that I didn't recognize. I knew he was on radio, he was a trained professional actor. (I knew) he did other things, too — was a singer, read poetry and did newscasts. Eventually, that projected voice became his normal voice."

Brace Beemer became a legend with that booming voice. Not many adults will have forgotten the familiar strains of the William Tell Overture and then the announcer saying:

"A fiery horse with the speed of light, a cloud of dust and a hearty 'Hi-yo, Silver,' The Lone Ranger!.

"With his faithful Indian companion, Tonto (played by John Todd throughout the life of the series) *the daring and resourceful masked rider of the plains led the fight for law and order in the early western United States.*

"Nowhere in the pages of history can one find a greater champion of justice. Return with us now to those thrilling days of yesteryear. From out of the past come the thundering hoofbeats of the great horse, Silver. The Lone Ranger rides again!"

And then Beemer's booming voice . . .

Pride/Silver died in the Spring of 1966 at age 29, according to Bob Beemer.

Brace Beemer's three sons learned their lessons well. They also are excellent astride horses.

Bob's two brothers are J. D., a professional horseman in Germantown, Md., and Richard, an attorney in Farmington. J.D. also followed in his father's foosteps, appearing in rodeos and various television shows.

Asked why his father didn't follow the Lone Ranger into the world of television, Bob Beemer says, "He didn't like TV. He thought it (the show) was the cheapest series ever made for TV. They used stock shots . . . he was a trained professional actor."

He says he also thinks his father figured he was too old and "not too realistic" for the part.

A Grosse Pointe and Delray Beach, Fla., sculptor, Frank Varga, has been commissioned by the Lone Ranger Memorial Committee to create a ¾-scale statue of Brace Beemer on a rearing horse.

In the meantime, Varga has made a 16-inch-tall replica of the statue, which is a key to the fund-raising campaign.

A 47-pound solid bronze original of the miniature was auctioned by the committee at a public showing May 1 at the Oxford High School. Successful bidder for $1,300 was Oxford Co-op Elevator.

In addition, the committee commissioned a limited edition of 500 cold cast replicas which are being sold to fans. The price tag for each is $150, which includes a numbered certificate.

According to Bob Beemer, Lone Ranger fans are legion. "Among ardent collectors of Lone Ranger memorabilia are two Pennsylvania residents, Jim Rosch, who has the major collection, and Lee Felbeinger, who has authored a book about Lone Ranger memorabilia."

In fact, he said, there was a large gathering of collectors in June.

They were attending dedication ceremonies of a memorial library to the late Fran Striker near Buffalo, N.Y. Striker, creator of the Lone Ranger who authored the scripts, had donated property to a church there, and the church established a camp for children on the grounds. The ceremonies were broadcast locally in Buffalo.

When Superman turned 50, the birthday bash was a huge success. The festivities included a television special, cover story in *Time* magazine, and news stories in top papers across the country. A special tribute was held in the Cleveland home of the 1938 creators of this character.

By comparison, the Lone Ranger turned 50 in 1983; unfortunately, there was very little fanfare or national coverage of the event. The Wrather Corporation had no Ranger to help promote the golden anniversary because of the 1981 film, *Legend of the Lone Ranger*, which bombed at the box office and was boycotted by fans of the original masked rider. A legal battle with Clayton Moore over his wearing of the Lone Ranger's mask also was a contributing factor in the decision to quietly let the Lone Ranger ride into the setting sun, rather than to promote his 50th anniversary.

However, there were two projects that I was involved in during this anniversary year of the Lone Ranger. On behalf of Wrather Corp., I developed a Lone Ranger mini-museum, incorporating my vast collection of memorabilia on the masked man. This display was exhibited at a special collectibles show at Valley Forge, Pennsylvania, in March of 1983. Also on hand, assisting me, was Fran Striker Jr.

The response and media coverage were overwhelming. It was obvious that a great many individuals still remember and enjoy the Lone Ranger, regardless of the version...radio, television, or movie.

In June of the same year, I joined with Fran in developing a special anniversary celebration in Arcade, New York. We consulted with the Wrather Corp. on their plans for celebrating the event, and were told there were not any plans in progress. We then decided to promote the birthday ourselves.

Working on a shoestring budget, we were able to successfully pull off a 50th anniversary celebration at the former home of Fran Striker, where many of the Lone Ranger adventures were penned by Striker.

In addition to celebrating the Lone Ranger birthday, a special dedication of a Fran Striker Memorial Study was held. This three-day event took place at Fran Striker's farm, located approximately 50 miles south of Buffalo, purchased as a summer home. The home was sold to the Children's Evangelica Fellowship (CEF) in 1962 after Striker's death. CEF agreed to let us use the facilities for our Lone Ranger anniversary celebration on June 24, 25, and 26, 1983.

Although attendance was not as good as we expected, those individuals participating in our celebration were rewarded with an enjoyable weekend of old movies, memorabilia displays, special guests, a radio listening room, collector's/dealer's flea market, and a special old-time radio broadcast on station WEBR. The radio broadcast used a revised script of the very first Lone Ranger radio show. It was an unusual and most enjoyable event for collectors and fans of old-time radio and especially memorable for Lone Ranger fans.

During the past 64 years, The Lone Ranger has brought about a new and accepted concept of cowboys and western life during the frontier days. He emphasizes honesty, cleanliness, and tolerance as the signs of strength, rather than brutality and coarseness. The important influence exercised by The Lone Ranger on American youth has been recognized by many leading national institutions and individuals.

Since 1937, The Lone Ranger has received 18 national citations for "Best Program" from organizations including the National Federation of Women's Clubs, American Legion, National Safety Council, and Parent-Teacher Association.

Such noted figures as Bernard Baruch, J. Edgar Hoover, Eleanor Roosevelt, Babe Ruth, and Senator Homer Ferguson proclaimed it their favorite program through the years.

As a force of good, The Lone Ranger has been mentioned in the Congressional Record, and praised for its beneficial influence on American youth.

While in command of the Pacific World War II forces, General Douglas MacArthur found time to have his son enlisted in The Lone Ranger Safety Club and later took him to meet the masked figure during a personal appearance at Madison Square Garden.

The Lone Ranger has been the subject of the commencement day address by Warren Austin at Syracuse University graduations.

Three times the Congressional Record has carried citations for The Lone Ranger from the program's work on behalf of youth betterment and in combating juvenile delinquency.

The Lone Ranger has been made an honorary Deputy Sheriff by more than 60 sheriffs throughout the United States.

Perhaps no greater tribute has ever been paid to an entertainment figure by a government agency, than the selection of the Lone Ranger by the U.S. Treasury Department to head the 1958 Savings Stamp and Bond Program.

With U.S. Treasury Secretary Robert B. Anderson and Postmaster General Arthur E. Sommerfield, the Lone Ranger inaugurated the Savings Stamp drive at a giant rally on the grounds of the Washington Monument.

The Lone Ranger, it is estimated by treasury officials, through his Lone Ranger Peace Patrol has reached an estimated four million school children through 50,000 U.S. public schools and 20,000 post offices.

More than three million children, through the purchase of Savings Stamps, enrolled as members of this famous Lone Ranger Peace Patrol.

During the years the Lone Ranger has appeared before more than 21 million people in personal appearances. His appearances have spanned the United States several times as well as appearances in England, Scotland, Wales, and Ireland, as well as Canada.

The Lone Ranger has received more than five million fan letters or "friend letters" as he prefers to regard them. The letters, not restricted to the United States alone, are received from all parts of the world.

A spokesman for The Lone Ranger, Inc., the organization that produces the adventure series, recently acknowledged these many citations and promised "The Lone Ranger will continue to avoid sensationalism; it will avoid emphasis on violence and stress action and clean adventure. It will uphold the principles of truth, righteousness and the supremacy of right over might which has been handed down as the keystone of our American Heritage."

Unfortunately, in 1981, the producers of the *Legend of the Lone Ranger* thought they could update the character to the values of the 1980s and ended up tarnishing both the character's silver bullets and reputation.

However, the real Lone Ranger is safe in the past of radio where his "silver" can never be tarnished. So with a cloud of dust and a hearty "Hi-Yo Silver" the Lone Ranger gallops into his 65 anniversary year — May he ride long and far!

This limited edition 50th Anniversary poster showing the Rangers from 1933 to 1983, printed in black and gold on a glossy paper, was designed by the author.

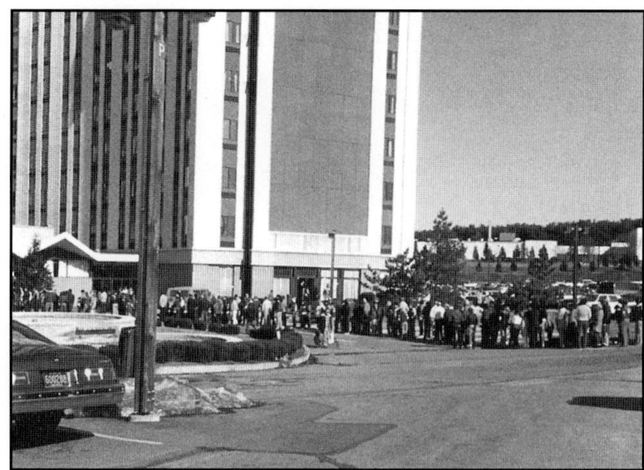

Photo shows the long line to enter the Sheraton Valley Forge Convention Center where the collectibles show and Lone Ranger mini-museum were the big attraction.

The author, Lee Felbilnger and his wife, Suzanne, hold the large Lone Ranger standee that was used by theatres to promote the Lone Ranger movie in 1956.

The Lone Ranger display and mini-museum was exhibited at Valley Forge, Pennsylvania, in March of 1983. Photo shows the author, Lee Felbinger on left, with Fran Striker Jr., holding a copy of the author's first Lone Ranger pictorial scrapbook.

FINALLY, THE DATES ARE SET...THE PLANS ARE CAST...JOIN US AND...

Celebrate an American Heritage

DEDICATING A *FRAN STRIKER* MEMORIAL STUDY

COMMEMORATING 50 YEARS OF *THE LONE RANGER*

THE TIME ....**JUNE 24, 25 AND 26, 1983**
THE PLACE ....**ARCADE, NEW YORK**

(JUST ABOUT 45 MINUTES FROM BUFFALO, N.Y.)

DETAILS —

In 1932, Fran Striker, radio dramatist in Buffalo, N.Y., received a letter from one of his regular customers. The letter requested that he "...come up with a western..." That was the beginning of the Lone Ranger. The customer was of course, station WXYZ in Detroit, Michigan. That's how it all began over fifty years ago.

As the character Striker created and wrote about gained popularity the writer subsequently moved to the Detroit area, but not before purchasing a tract of land in western New York state that would become the family summer home.

After his death in 1962, the property was sold to the Child Evangelism Fellowship (CEF) who made it into a camp for underpriviledged children. Efforts have been on-going, by fans in the Buffalo area, to refurbish Fran Striker's office at the camp and make it into a memorial study. The CEF has made the entire 100 plus acre camp available to Fran Striker, Jr. for the purpose of hosting an appropriate dedication ceremony and festival. Proceeds of the event will go, in part, to the CEF for the continuation of the children's camp.

This will be an unusual and most enjoyable event for all who are fans of old time radio, and The Lone Ranger in particular.

NOTE —

This is a special advanced information mailing that has been sent to people such as yourself who have been kind enough to express an interest in this celebration, or who are known to be Ranger fans and/or collectors. In a few weeks regular advertising of the event will commence so if you are interested in attending and staying on-site, please send in your reservation as soon as possible as space is limited and will be assigned on a first come first serve basis. Your remittance in full must accompany your reservation.

There will be extensive radio advertising in the Metropolitan Buffalo, N.Y. area as well as in selected publications.

FEATURING —

— Old time radio nostalgia.
— The world's most complete Lone Ranger memorabilia display.
Dealer/trader/collector tables.
— Appropriate movies.
— Radio listening room.
— Camping on the old Striker property.
— Special events.

SPECIAL FEATURE —

Radio station WEBR (Buffalo) will be broadcasting LIVE from the celeration on Saturday. The broadcast will include the dedication ceremony and a dramatic script written by the senior Fran Striker in the early 1930's and originally broadcast by WEBR at that time the broadcast will be **produced at the festival in front of a live audience.** This is your chance to see how it was done in the good ol' days.

SPECIAL GUESTS —

Although the guest list continues to grow, here are a few of the people who have already indicated that they will attend and participate.

— **Lee Allman** (Radio actress. First played Lenore Case on The Green Hornet series.)
— **R. Brace Beemer** (Son of Beemer The Radio Ranger from 1941 until 1954.)
— **Lee Felbinger** (Ranger historian and owner of what is considered to be the world's most complete collection of Lone Ranger memorabilia.)
R.E. (Dick) Osgood (Writer, actor, and radio personality at WXYZ during the golden age of radio.)
Fran Striker, Jr. (Your host and son of the man who created and wrote The Lone Ranger series.)

For Further Information Write:
FRAN STRIKER JR.
P.O. Box 832
Lansdale, PA. 19446

Special ad flyer that was used to promote the 50th Anniversary.

Lone Ranger Collectibles

Mask, 1940, Buchan's Bread Premium, $75.00 – 155.00.

Hi-Yo Silver mask, 1941, Schulze Butter-Nut Bread Premium, $75.00 – 125.00 each.

Bread labels, 1950, Merita Bread premiums, $10.00 – 25.00.

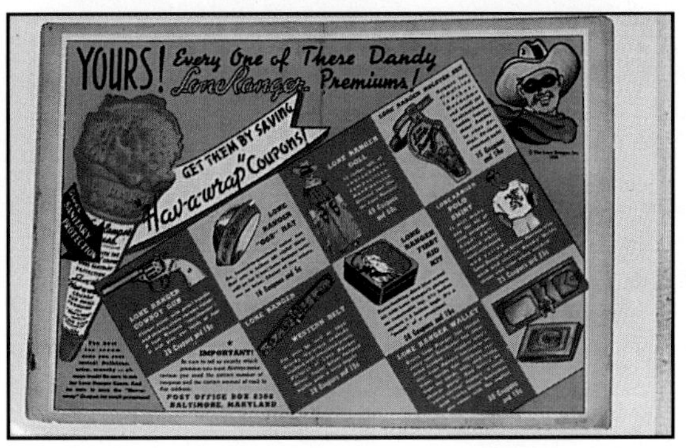

Advertisements, 1938, ice cream premium lists, rare, $125.00 – 185.00 each.

Valentine card, 1940, Merita Bread premium, $125.00 – 150.00.

DEAR LONE RANGER SAFETY SCOUT:

I can call you that now, for you have been enrolled as one of my helpers.

Here is your Lone Ranger Safety Scout Badge. Isn't it a dandy though? Put it on and wear it. You can be mighty proud of it, for those who see it will say to themselves, "There is a comrade of the Lone Ranger and one of his right hand helpers . . . brave and dependable."

REMEMBER, you are NOT to wear this badge of honor, if you fail to keep your Lone Ranger Safety Scout pledge.

By working together just think of the good we can do . . . how many children, yes and grown-ups too, we can save from being hurt by autos and trucks. Think of the great help we can be to each other, for you know we are all comrades.

Read your Lone Ranger Safety Scout pledge often and live up to it everyday.

I am counting on you. Don't disappoint me.

Your comrade,

The Lone Ranger

Oke Tonto

"TONTO HIM KNOW YOU KEEP 'EM PLEDGE TO LONE RANGER"

Folder, 1940, Silvercup Bread premium, $75.00 – 150.00.

Six Lone Ranger cast photo cards, 1938, Cobakco Bread premium, $250.00 – 350.00 set.

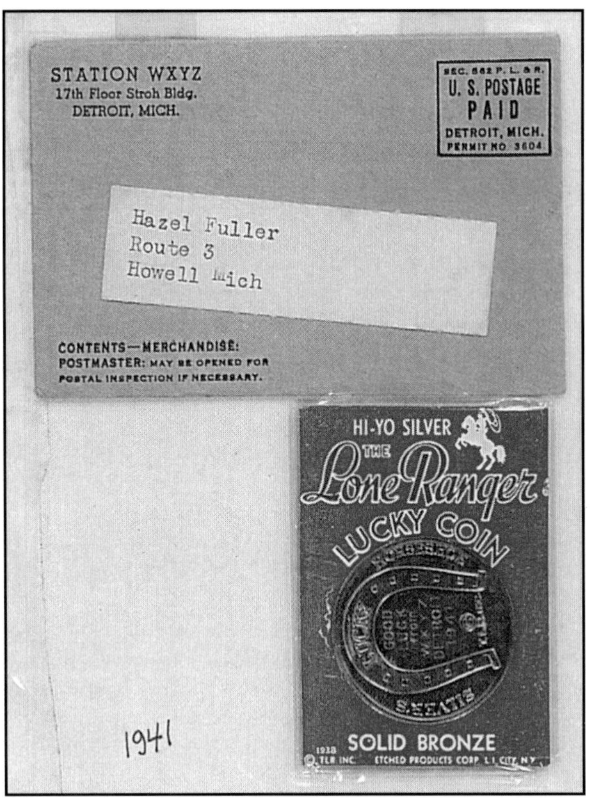

Lucky Coin, 1941, radio station WXYZ premium, $150.00 – 350.00 complete.

Rodeo card, 1950, personal appearance, $65.00 – 95.00.

Pinback button, 1946 – 1948, sold at circus appearances, because button shows dark horse instead of white horse and rider does not have a mask, very rare mistake item, $125.00 – 250.00.

Color pinback button, 1950, $35.00 – 65.00.

Pinback buttons, 1938 – 1950, $35.00 – 75.00 each.

Secret compartment, 1942, early prototype that was not used, limited number were made up for review. Regular second version with sliding top was then presented and produced. $250.00 – 850.00, rare item; mint $2,500.00.

Pinback buttons, 1960, Clayton Moore photos, $25.00 – 45.00.

Buchan's Bread buttons, 1938, complete set, $250.00 – 350.00.

Captain Action rings, 1960, $25.00 – 45.00.

White plastic ring, 1970s, $35.00 – 55.00.

Magazine photos, 1938 – 1940, Brace Beemer, $35.00 – 65.00 each.

Cardboard sign, 1950, $125.00 – 250.00.

Savings bonds membership card and coin, 1957, $125.00 – 175.00.

Spoon, 1938, $75.00 – 95.00.

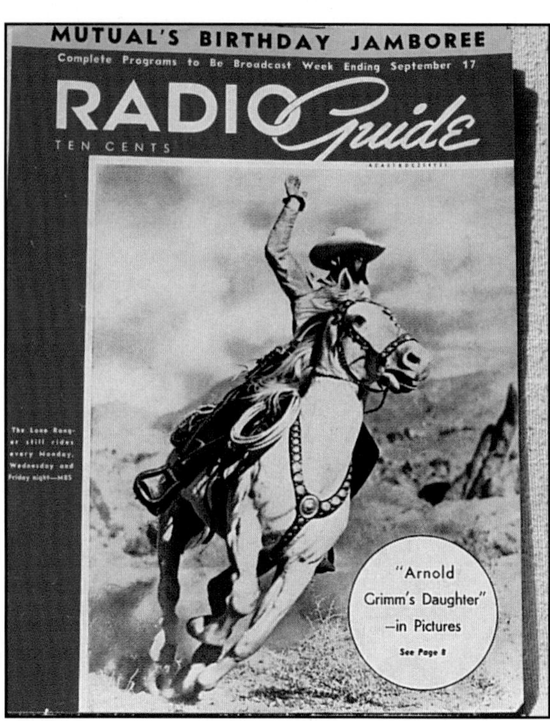

Radio guide, Lone Ranger Story, 1939, $65.00 – 95.00.

Pocket watch, 1970, $75.00 – 95.00.

Wristwatch, 1938, $125.00 – 175.00.

Large tin sign, full color embossed, $750.00 – 1,500.00.

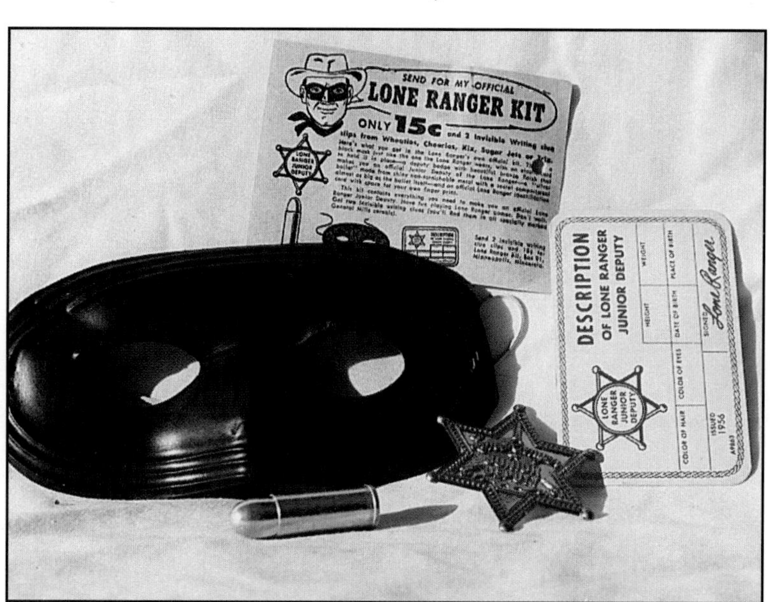

Deputy kit, 1956, radio premium, $125.00 – 175.00.

Pilot radio, adult, 1940, $750.00 – 1,500.00 rare.

Cereal premium advertisements, 1945 – 1954, $35.00 – 55.00.

First aid kit, Victory Corp., 1942, $75.00 – 95.00.

Cone papter wrapper, 1940, $75.00 – 125.00.

Large 24" doll, 1940, $975.00 – 1,500.00.

Ice cream comic, 1938, rare first comic, $1,750.00 – 3,200.00, fine condition.

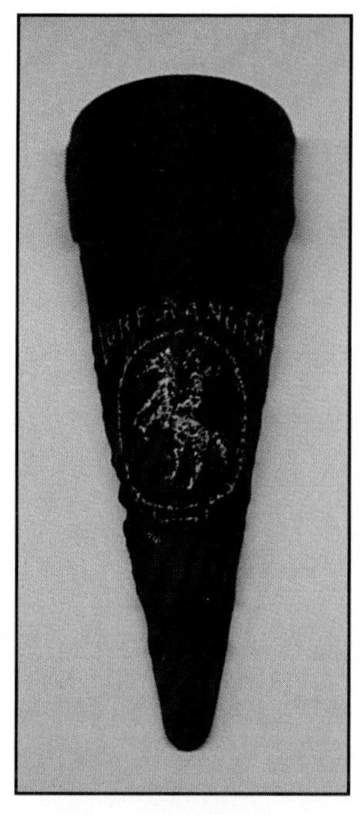

Cast iron die for cones, 1940, rare, $350.00 – 450.00.

Ice cream cone box, 1940, $350.00 – 750.00.

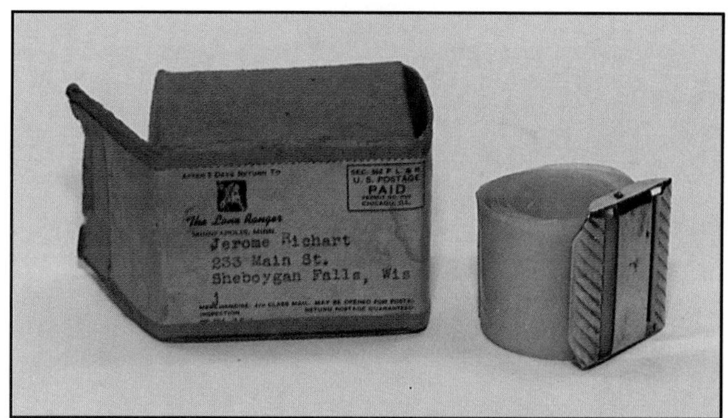

Glow-in-the-dark belt, 1943, rare, $150.00 – 250.00.

Tonto beaded belt, 1956, premium, rare, $125.00 – 175.00.

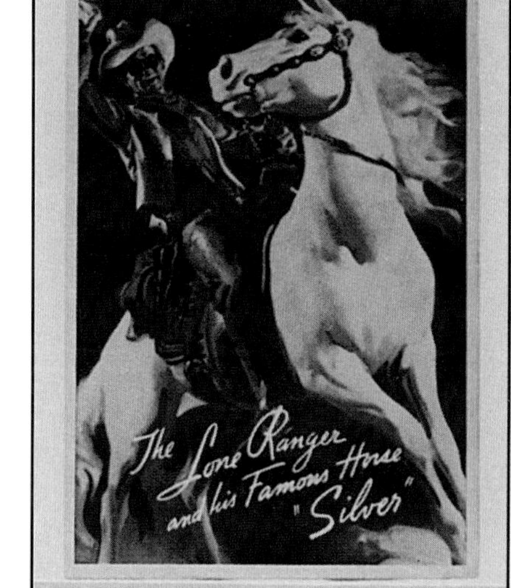

Newspaper photo card, 1938, $35.00 – 75.00.

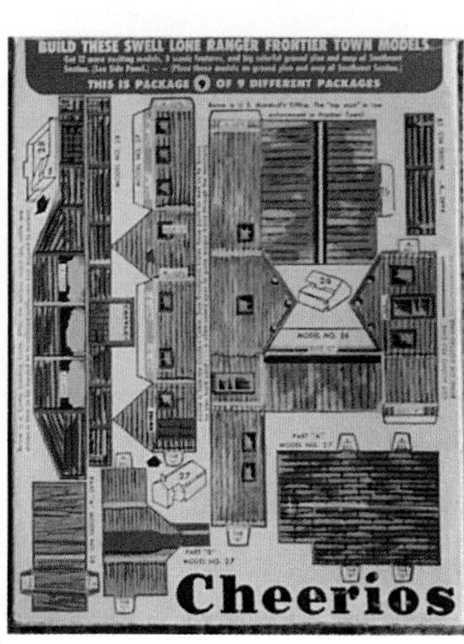

Frontier town, rare, four sections complete with 72 models, $1,500.00 – 2,000.00.

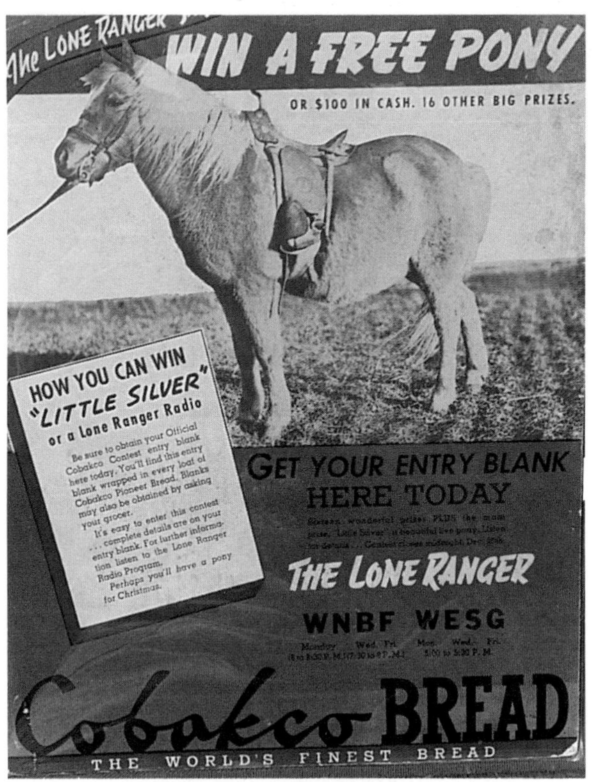

Store ad for pony, 1940, $95.00 – 150.00.

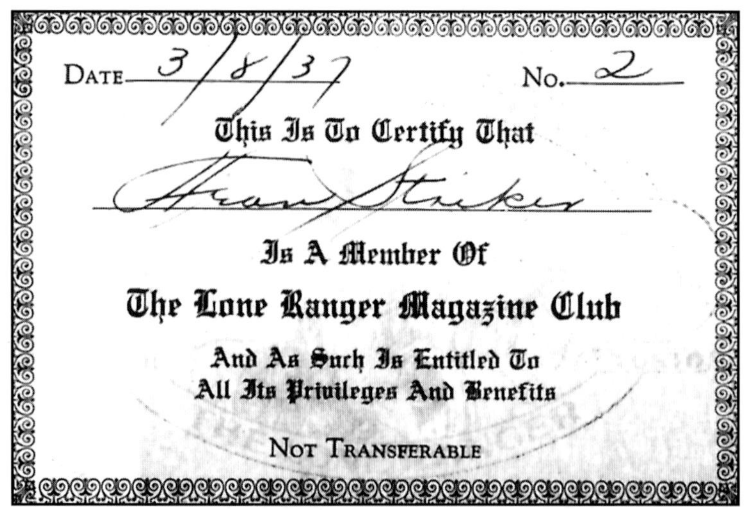
Date 3/8/37 No. 2

This Is To Certify That

[signature]

Is A Member Of

The Lone Ranger Magazine Club

And As Such Is Entitled To
All Its Privileges And Benefits

Not Transferable

Pulp magazine club, 1939, membership card permium, $150.00 – 250.00.

Saddle ring with film, 1951, $125.00 – 175.00.

Face masks, 1957, $25.00 each, $350.00 set.

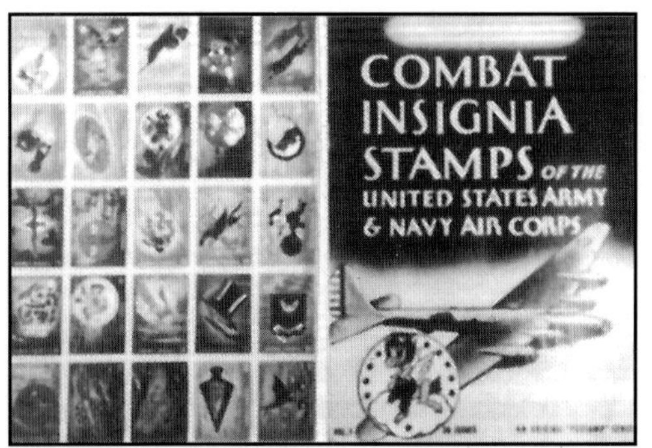

Combat stamps, 1942, $125.00 – 175.00.

Pedometer, 1947, $55.00 – 95.00.

Manual, 1940, $125.00 – 175.00.

Frontier Town newspaper ad, 1948, $35.00 – 55.00.

Advertising folder, 1938, ice cream giveaway premiums, $150.00 – 250.00.

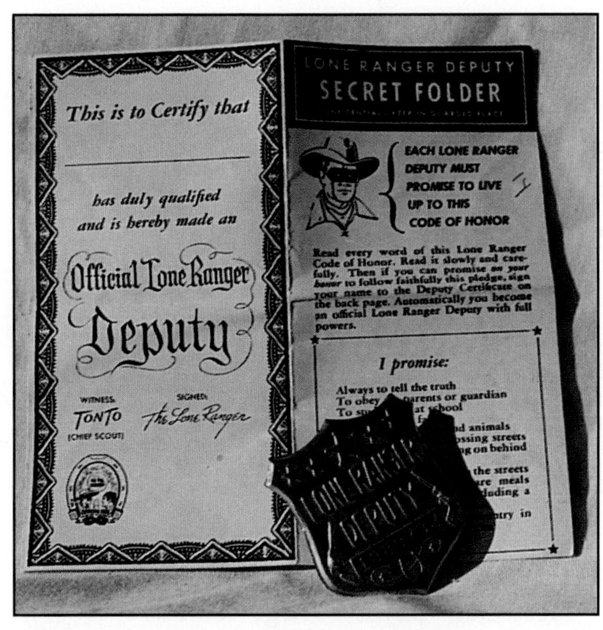

Deputy badge with secret component, 1951, $125.00 – 175.00.

Marx clicker pistols, serial giveaway, 1939, $125.00 – 175.00 each.

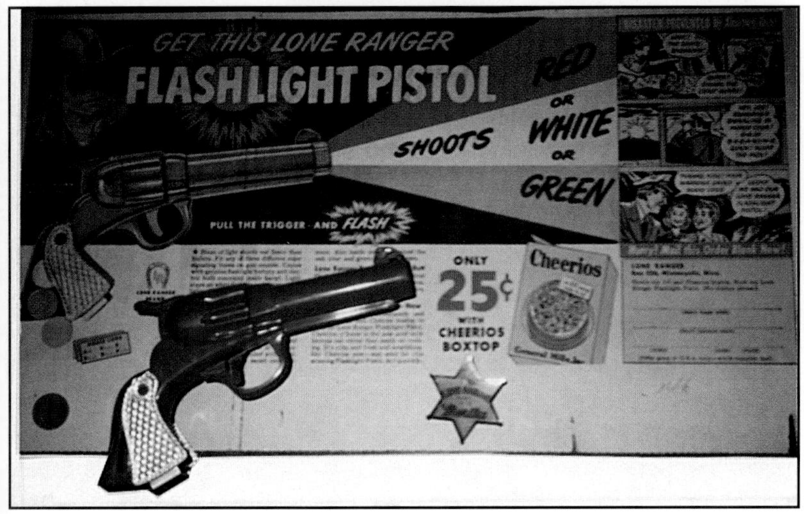

Flashlight pistol, 1948, $125.00 – 150.00.

Flashlight ring, 1947, $125.00 – 150.00.

Cheerios box, 1956, revolver premium, $150.00 – 175.00.

Six-gun ring, 1948, $150.00 – 175.00.

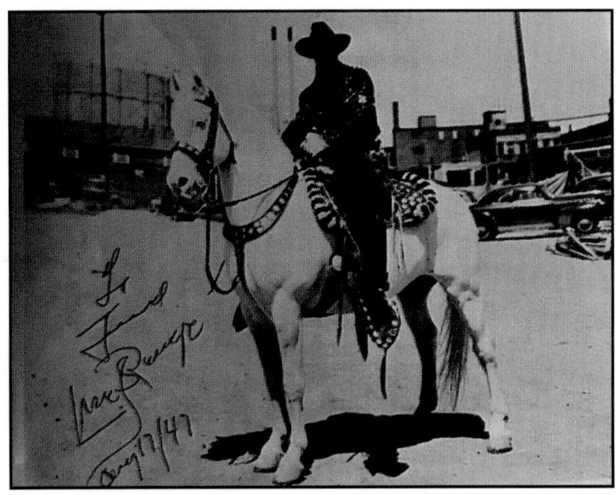

Black and white photo, giveaway, 1947, actor unknown, $75.00 – 175.00.

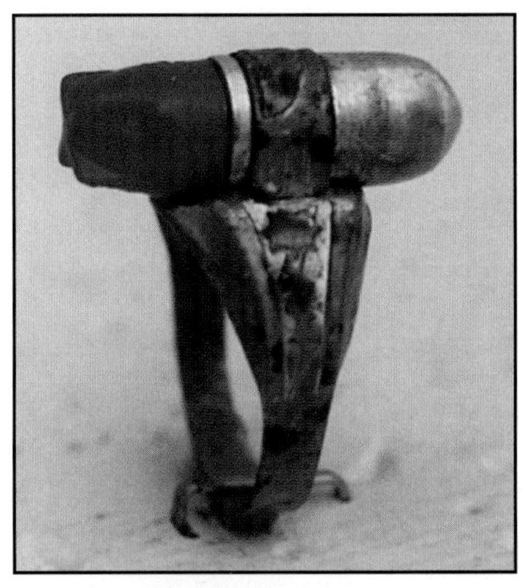

Atomic bomb ring, 1946, $95.00 – 125.00.

Bond Bread giveaway, color painting, 1938 – 1940, $50.00 – 75.00.

Comic booklets, 1951, $35.00 – 55.00 each.

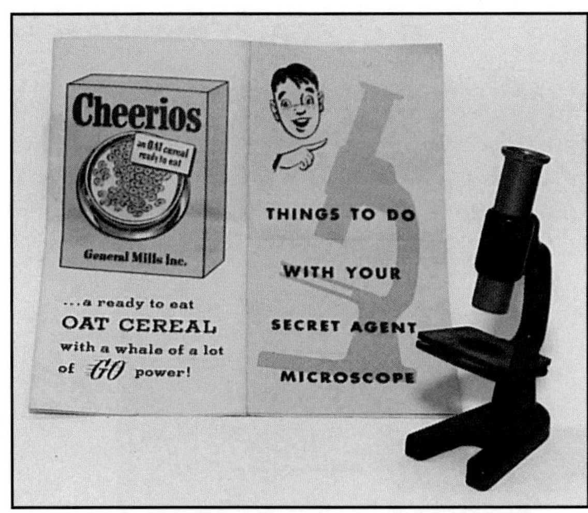

Cheerios secret agent microscope, 1947, $125.00 – 150.00.

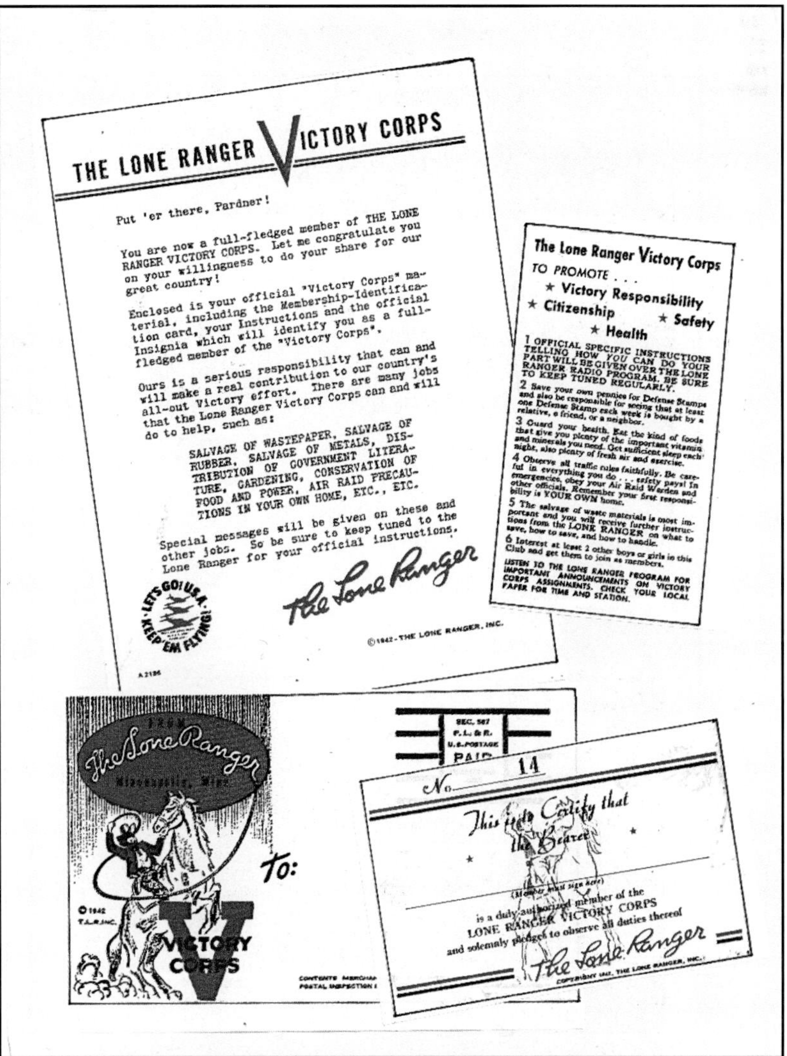

THE LONE RANGER VICTORY CORPS

Put 'er there, Pardner!

You are now a full-fledged member of THE LONE RANGER VICTORY CORPS. Let me congratulate you on your willingness to do your share for our great country!

Enclosed is your official "Victory Corps" material, including the Membership-Identification card, your Instructions and the official Insignia which will identify you as a full-fledged member of the "Victory Corps".

Ours is a serious responsibility that can and will make a real contribution to our country's all-out Victory effort. There are many jobs that the Lone Ranger Victory Corps can and will do to help, such as:

SALVAGE OF WASTEPAPER, SALVAGE OF RUBBER, SALVAGE OF METALS, DISTRIBUTION OF GOVERNMENT LITERATURE, GARDENING, CONSERVATION OF FOOD AND POWER, AIR RAID PRECAUTIONS IN YOUR OWN HOME, ETC., ETC.

Special messages will be given on these and other jobs. So be sure to keep tuned to the Lone Ranger for your official instructions.

The Lone Ranger

LET'S GO! U.S.A. KEEP 'EM FLYING!

©1942 - THE LONE RANGER, INC.

A 2186

The Lone Ranger Victory Corps

TO PROMOTE . . .

★ Victory Responsibility
★ Citizenship ★ Safety
★ Health

1 OFFICIAL SPECIFIC INSTRUCTIONS TELLING HOW *YOU* CAN DO YOUR PART WILL BE GIVEN OVER THE LONE RANGER RADIO PROGRAM. BE SURE TO KEEP TUNED REGULARLY.

2 Save your own pennies for Defense Stamps and also be responsible for seeing that at least one Defense Stamp each week is bought by a relative, a friend, or a neighbor.

3 Guard your health. Eat the kind of foods that give you plenty of the important vitamin and minerals you need. Get sufficient sleep each night, also plenty of fresh air and exercise.

4 Observe all traffic rules faithfully. Be careful in everything you do . . . safety pays! In emergencies, obey your Air Raid Warden and other officials. Remember your first responsibility is YOUR OWN home.

5 The salvage of waste materials is most important and you will receive further instructions from the LONE RANGER on what to save, how to save, and how to handle.

6 Interest at least 2 other boys or girls in this Club and get them to join as members.

LISTEN TO THE LONE RANGER PROGRAM FOR IMPORTANT ANNOUNCEMENTS ON VICTORY CORPS ASSIGNMENTS. CHECK YOUR LOCAL PAPER FOR TIME AND STATION.

FROM The Lone Ranger Minneapolis, Minn.

To:

VICTORY CORPS

SEC. 567 P.L. & R. U.S. POSTAGE PAID

No. 14

This is to Certify that the Bearer

(Member must sign here)

is a duly authorized member of the LONE RANGER VICTORY CORPS and solemnly pledges to observe all duties thereof

The Lone Ranger

COPYRIGHT 1942, THE LONE RANGER, INC.

Victory Corps, 1942, $75.00 – 150.00.

Life-size figures, paper, 1957, $600.00 – 850.00 set.

Victory circus, 1942, $65.00 – 125.00.

Silver's lucky horseshoe badge, 1940, $75.00 – 125.00.

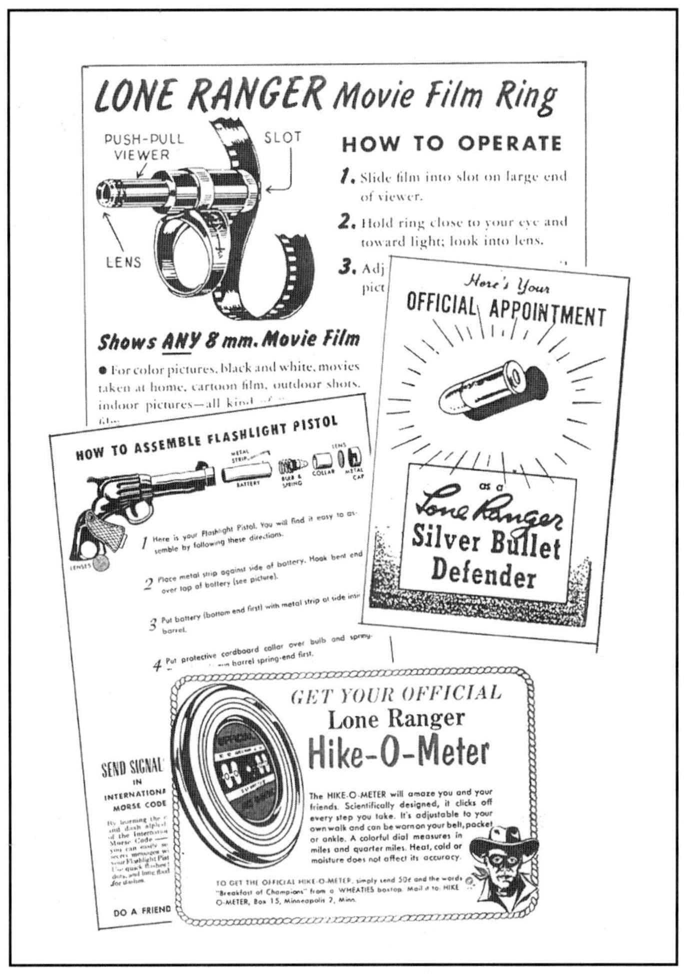

Cereal premium flyers, $25.00 – 75.00.

Coloring contest card, 1951, $65.00 – 95.00.

Movie telescope ring with film, 1951, $175.00 – 250.00.

Silvercup badge, 1935, $125.00 – 250.00 each.

Circus program, first public appearance outside Detroit, rare, 1940, $95.00 – 150.00.

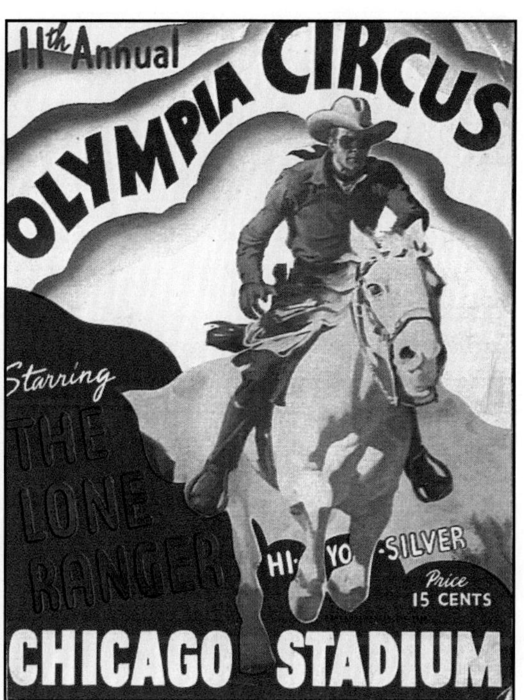

Rodeo and Ranch Exposition program, last rodeo appearance, 1950, $95.00 – 150.00.

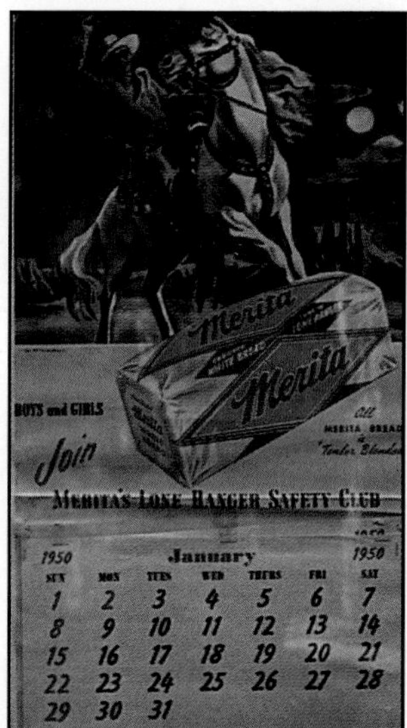

Merita bread calandar, 1938 – 1940, $60.00 – 225.00.

Coloring contest pictures from cereal boxes, rare, 1951, $45.00 – 95.00 each.

Good luck token, 1938 – 1940, $85.00 – 125.00.

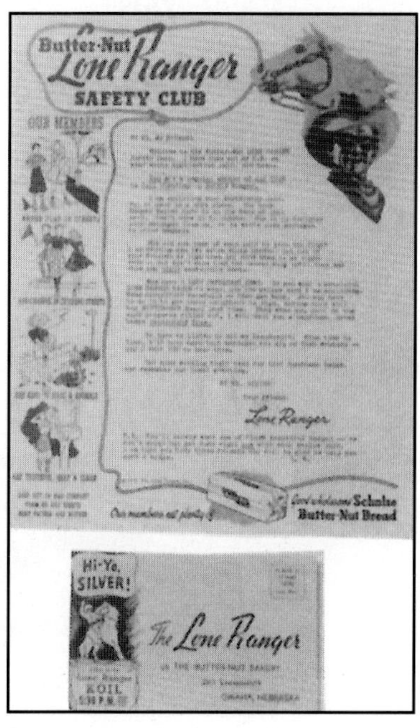

Safety club, 1940, $85.00 – 125.00.

Cereal boxes, 1940 – 1957, $75.00 – 175.00.

Morton salt premium, 1940, $150.00 – 250.00.

Weber Bread wrapper, 1940, $25.00 – 65.00.

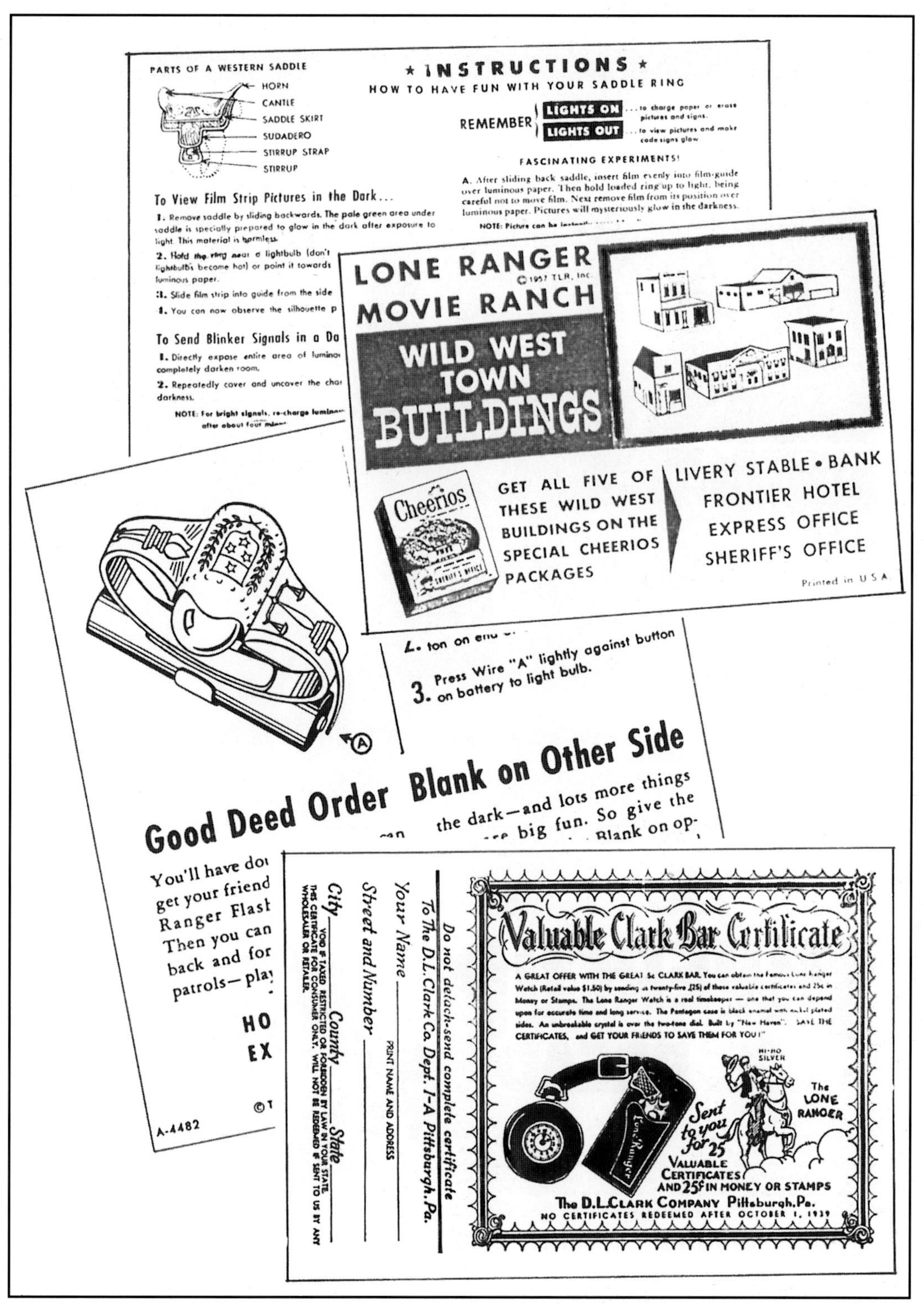

Cereal premium flyers, 1940 – 1952, $25.00 – 75.00.

WHERE'S THE LONE RANGER?

Here Is Your
LONE RANGER HUNT MAP
LISTEN TO THE LONE RANGER
Monday, Wednesday and Friday Evenings
SILVERCUP
THE WORLD'S FINEST BREAD
WXYZ
WOR
WGN

"Try SILVERCUP The World's Finest BREAD"

Here's the bread that youngsters and grown-ups go for... it tastes so good. And it's good *for* them, too. Practically half, 42 per cent, of every loaf is rich, whole, liquid milk. Only natural wheat flour, aged and mellowed for 14 weeks, is used in Silvercup. The result is "the world's finest bread." And Silvercup is always delivered in *two* jackets... *both* sealed ... to fully guard its wholesome freshness. And it always makes delicious toast. Try a golden loaf of Silvercup, the world's finest bread. You'll go for it, too!

GORDON BAKING COMPANY · DETROIT, NEW YORK, CHICAGO

Hunt map premium, 1941, rare, $175.00 – 250.00 complete.

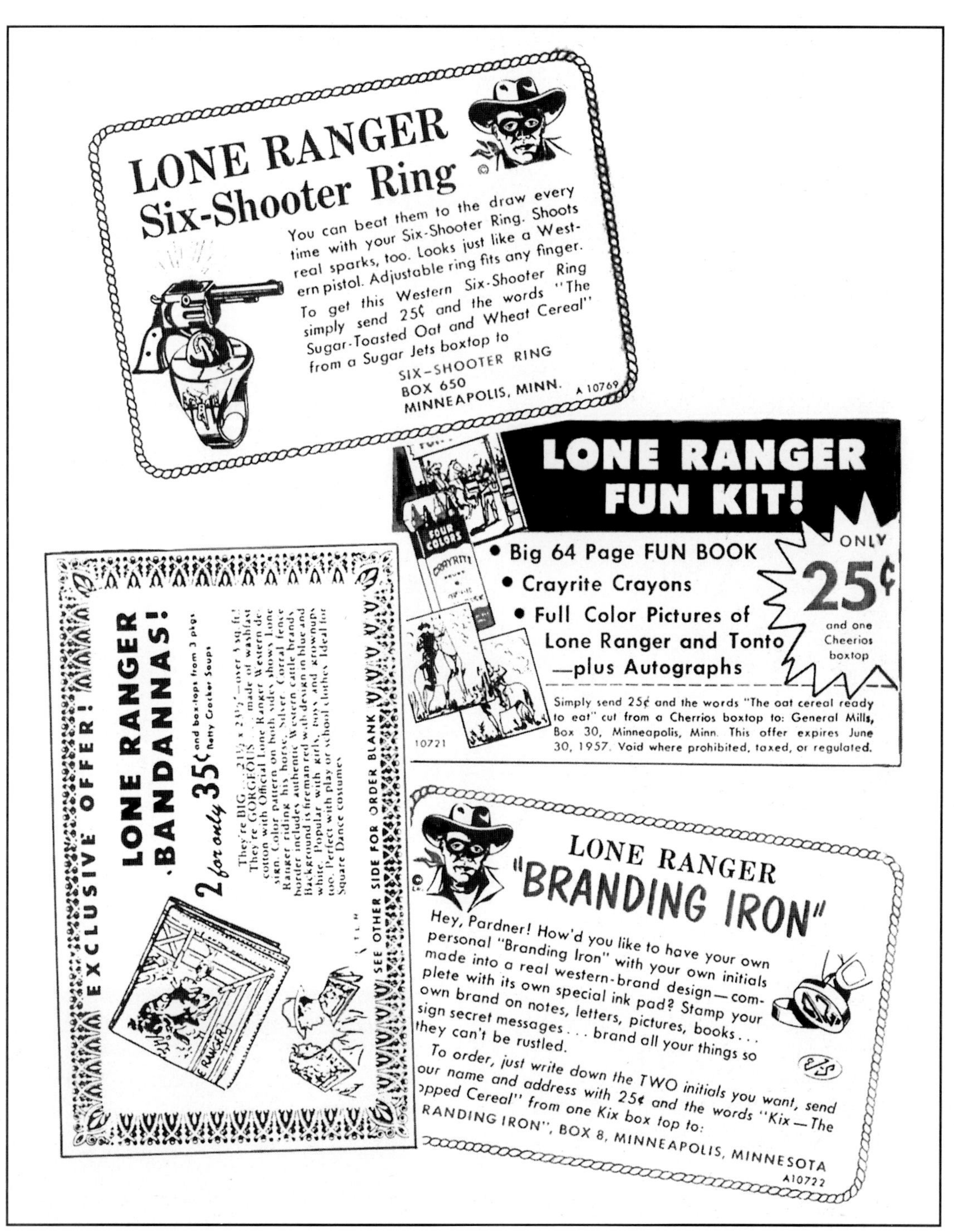

Cereal premium flyers, 1945 – 1952, $25.00 – 65.00.

Photo giveaways, premiums, 1936 – 1940, $65.00 – 125.00.

CHARTER

LONE RANGER SAFETY CLUB

SPONSORED BY Merita BREAD AND CAKES

We, the undersigned, pledge ourselves to support the principles and ideals of the Lone Ranger, to always obey his ten safety rules and to help promote safety at every opportunity.

MEMBERS

Countersigned Lone Ranger

Safety club charter, 1938, Merita bread premium, $75.00 – 95.00.

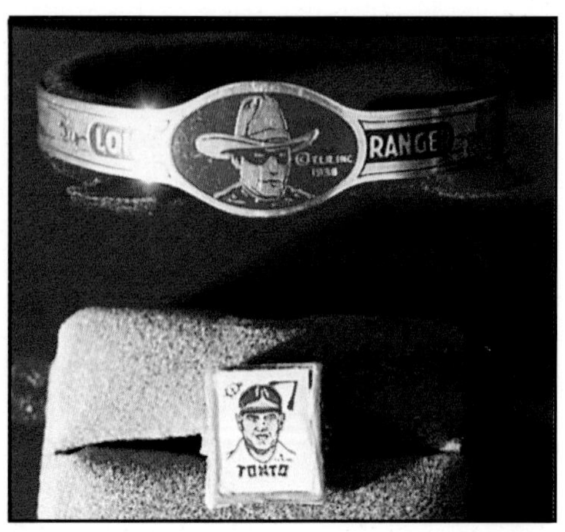

1938, rare ice cream premiums, Tonto ring, $75.00 – 150.00; Lone Ranger bracelet, $125.00 – 200.00.

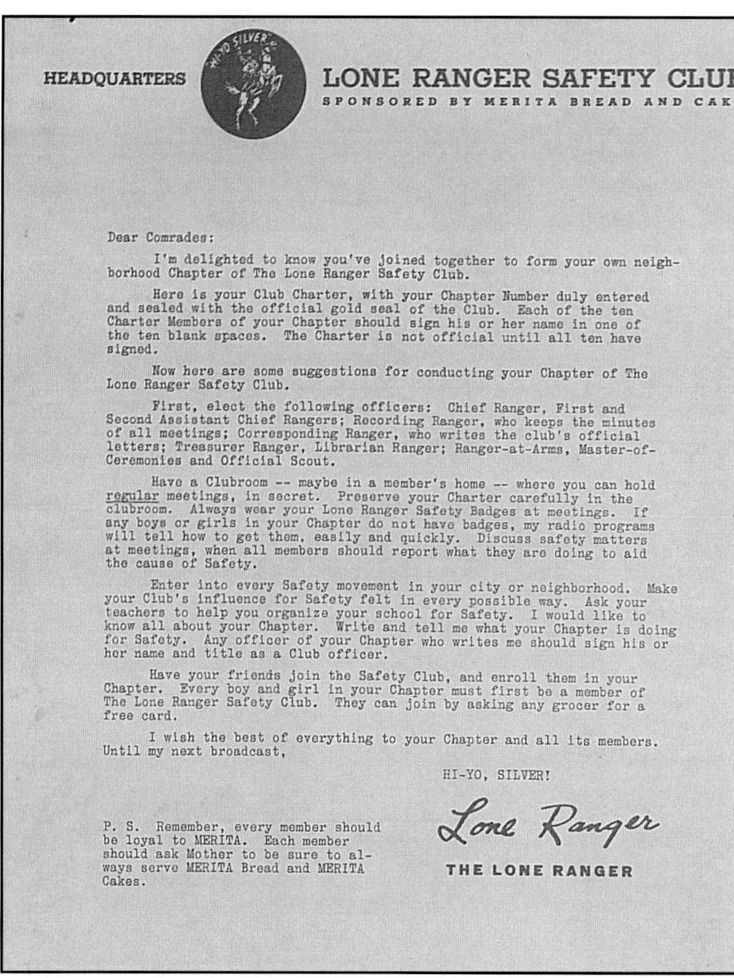

HEADQUARTERS

LONE RANGER SAFETY CLUB

SPONSORED BY MERITA BREAD AND CAK

Dear Comrades:

I'm delighted to know you've joined together to form your own neighborhood Chapter of The Lone Ranger Safety Club.

Here is your Club Charter, with your Chapter Number duly entered and sealed with the official gold seal of the Club. Each of the ten Charter Members of your Chapter should sign his or her name in one of the ten blank spaces. The Charter is not official until all ten have signed.

Now here are some suggestions for conducting your Chapter of The Lone Ranger Safety Club.

First, elect the following officers: Chief Ranger, First and Second Assistant Chief Rangers; Recording Ranger, who keeps the minutes of all meetings; Corresponding Ranger, who writes the club's official letters; Treasurer Ranger, Librarian Ranger; Ranger-at-Arms, Master-of-Ceremonies and Official Scout.

Have a Clubroom -- maybe in a member's home -- where you can hold regular meetings, in secret. Preserve your Charter carefully in the clubroom. Always wear your Lone Ranger Safety Badges at meetings. If any boys or girls in your Chapter do not have badges, my radio programs will tell how to get them, easily and quickly. Discuss safety matters at meetings, when all members should report what they are doing to aid the cause of Safety.

Enter into every Safety movement in your city or neighborhood. Make your Club's influence for Safety felt in every possible way. Ask your teachers to help you organize your school for Safety. I would like to know all about your Chapter. Write and tell me what your Chapter is doing for Safety. Any officer of your Chapter who writes me should sign his or her name and title as a Club officer.

Have your friends join the Safety Club, and enroll them in your Chapter. Every boy and girl in your Chapter must first be a member of The Lone Ranger Safety Club. They can join by asking any grocer for a free card.

I wish the best of everything to your Chapter and all its members. Until my next broadcast,

HI-YO, SILVER!

Lone Ranger

THE LONE RANGER

P. S. Remember, every member should be loyal to MERITA. Each member should ask Mother to be sure to always serve MERITA Bread and MERITA Cakes.

Safety club letter, 1938, Merita Bread premium, $35.00 – 55.00.

Advertisement, 1940, Merita Bread, paper, $45.00 – 85.00.

Pocketknife, 1947, $45.00 – 75.00.

Sailor hat, 1938 – 1940, $25.00 – 75.00.

Victory tab, 1942, $95.00 – 125.00.

Coloring book, 1950, Merita Safety/Health Club premium, $75.00 – 125.00.

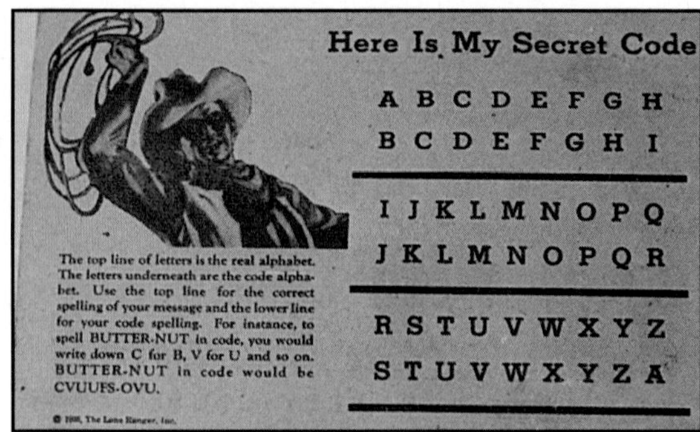

Here Is My Secret Code

A B C D E F G H
B C D E F G H I

I J K L M N O P Q
J K L M N O P Q R

R S T U V W X Y Z
S T U V W X Y Z A

The top line of letters is the real alphabet. The letters underneath are the code alphabet. Use the top line for the correct spelling of your message and the lower line for your code spelling. For instance, to spell BUTTER-NUT in code, you would write down C for B, V for U and so on. BUTTER-NUT in code would be CVUUFS-OVU.

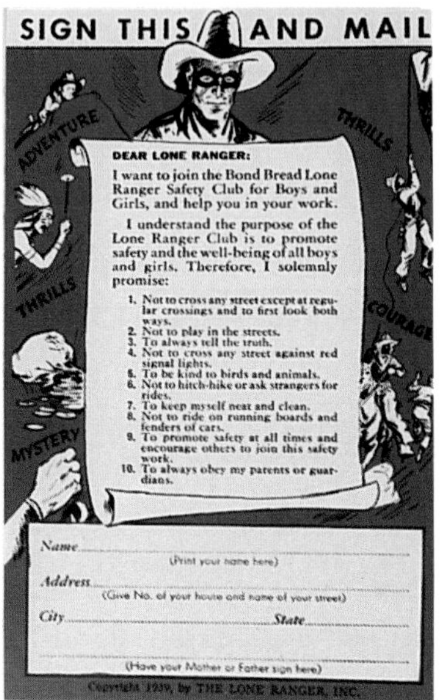

SIGN THIS AND MAIL

DEAR LONE RANGER:

I want to join the Bond Bread Lone Ranger Safety Club for Boys and Girls, and help you in your work.

I understand the purpose of the Lone Ranger Club is to promote safety and the well-being of all boys and girls. Therefore, I solemnly promise:

1. Not to cross any street except at regular crossings and to first look both ways.
2. Not to play in the streets.
3. To always tell the truth.
4. Not to cross any street against red signal lights.
5. To be kind to birds and animals.
6. Not to hitch-hike or ask strangers for rides.
7. To keep myself neat and clean.
8. Not to ride on running boards and fenders of cars.
9. To promote safety at all times and encourage others to join this safety work.
10. To always obey my parents or guardians.

Name .... (Print your name here)

Address .... (Give No. of your house and name of your street)

City .... State ....

.... (Have your Mother or Father sign here)

Copyright 1939, by THE LONE RANGER, INC.

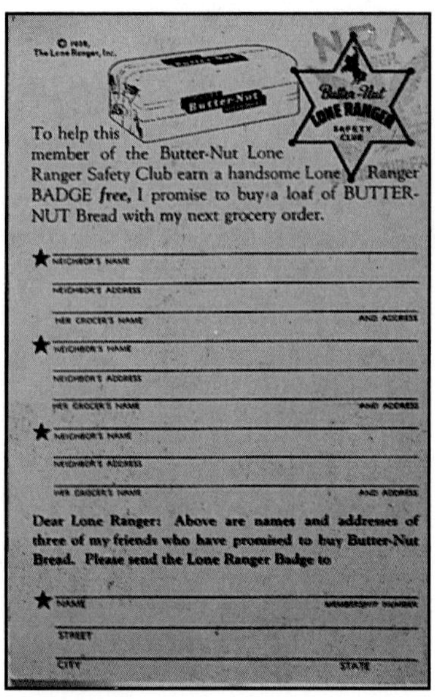

© 1938, The Lone Ranger, Inc.

To help this member of the Butter-Nut Lone Ranger Safety Club earn a handsome Lone Ranger BADGE *free*, I promise to buy a loaf of BUTTER-NUT Bread with my next grocery order.

★ NEIGHBOR'S NAME

NEIGHBOR'S ADDRESS

HER GROCER'S NAME AND ADDRESS

★ NEIGHBOR'S NAME

NEIGHBOR'S ADDRESS

HER GROCER'S NAME AND ADDRESS

★ NEIGHBOR'S NAME

NEIGHBOR'S ADDRESS

HER GROCER'S NAME AND ADDRESS

Dear Lone Ranger: Above are names and addresses of three of my friends who have promised to buy Butter-Nut Bread. Please send the Lone Ranger Badge to

★ NAME MEMBERSHIP NUMBER

STREET

CITY STATE

Safety club cards, 1938 – 1940, Butter Nut/Bond Bread premiums, $75.00 – 95.00 each.

Six-gun grocery store color poster, 1948, $50.00 – 250.00.

Flyers/banners, 1933, advertising Hi-Yo Silver of readio fame appearances, $350.00 – 750.00.

Gum card/painting, original, $1,500.00 – 2,500.00.

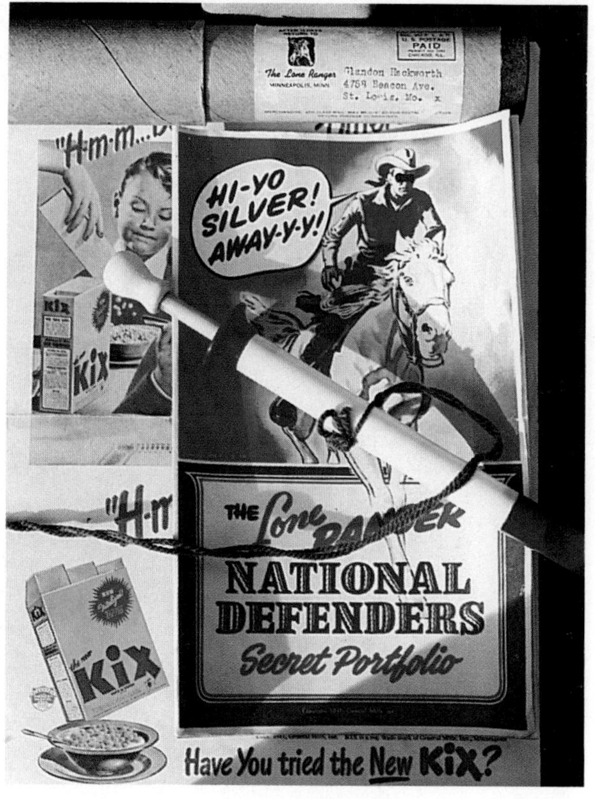

Signal Siren premium/mailer, portfolio, 1941, rare, $650.00 – 950.00.

Calendars, Merita bread, 1940 – 1950, $150.00 – 350.00 each.

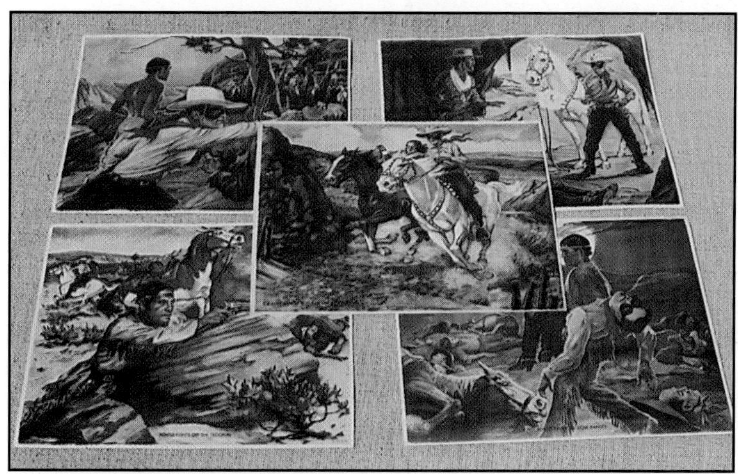

8"x10" color cards for Gum Inc., 1940, $350.00 – 600.00 set.

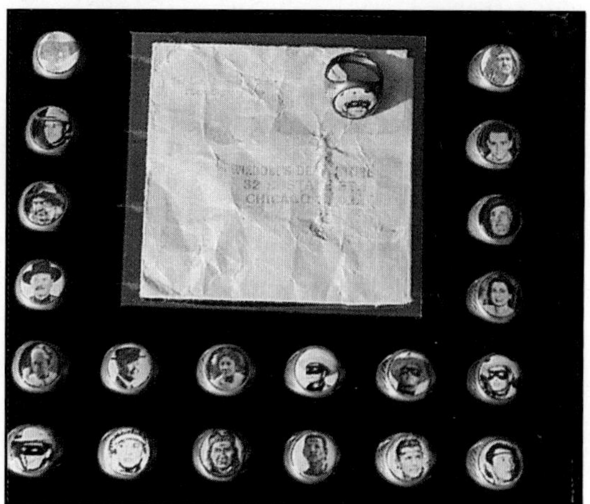

Rings, 1940 – 1950, Wiebolt's dept. store giveaways, photos of radio and television cast, $650.00 – 1,000.00.

Bandana, 1948 – 1950, premium, $75.00 – 125.00.

Color painting premium Merita bread, 1941, $175.00 – $225.00.

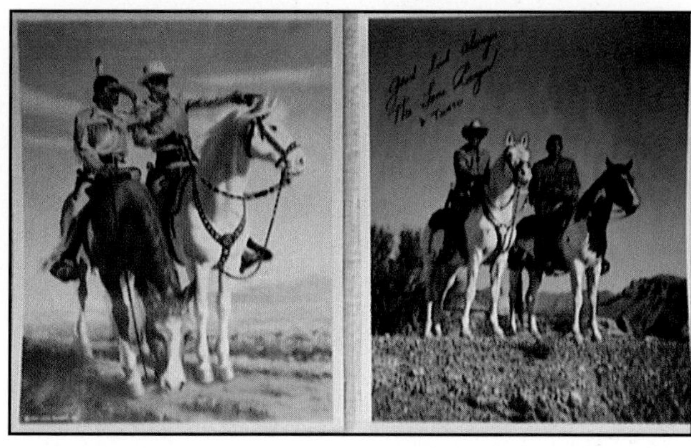

Premium photos, 1950s, full color, $55.00 – 85.00 each.

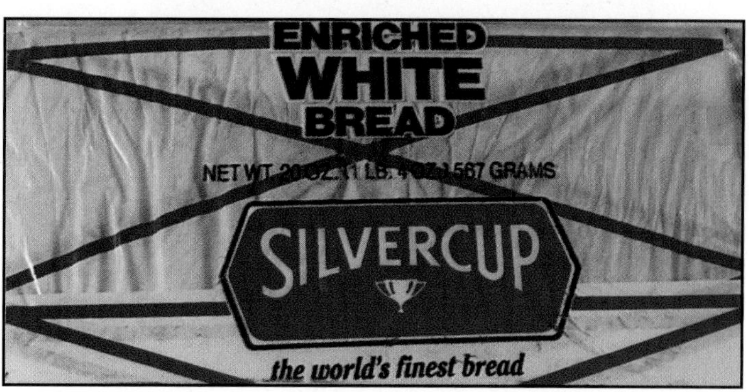

Silvercup bread wrapper, 1945, $65.00 – 75.00.

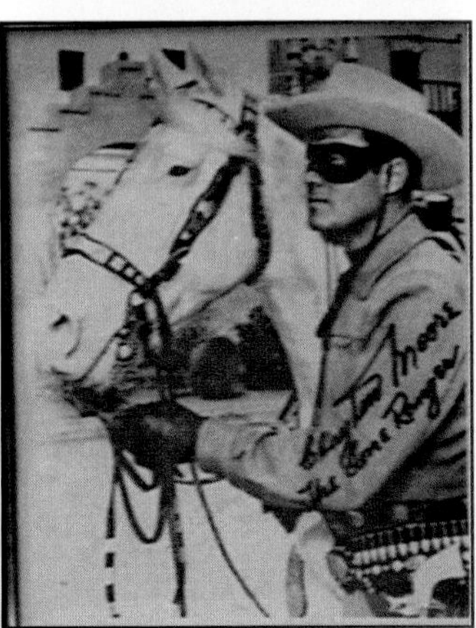

Autographed photographs: Chief Thundercloud, Bob Livingston, George Tendle, Brace Beemer, Clayton Moore, 1940 – 1950, $50.00 – 650.00.

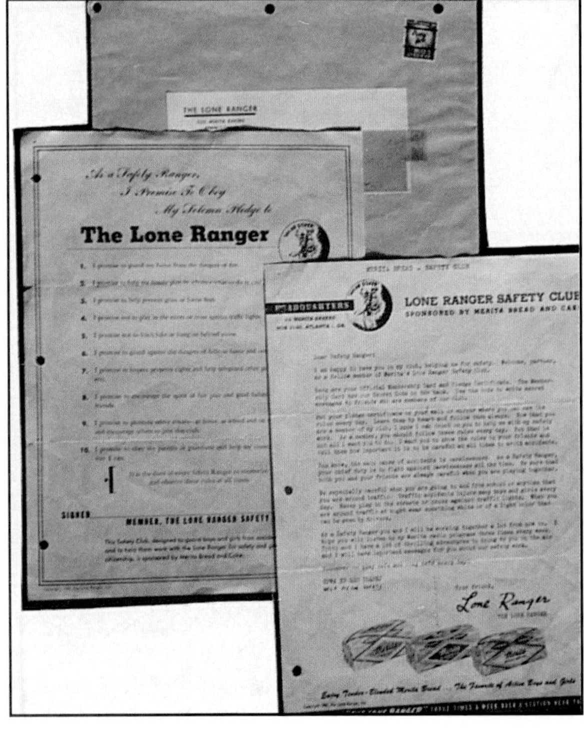

Merita Safety Club kit, 1940, $75.00 – 125.00.

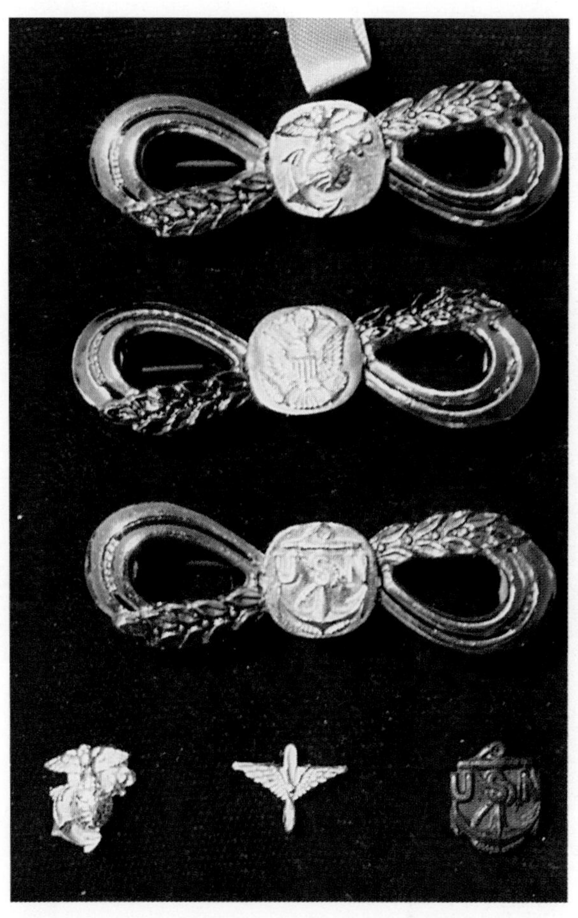

Military sweetheart pins for Army, Navy, and Marines, 1941, rare items, $150.00 – 250.00.

Advertising flyers, General Mills, 1940 – 1950, $25.00 – 45.00 each.

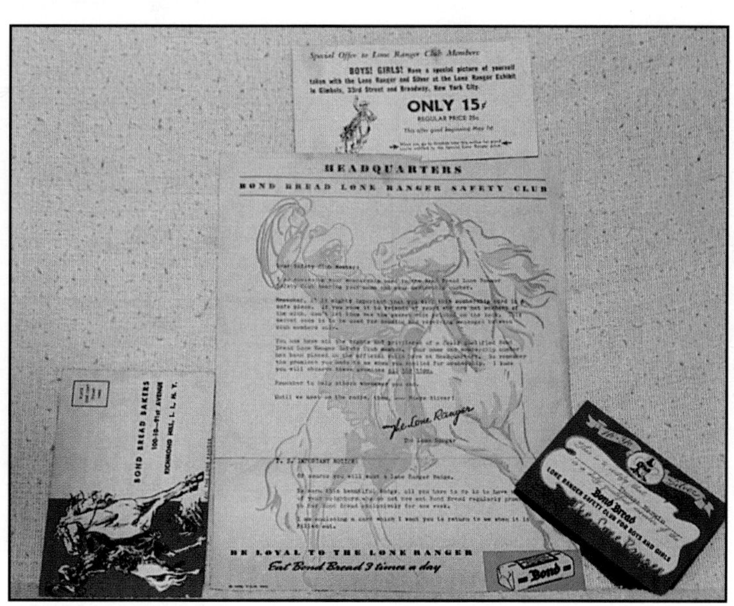

Safety Club kit, Bond bread, 1940s, $175.00 – 250.00 complete.

Merita bread premium, cardboard picture, 1950, $75.00 – 125.00.

Small metal sign, Merita bread, 1950, $250.00 – 450.00.

Merita bread cardboard sign, 1951, $175.00 – 250.00.

Bread wrapper for Bond bread, 1950, $75.00 – 125.00.

Holsum bread wrapper, 1939, $55.00 – 75.00.

Secret compartment ring, 1942, $175.00 – 250.00 with photo.

Schmidt's bread decal, 1940, rare, $125.00 – 175.00.

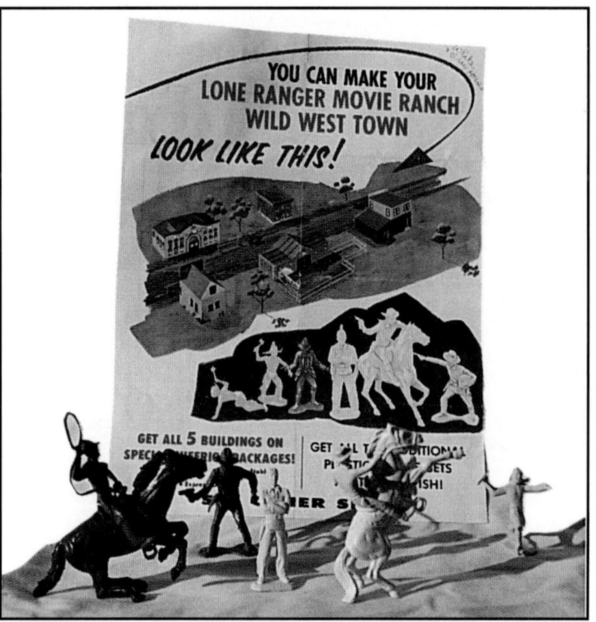

Figures, cereal premium, 1952, $95.00 – 145.00 set.

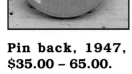

Pin back, 1947, $35.00 – 65.00.

Weather ring, 1947, $150.00 – 225.00.

Bullet key chain, 1970, $45.00 – 65.00.

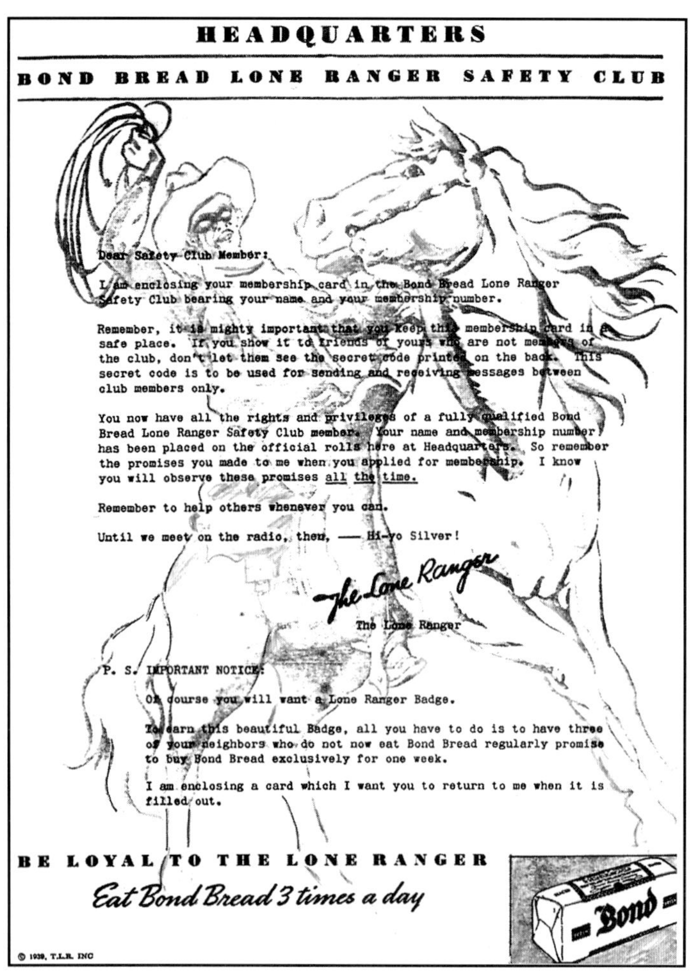

HEADQUARTERS

BOND BREAD LONE RANGER SAFETY CLUB

Dear Safety Club Member:

I am enclosing your membership card in the Bond Bread Lone Ranger Safety Club bearing your name and your membership number.

Remember, it is mighty important that you keep this membership card in a safe place. If you show it to friends of yours who are not members of the club, don't let them see the secret code printed on the back. This secret code is to be used for sending and receiving messages between club members only.

You now have all the rights and privileges of a fully qualified Bond Bread Lone Ranger Safety Club member. Your name and membership number has been placed on the official rolls here at Headquarters. So remember the promises you made to me when you applied for membership. I know you will observe these promises all the time.

Remember to help others whenever you can.

Until we meet on the radio, then, —— Hi-yo Silver!

The Lone Ranger

The Lone Ranger

P. S. IMPORTANT NOTICE:

Of course you will want a Lone Ranger Badge.

To earn this beautiful Badge, all you have to do is to have three of your neighbors who do not now eat Bond Bread regularly promise to buy Bond Bread exclusively for one week.

I am enclosing a card which I want you to return to me when it is filled out.

BE LOYAL TO THE LONE RANGER

Eat Bond Bread 3 times a day

Bond

© 1939, T.L.R. INC

Safety Club letter, 1939, $55.00 – 95.00.

Silver bullets, 1938 – 1952, $65.00 – 125.00.

Full color wood plaque, 1939, $75.00 – $125.00; color photo and frame, 1940, $75.00 – 95.00.

First photo giveaway for WXYZ, 1933, rare, $125.00 – 175.00.

Anniversary guest pin-back and ribbon, 1983, $50.00 – 65.00.

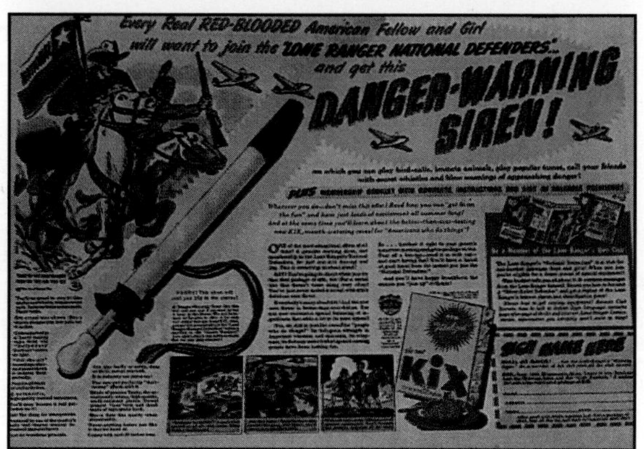

Premium ads, 1940 – 1950, $65.00 – 125.00 each.

Blackout kit, 5 items, complete kit with envelope, 1943, $125.00 – 225.00.

Cheerios war album with stamps and envelope, complete, 1943, $125.00 – 150.00.

Metal silver bullet pencil sharpener, 1938 – 1940, $85.00 – 125.00.

Autographed black & white photos, 1938 – 1940, $75.00 – 125.00.

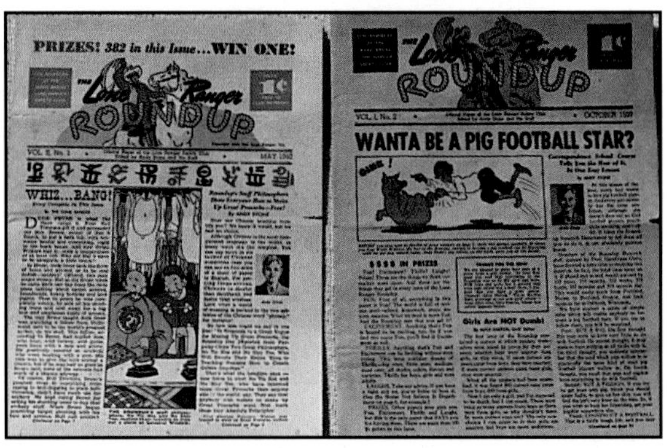

Safety Club newspapers, six issues, 1938 – 1940, rare paper items, $125.00 – 225.00.

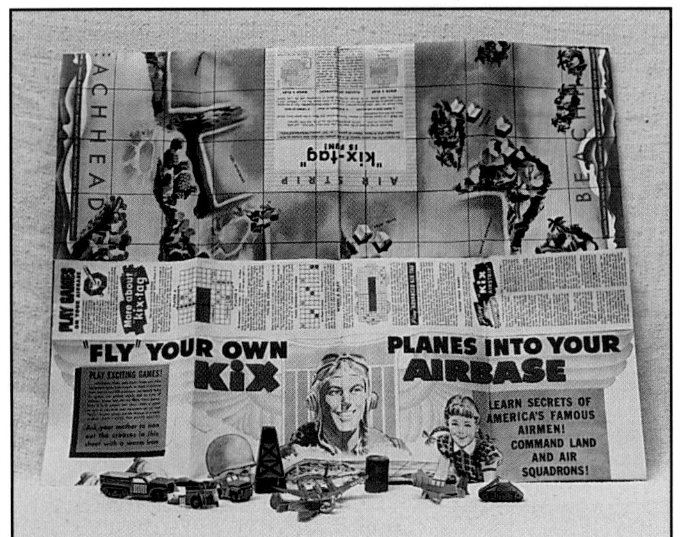

Kix airbase, 1943, rare, with all models, $175.00 – 350.00.

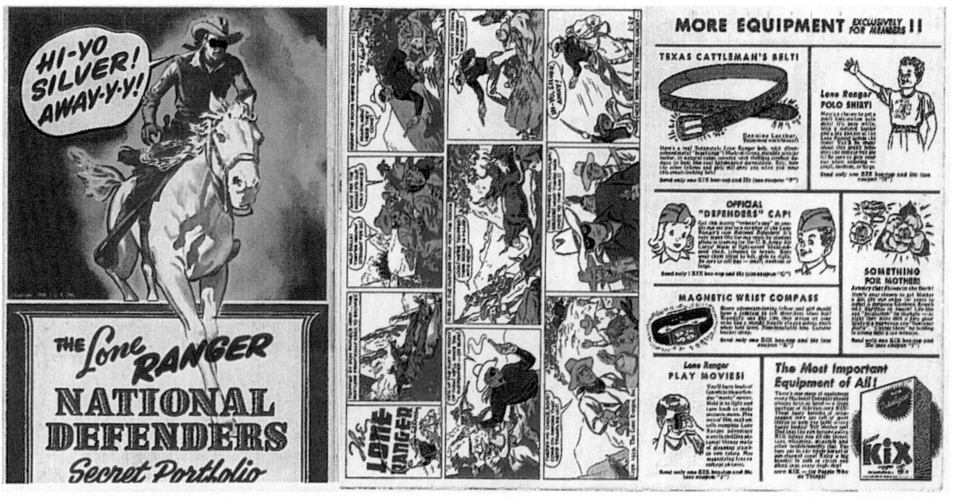

National Defenders secret portfolio, 1941, rare, $125.00 – 175.00.

Metal badge, 1950, $65.00 – 85.00.

Movie viewer, 1946, $95.00 – 125.00.

Tie rack, 1938, rare, $125.00 – 250.00.

Seven record set (Decca Records), 1951, $125.00 – 150.00.

Radio advertisement poster, 1940, $75.00 – 125.00.

Exhibit card display, 1940 – 1950, $75.00 – 150.00 each.

Mask and belt set, 1958, $75.00 – 95.00.

Deputy badge/card, 1966, $75.00 – 125.00.

Belt buckle, Clayton Moore, 1970, $75.00 – 125.00.

Lone Ranger and Silver Bullets game, unauthorized item, very rare, 1956, $125.00 – 225.00

Toy wrist watch, 1980, $65.00 – 95.00.

Ranch set, 1940, $350.00 – 450.00.

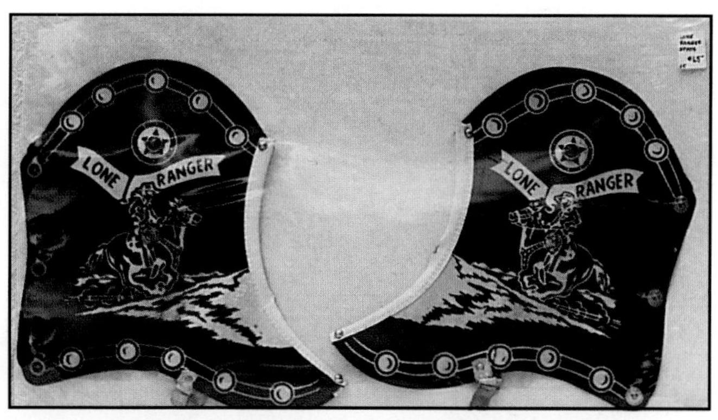

Boot spats, 1950, $65.00 – 95.00.

Rodeo set, 1940, $350.00 – 450.00.

Lone Ranger and Tonto figures, Marx, 1955, $125.00 – 175.00 complete.

Transfer decal, 1945, $35.00 – 45.00.

Figure pin (12 in series), 1970, $75.00 – 125.00, card set $45.00 each pin.

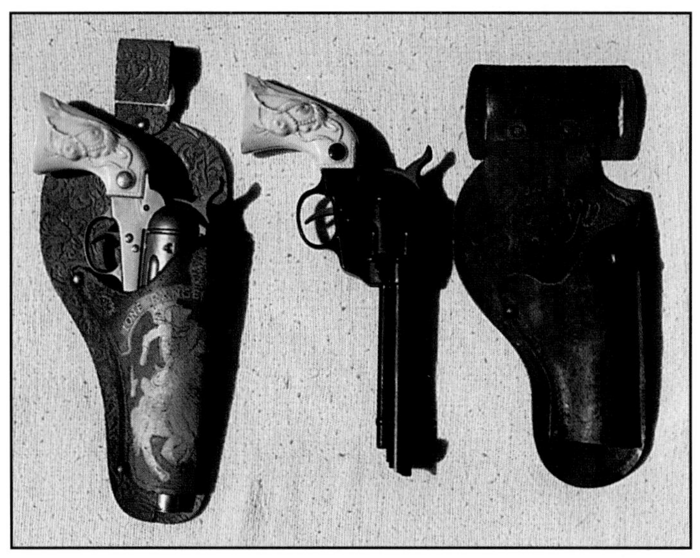

Smoking six-gun and holster, Marx, 1950s, $75.00 – 125.00 each.

Beanie cap, 1940, $75.00 – 95.00 each.

Room advertisement, Armstrong Flooring, 1940, $25.00 – 45.00.

Cast-iron six-gun with holster, Kilgore, 1938, $250.00 – 375.00.

Window card, 1956, $55.00 – 75.00.

Tonto outfit, 1946, $150.00 – 195.00.

Shirt, 1950, $75.00 – 125.00.

Lone Ranger and Tonto color print, 1,500 signed copies, 1980, $450.00 – 650.00.

Wall clock, $125.00 – 175.00.

Costume, complete, 1978, $75.00 – 95.00.

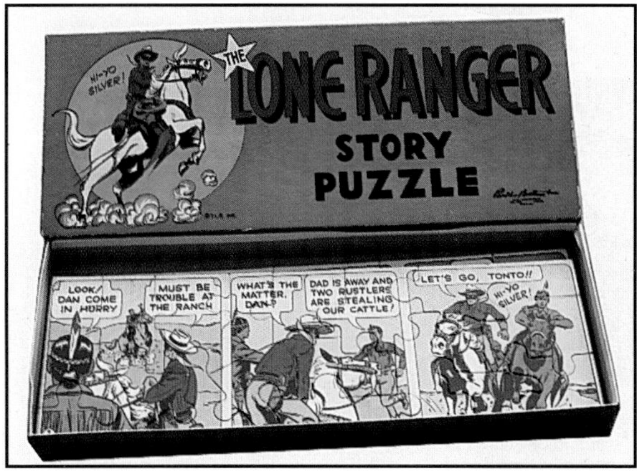

Puzzle set, four comic strips, 1945, $175.00 – 250.00.

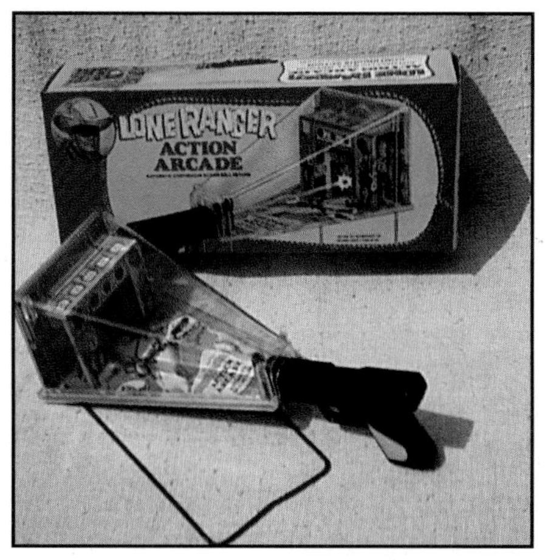

Action arcade, 1975, $95.00 – 125.00.

Playsuit and box, 1945 – 1947, $250.00 – 350.00.

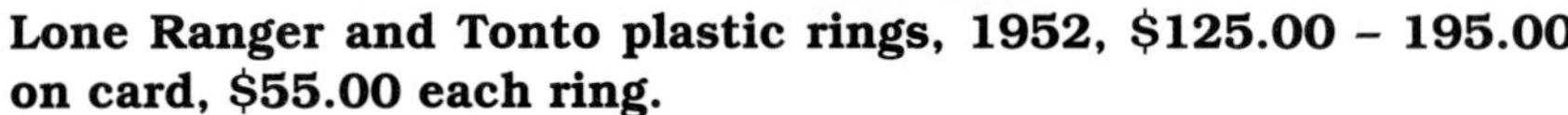

Lone Ranger and Tonto plastic rings, 1952, $125.00 – 195.00 on card, $55.00 each ring.

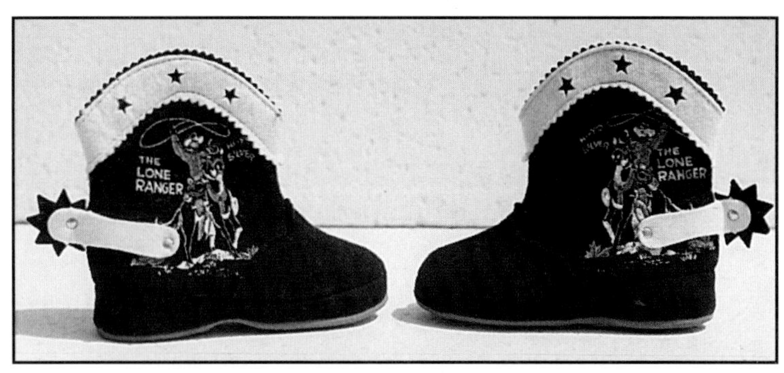

Slippers, 1950, $150.00 – 200.00.

Hi-Yo! Silver game, 1956, $95.00 – 150.00.

Parker Brothers Lone Ranger game, 1938, $95.00 – 150.00.

Lone Ranger/Tonto model, 1977, $50.00 – 75.00 each.

Game/boxed puzzle, 1966, $75.00 – 125.00.

Sports kit, complete, 1940, $250.00 – 295.00.

Gym bag and school bag, 1950s, $125.00 – 200.00.

Hand puppets with box, 1947, $175.00 – 200.00.

Holster, 1956, $125.00 – 175.00; gun, 1956, $75.00 – 125.00.

Bicycle, rare, date and price unknown.

Chuckwagon lantern, 1945, $175.00 – 225.00.

Marx tin wind-up, 1940, $350.00 – 750.00 with box.

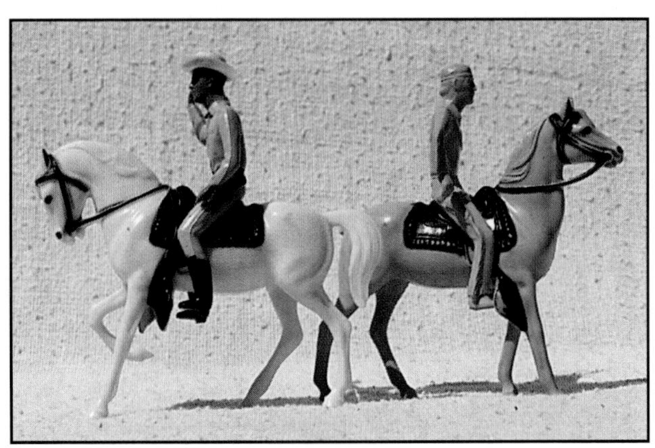

Small Hartland figures, 1950, rare, $95.00 – 125.00 each.

Large Hartland figures, 1950, $125.00 – 175.00 each (complete).

Plate and glass, 1939, $125.00 – 150.00 plate, 95.00 glass.

Wooden figure, very detailed, rare, 1938 – 1940, $750.00 – 900.00.

Plate, 1945, rare, $125.00 – 150.00.

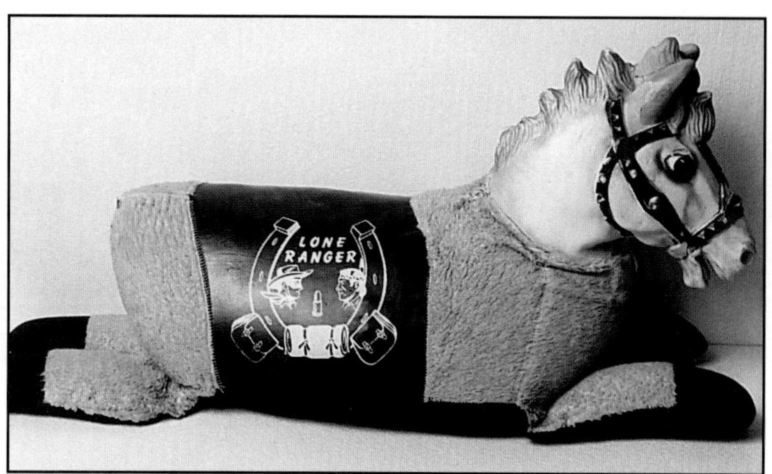

Silver, 1950, $150.00 – 225.00.

Cowboy hat, 1940, rare, $150.00 – 250.00.

Target and gun, small size, 1938, $125.00 – 175.00.

Wood record player, 1950, $225.00 – 275.00.

Handmade metal balance toy, rare, date unknown, $175.00 – 225.00.

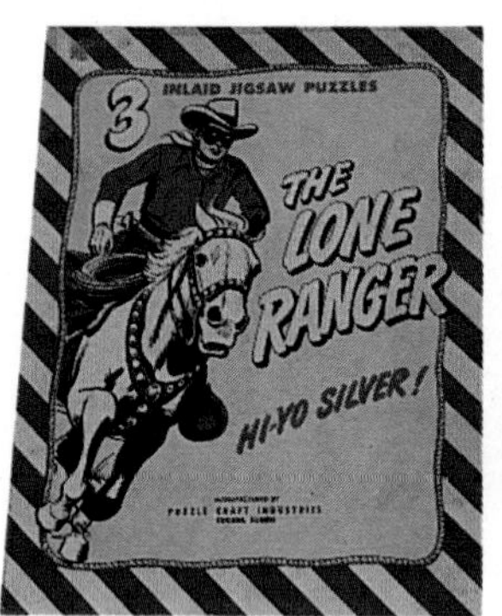

Puzzle set, four puzzles, 1945, $175.00 – 250.00.

Pencil boxes, 1947, $95.00 – 125.00 each.

Pistol, unauthorized, 1944, rare, $125.00 – 175.00.

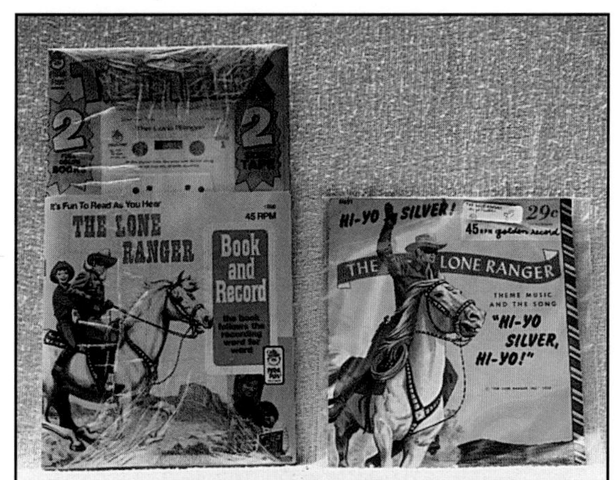

Record and book, 1970, $15.00 – 25.00; song record, 1958, $35.00 – 50.00.

Lunch box, 1946, $350.00 – 600.00.

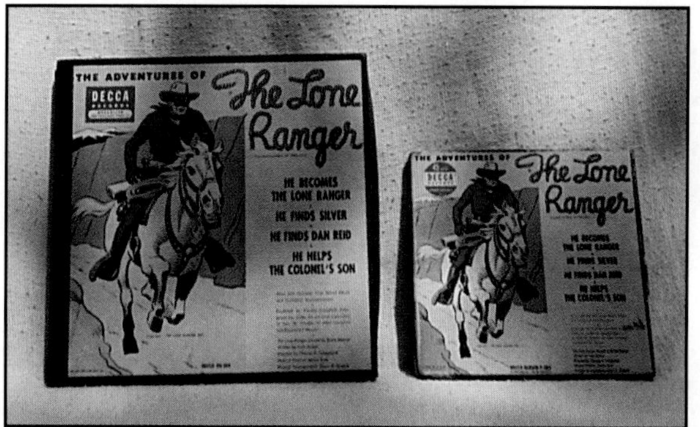

Record sets, 1951, $150.00 – 200.00 each.

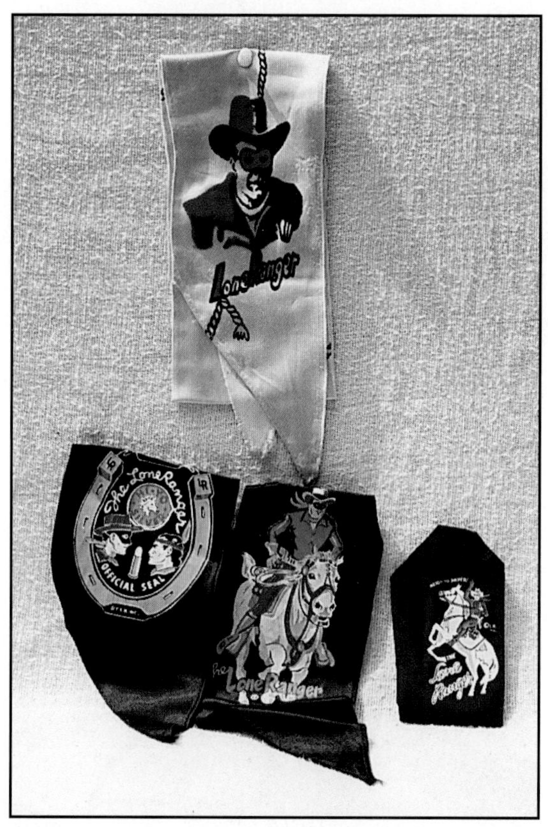

Ties, 1938 – 1952, $65.00 – 125.00 each.

Puzzles, 1958 – 1970, $35.00 – 75.00.

45-gun on card, 1958, $65.00 – 95.00.

Wallet with box, 1947, $125.00 – 175.00.

Clicker pistol with box, 1940, $150.00 – 225.00.

Punch-out set, complete, 1947, $175.00 – 250.00.

Suspenders, 1947, $35.00 – 65.00.

Tie, 1950, $125.00 – 150.00.

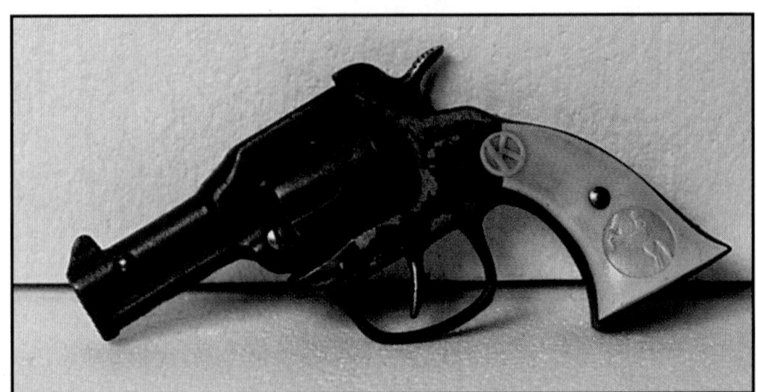

Metal cap gun, small size, 1938, $125.00 – 175.00.

Punch board, 1940, rare, $85.00 – 125.00.

Harmonica with box, 1947, $75.00 – 125.00.

Pocket watch, 1970, $85.00 – 125.00.

Cowboy slippers, 1940s, $125.00 – 150.00.

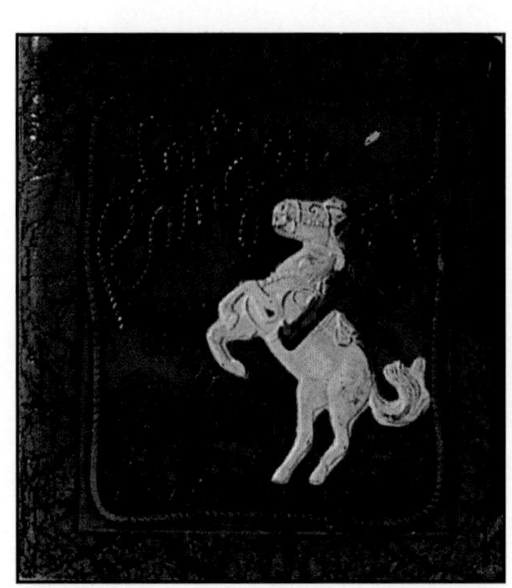

Bank, metal, 1938, $150.00 – 250.00.

Bib overalls, 1938, $125.00 – 250.00.

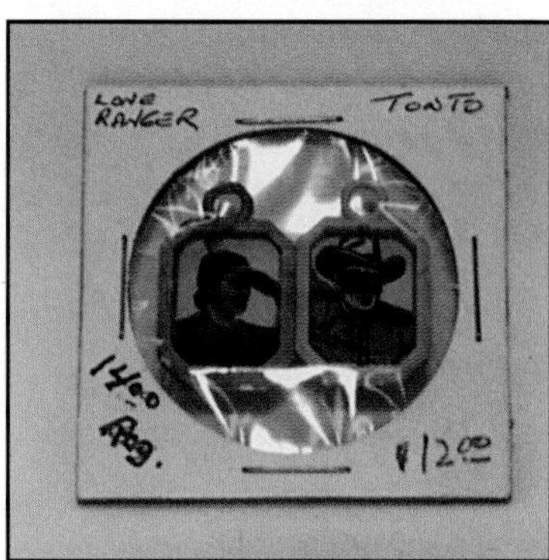

Picture charms, 1950, $20.00 – 35.00 each.

Full-page ad promoting comic with first Sunday page, dated Sept. 11, 1938, $150.00 – 350.00.

Card packs with ad for bubble gum, 1940, $350.00 – 600.00.

Paper gun promoting comic strip, 1938, $75.00 – 150.00.

Republic serial pin back, 1938, $65.00 – 195.00.

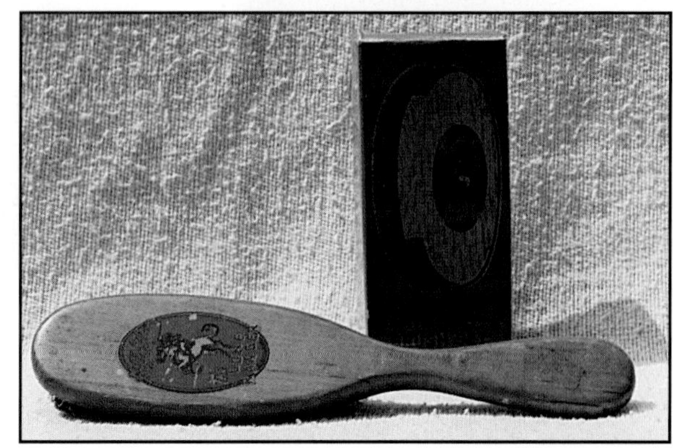

Small hairbrush with box, 1938, $125.00 – 150.00; large hairbrush, 1938, $75.00 – 125.00.

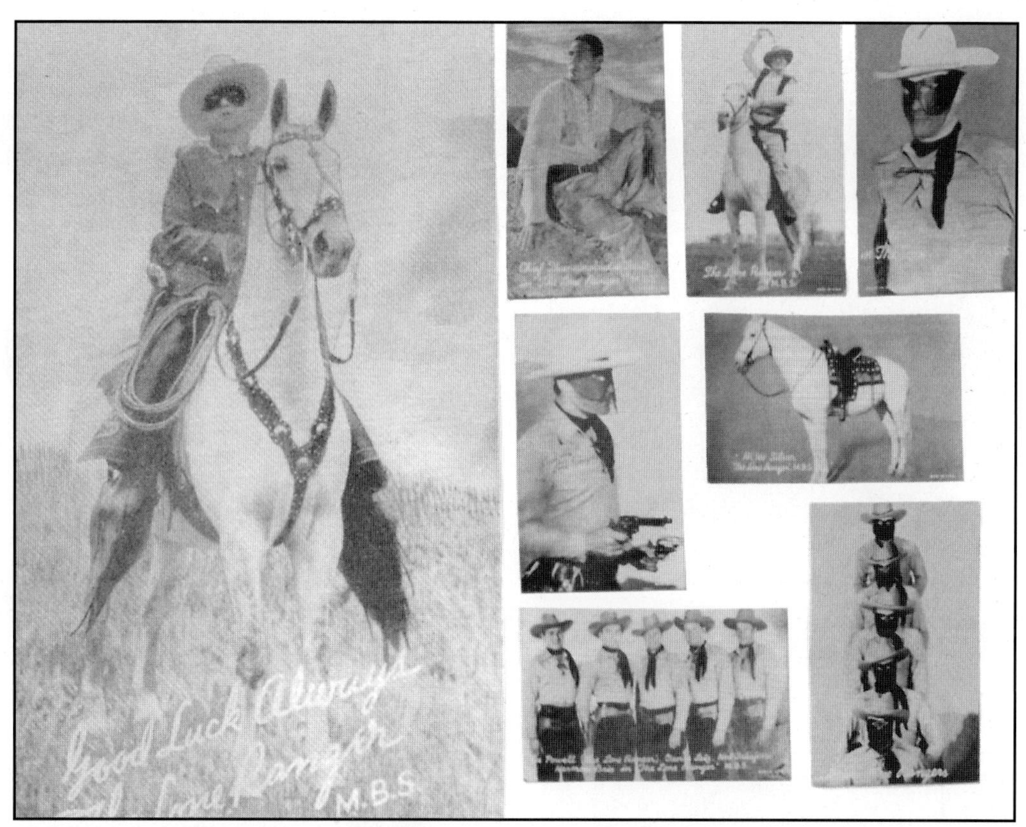

Exhibit cards, 1940 – 1950, $12.00 – 18.00 each.

Gum cards, 1940, $15.00 – 40.00 each.

Mask and watch set, 1960, $45.00 – 65.00.

Lone Ranger figure and Silver on card, 1974, $65.00 – 125.00.

Crayons with tin, 1953, $65.00 – 95.00.

Chalk figures, 1940s, $85.00 – 150.00.

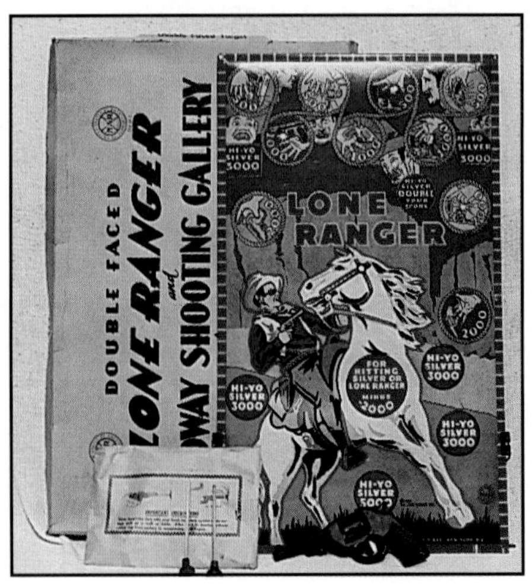

Small and large tin targets, Marx, 1938, $125.00 – 225.00.

Single holster 6-gun outfits, 1970, $125.00 – 250.00.

Pocket watches, 1940s, $350.00 – 600.00.

School bags, 1946 – 1950, $75.00 – 145.00.

Mexican toys, 1984, $65.00 – 85.00 each.

Captain Action dolls, red and blue shirt, 1960, $250.00 – 450.00 each.

Hobby horse, 1940, rare, $250.00 – 350.00.

Famous rider, 1938, rare, $350.00 – 750.00.

Metal badge, 1950, $35.00 – 55.00.

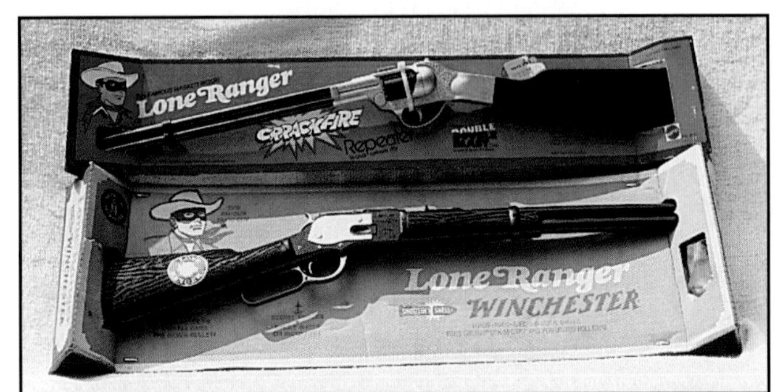

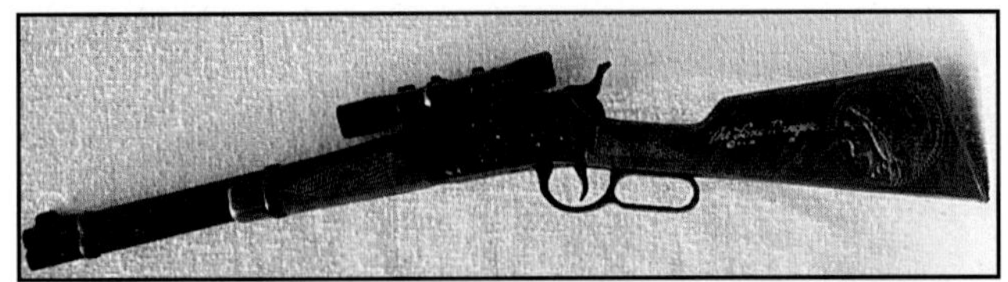

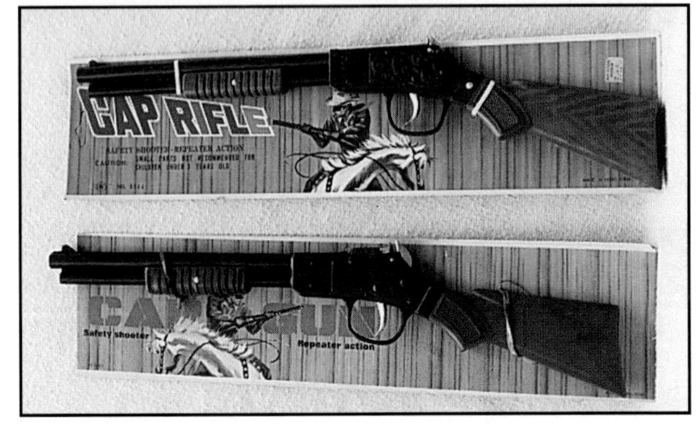

Rifles, 1970, $85.00 – 195.00.

Guitar, 1956, $150.00 – 195.00.

Chenille bed spread, 55" x 72", 1950, $150.00 – 200.00.

Official outfit, 1940, $250.00 – 350.00.

TV puzzles, 1958 – 1960, $45.00 – 75.00.

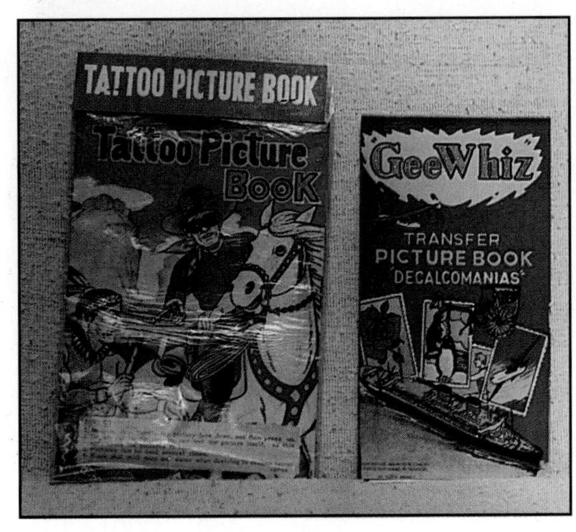

Transfer decals, 1950, $55.00 – 85.00.

Blanket, 68" x 72", 1940s, $175.00 – 250.00.

Child's quilt, 36" x 42", 1938 – 1940, rare, $250.00 – 350.00.

Tin wind-up toy, 1951, $250.00 – 450.00 each.

Pillow case, Flander's Art, 1945, $125.00 – 175.00.

Boots, 1947, $125.00 – 225.00.

Holster sets, 1965, $125.00 – 200.00 single, $350.00 – 650.00 double.

Plastic puppet, 1960, $125.00 – 150.00.

Talking doll, 1960, $150.00 – $350.00; small doll, 1960, $75.00 – 125.00.

TV cards, 1950, $12.00 – 20.00 each.

Color exhibit cards, 1950s, $12.00 – 18.00 each.

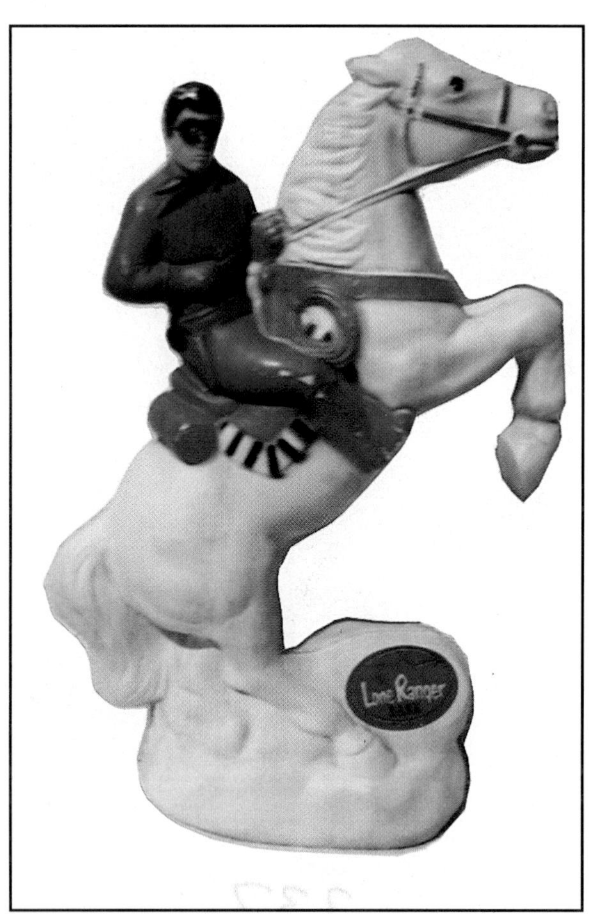

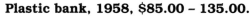

Plastic bank, 1958, $85.00 – 135.00.

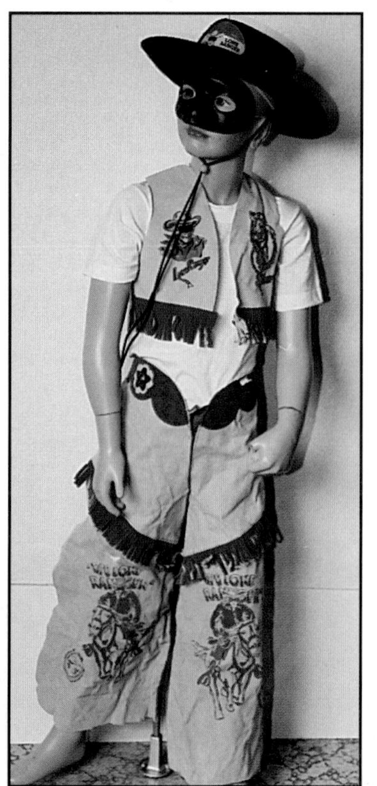

Lone Ranger and Tonto cowboy outfits, 1945, $125.00 – 200.00 each.

Water guns on card, 1975, $85.00 – 95.00 each.

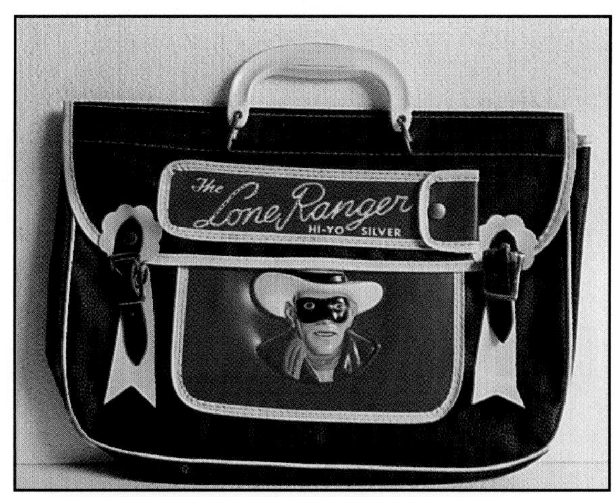

School bag, 1950s, $150.00 – 200.00.

Lone Ranger and Tonto cowboy set, 1967, $75.00 – 125.00.

Red plastic cup, 1947, $125.00 – $150.00; restaurant cup, 1962, $95.00 – 125.00.

Four transfer gum wrappers, $25.00 each.

Large movie viewer, 1940, $195.00 – 250.00 complete.

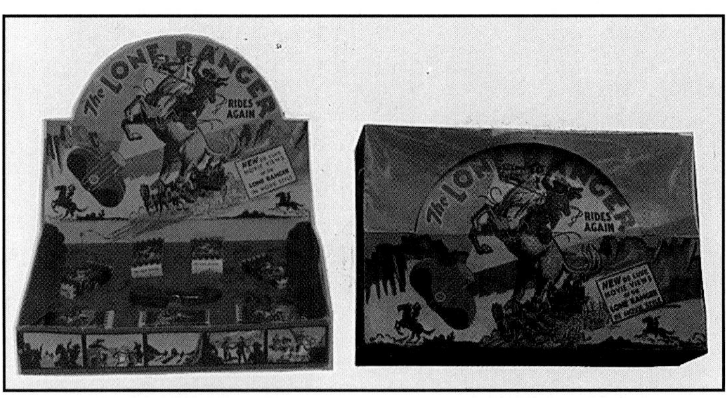

Small movie viewer, 1938 – 1940, $125.00 – 200.00 complete.

May Company Christmas booklet, 1940, rare, $150.00 – 250.00.

Ice cream cone match books, 1940, two different types, $125.00 – 175.00.

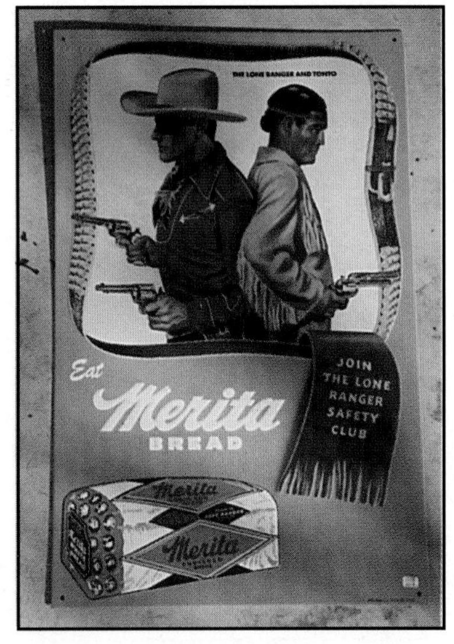

Merita bread sign from serial, 1938 – 1940, $250.00 – 750.00.

Gun/holster cuffs and rope set, 1938 – 1940, $195.00 – 350.00.

Herald Examiner pinback button, 1938 – 1940, $125.00 – 150.00.

Pens and belt holder, 1947, $125.00 – 175.00.

School tablet, 1956, $35.00 – 55.00.

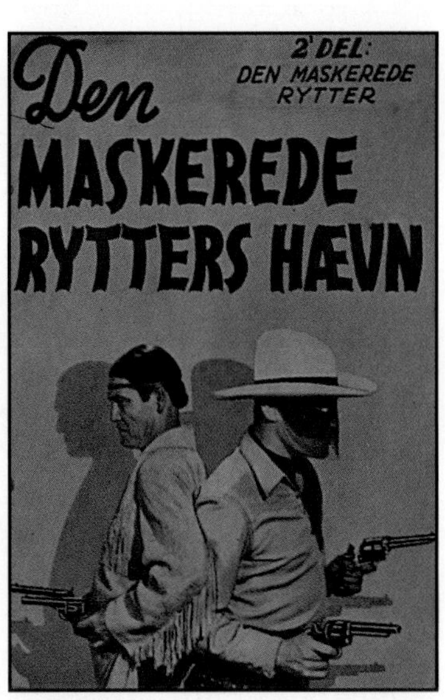

Movie poster, Denmark, 1958, $125.00 – 175.00.

Airline radio, 1951, $450.00 – 875.00.

Tin cookie can, 1952, England, $95.00 – 125.00.

Badges and card, 1955, $55.00 each, complete with card $150.00 – 250.00.

Sleeping bag, 1975, $75.00 – 125.00.

Pop guns, 1940 – 1950, $125.00 – 175.00.

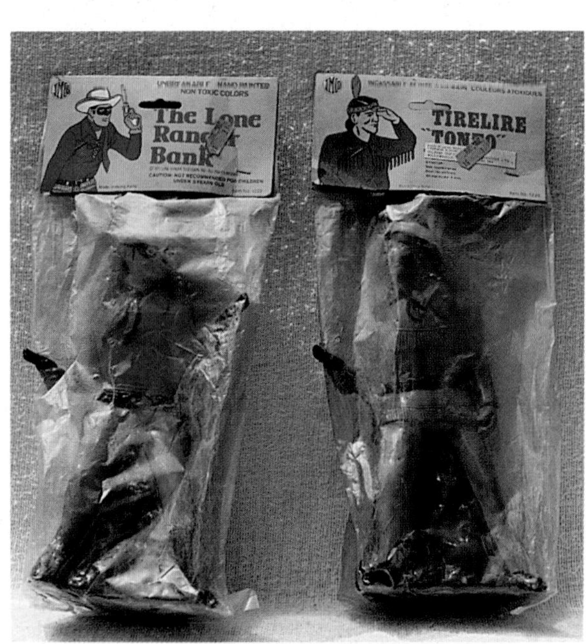

Banks, 1975, $65.00 – 95.00 each.

Felt pennant, 1946, $150.00 – 250.00.

Ink blotter, 1938, $65.00 – 95.00.

Game, 1967, $75.00 – 125.00.

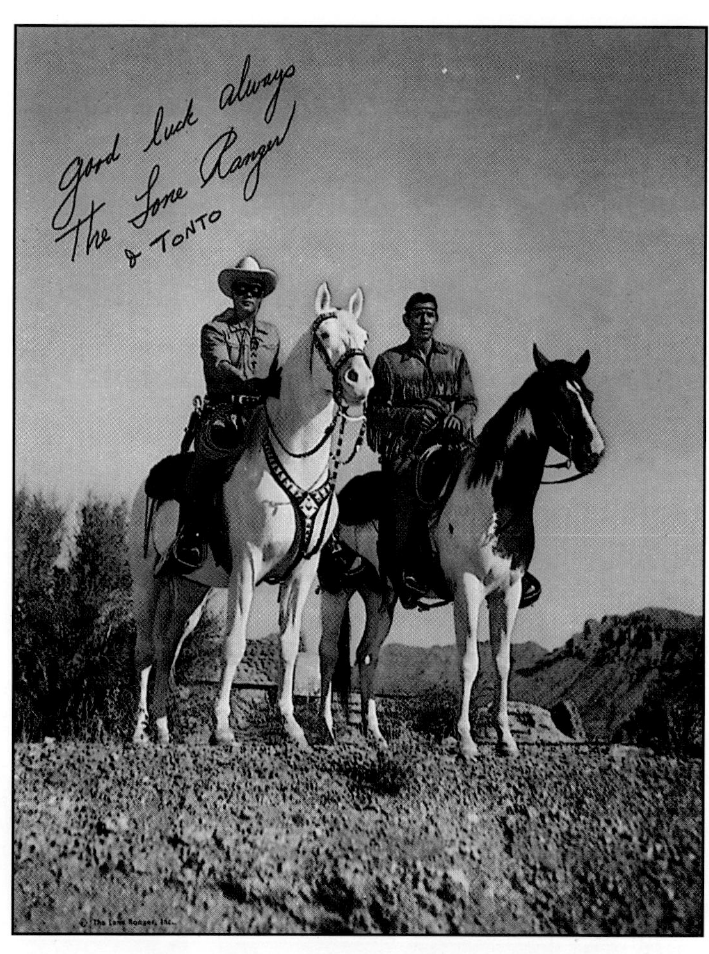

Color photo, 1956, $55.00 – 75.00.

Felt pennant, 1956, $65.00 – 95.00.

Hi-Yo Silver movie poster, 1940, $350.00 – 1,200.00.

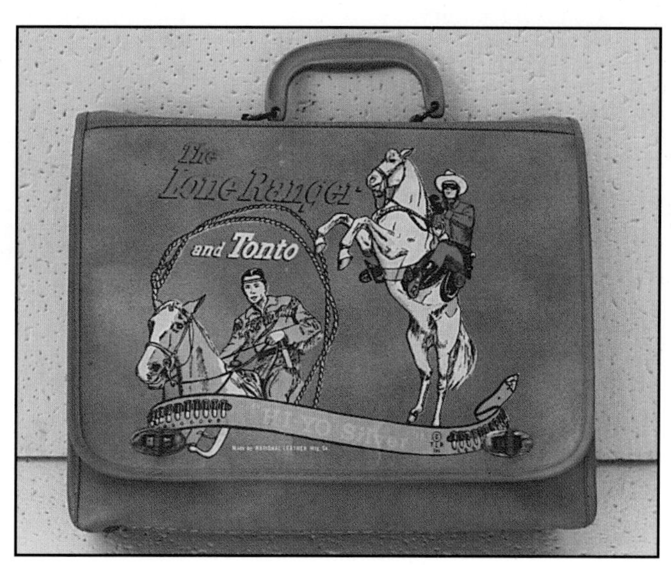

The
Lone Ranger
and Tonto
HI-YO Silver

School bag, 1958, $55.00 – 75.00.

Book jacket, 1940, rare, $95.00 – 125.00.

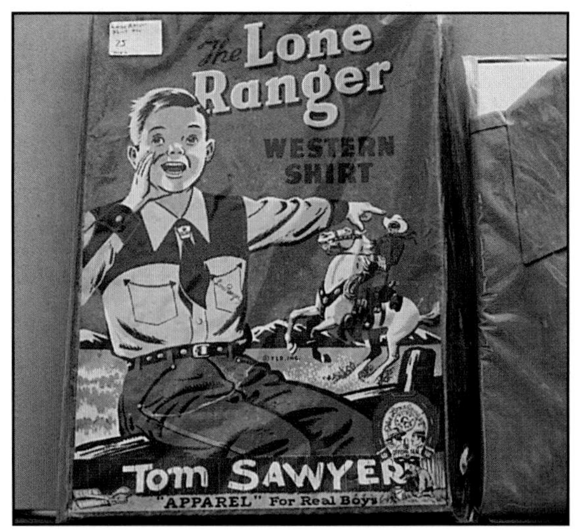

Shirt and box, 1950s, $75.00 – 150.00.

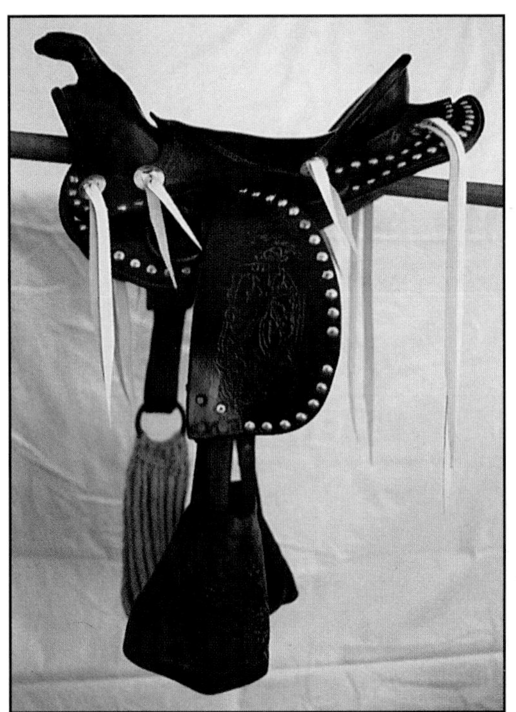

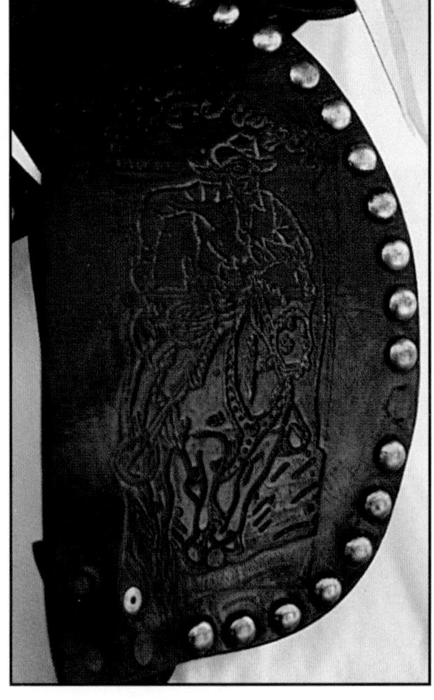

Child's saddle, giveaway and store item, 1950s, $300.00 – 800.00.

Guitar, 1951, $95.00 – 150.00.

Tin wind-ups, 1944, $450.00 – 800.00.

Lead toys, 1940, $95.00 – 125.00 set of three.

Tin horns, 1950, $15.00 – 25.00.

Official holster set, 1945, $350.00 – 450.00.

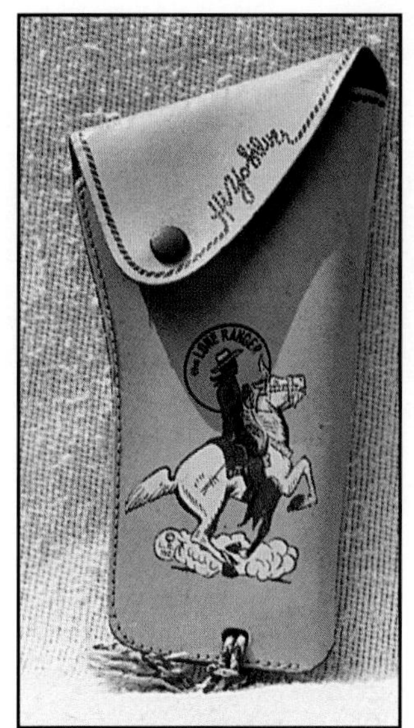

Holster pencil case, 1945, $75.00 – 125.00.

Cowboy hat, 1960, $55.00 – 75.00.

Wallpaper, 1945, rare, $150.00 – 225.00 roll.

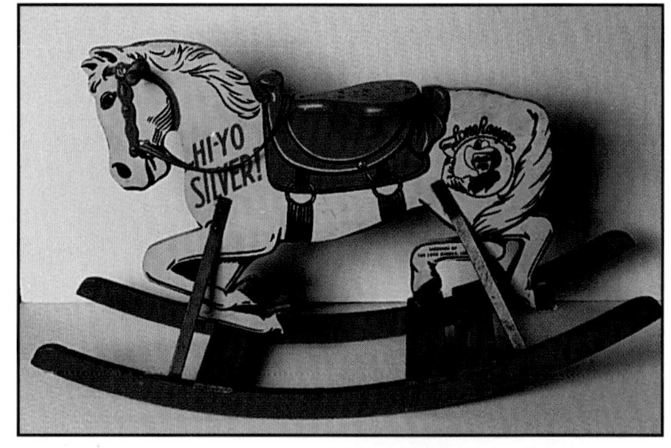

Rocking horse, 1940, $350.00 – 600.00.

Sunday comic pages, $10.00 – 15.00 each, original art, $75.00 – 1,500.00.

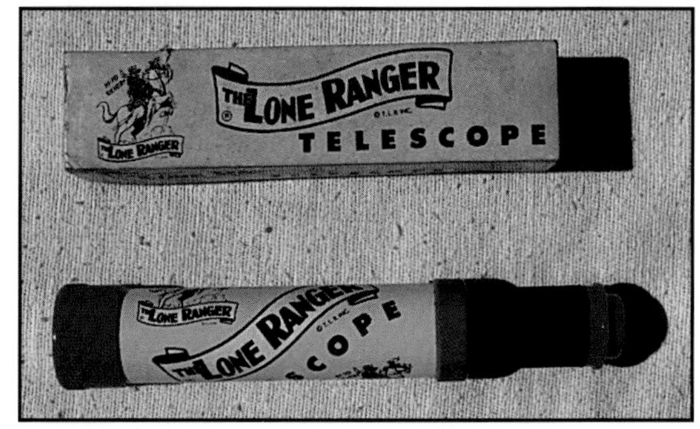

Telescope, 1946, $150.00 – 200.00.

Grosset and Dunlap books with DJ, 18 in set, $25.00 – 50.00 each.

Cardboard sign for trading cards, 1950, $125.00 – 150.00.

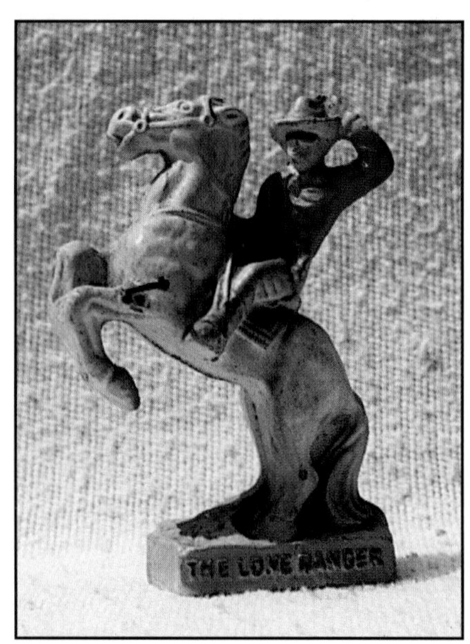

Toothbrush holder, 1938, $75.00 – 125.00.

Wood guitar (not a toy), 1940, two different models, $250.00 – 325.00.

Lone Ranger and Tonto outfit and box, 1950, $95.00 – 225.00.

Movie poster, 1956, $95.00 – 250.00.

Card game, 1960, $55.00 – 95.00.

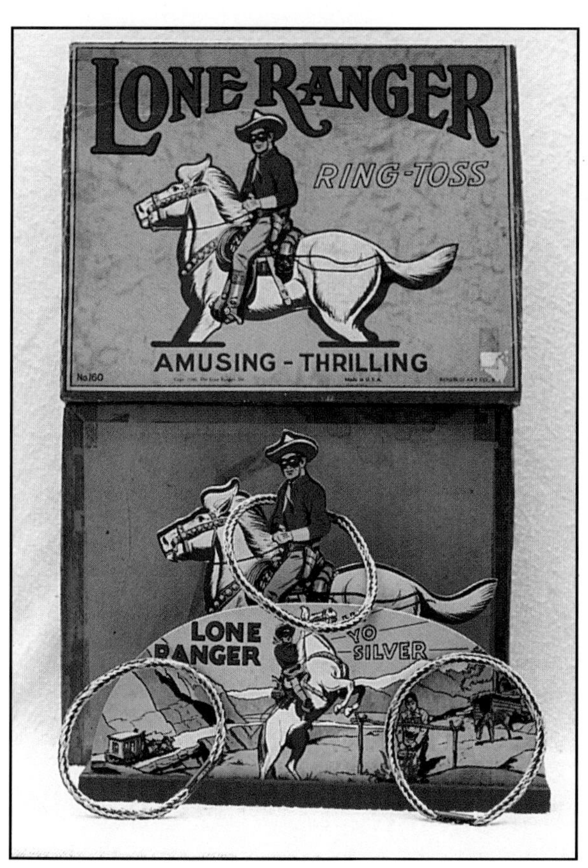

Ring toss game, 1943, $350.00 – 450.00.

Statue of Silver, chalk-like material, 1940s, rare, $150.00 – 350.00.

Records, 1960 – 1970, $25.00 – 65.00.

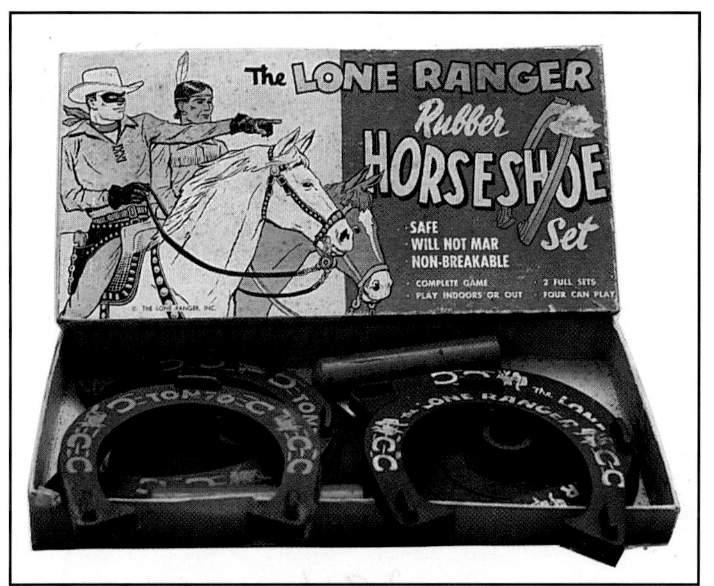

Horseshoe set, 1950, $150.00 – 225.00.

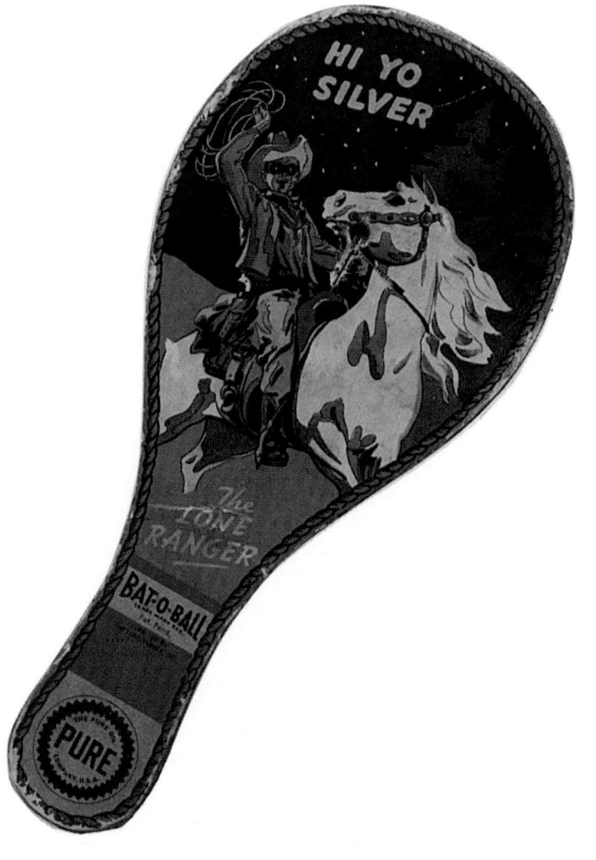

Paddle ball premium, 1940, $75.00 – 125.00.

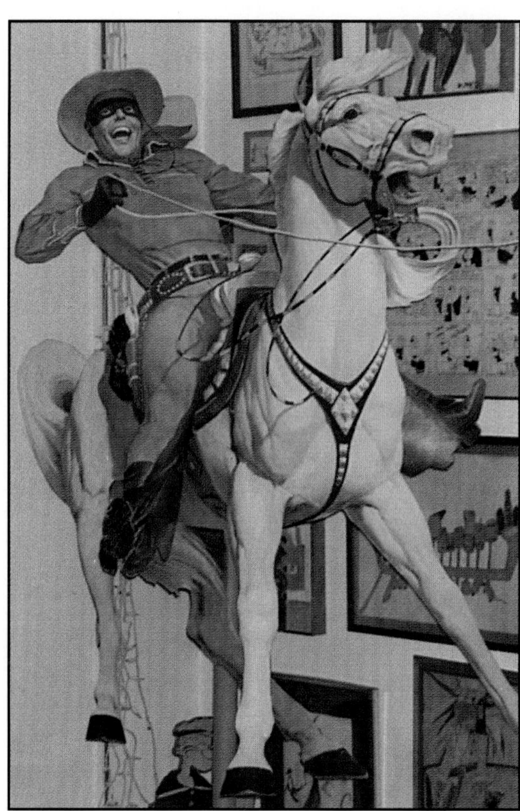

General Mills standee grocery stores for display, 1957, $450.00 – 2,500.00.

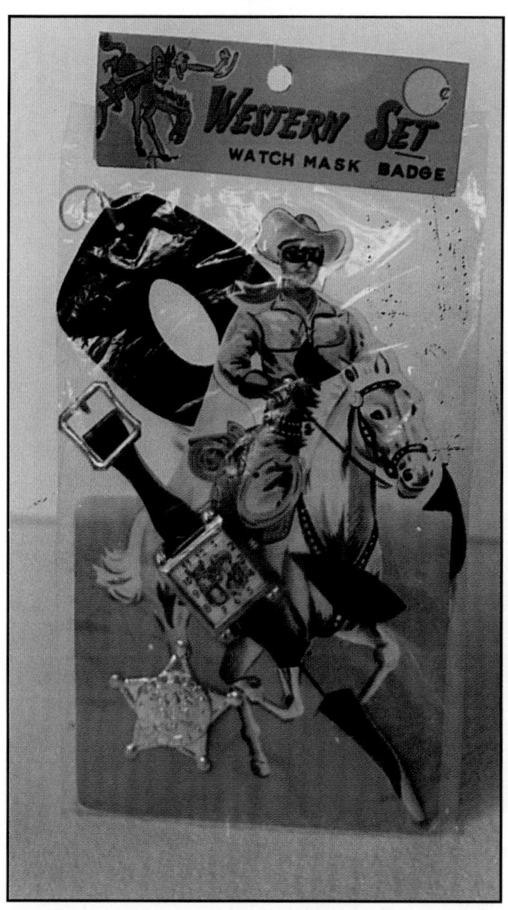

Western watch and badge set, 1970, $50.00 – 75.00.

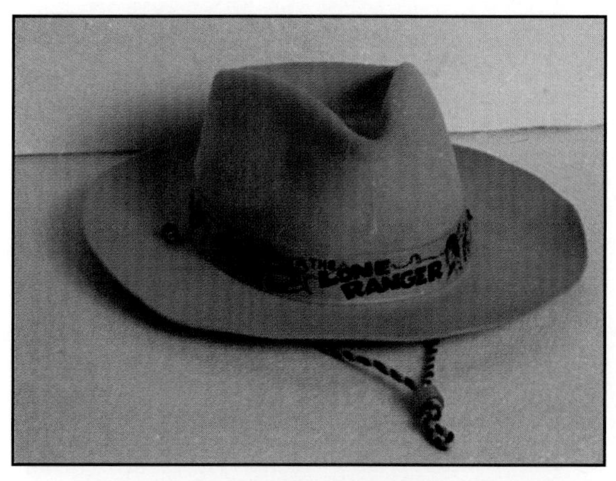

Cowboy hat, 1948, $35.00 – 75.00.

Tie rack, 1940, rare, $95.00 – 125.00.

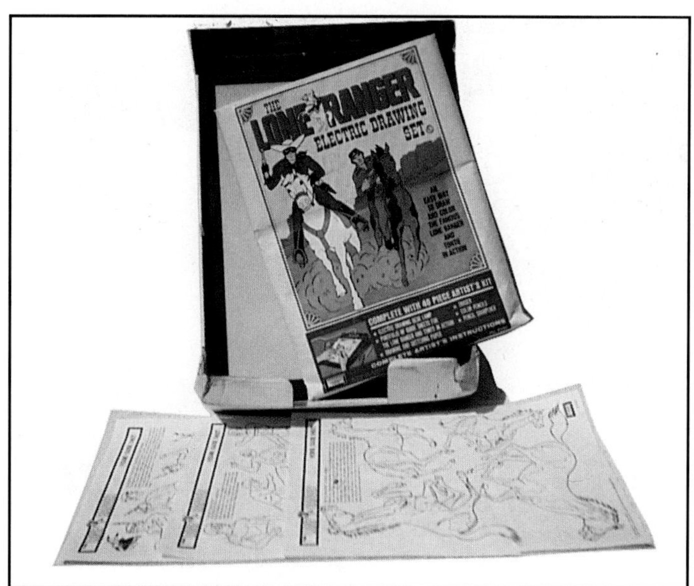

Electric drawing set, 1968, $125.00 – 150.00.

Movie standee, 1956, $750.00 – 1,200.00.

Plastic action bank, 1948 – 1950, rare, $50.00 – 150.00.

Lamp and shade, 1950, $125.00 – 200.00.

Restaurant poster, 1958, rare, $125.00 – 250.00.

Jail keys, 1945, $65.00 – 95.00.

Press action toy with box, 1939, $125.00 – 175.00.

Pinback buttons, bread company premiums, 1941 – 1945, $65.00 – 150.00.

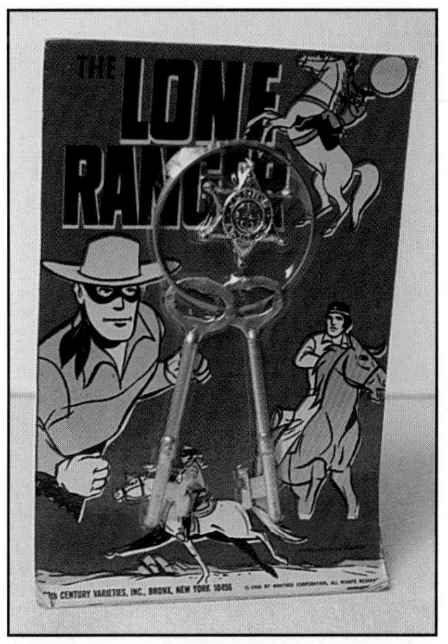

Jail keys and badge, 1966, $35.00 – 65.00.

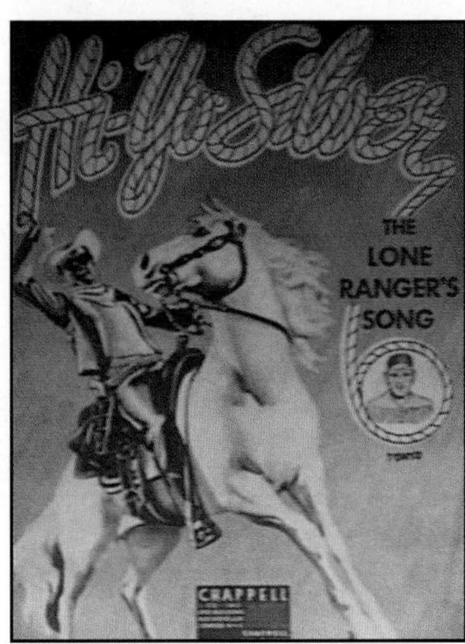

Sheet music, 1938, $75.00 – 95.00.

Health and Safety Scout booklet, 1954, $65.00 – 75.00.

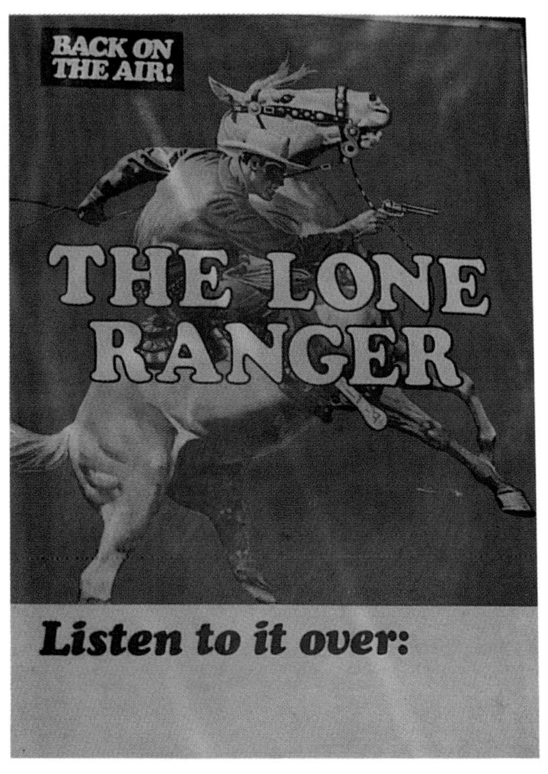

Cardboard sign, 1960, $45.00 – 65.00.

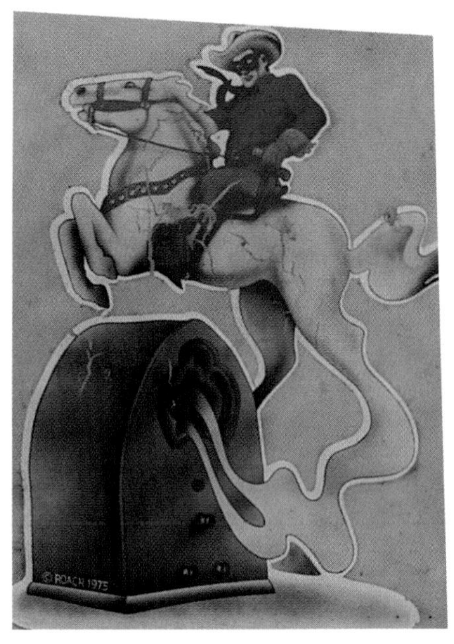

Decal for T-shirt, 1975, $60.00 – 75.00.

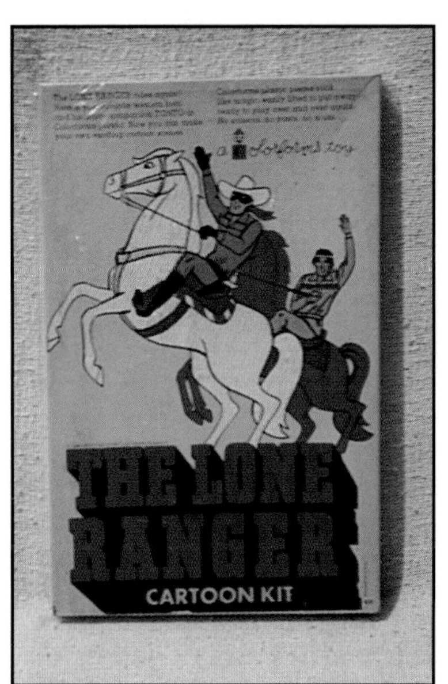

Cartoon kit, 1966, $65.00 – 95.00.

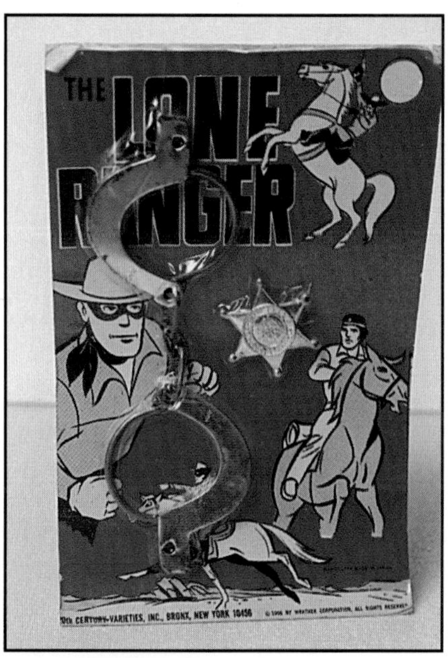

Handcuffs and badge, 1966, $35.00 – 65.00.

Hartland lamp and shade, only 200 were made, 1950, rare, $350.00 – 650.00.

Paperback books, series of 8, 1981, $10.00 – 15.00 each.

Rare comics, feature book 24 and 21, 1940, $75.00 – 650.00 each.

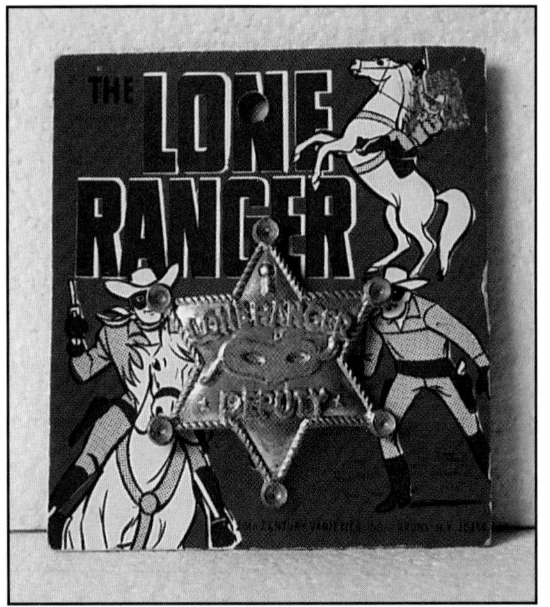

Deputy badge, 1960, $25.00 – 45.00.

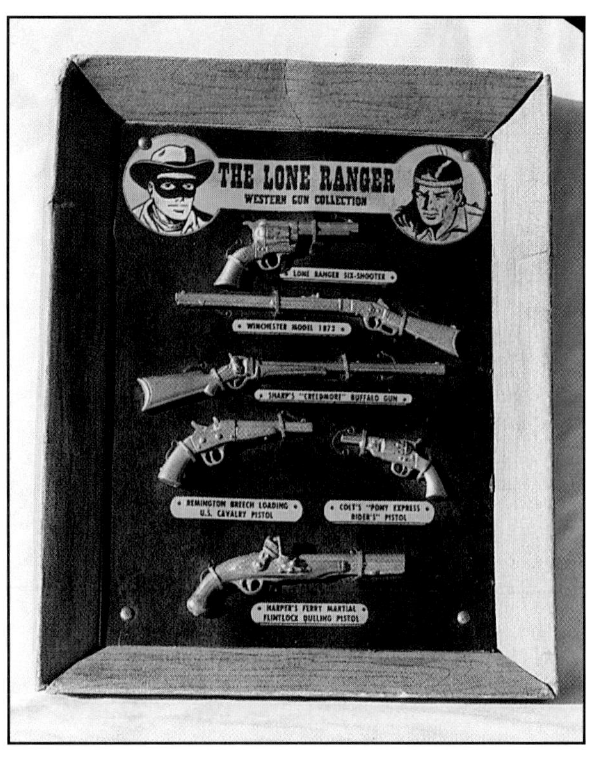

Gun collection, 1946, $175.00 – 250.00 complete.

Signal flashlight with box, 1945, $95.00 – 150.00.

China lamp and shade, 1940s – 1950, $250.00 – 350.00.

Tin puzzles, complete with box, 1944, $150.00 – 250.00.

Card game, 1938, $75.00 – 125.00.

Pulp magazines, 1940, $95.00 – 250.00 each.

Sticker fun, 1952, $75.00 – 95.00.

Coloring books, 1938 – 1945, $125.00 – 150.00.

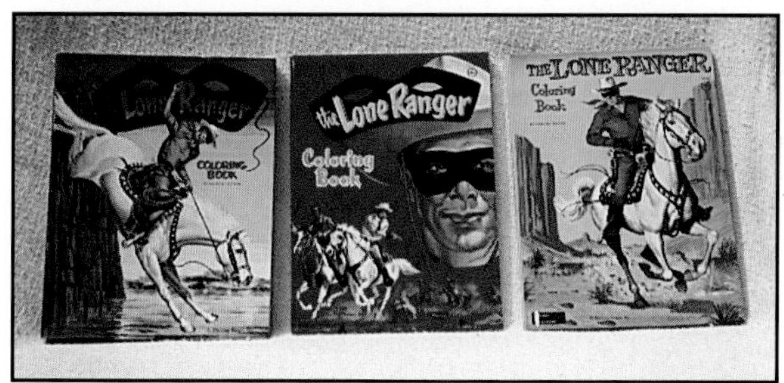

Coloring books, 1945 – 1957, $65.00 – 95.00.

Coloring books, 1946 – 1951, $65.00 – 85.00.

Hi-Yo Silver coloring book, 1960, $65.00 – 85.00.

Coloring book set, 6, 1951, $125.00 – 175.00.

Coloring books, 1951, $75.00 – 95.00.

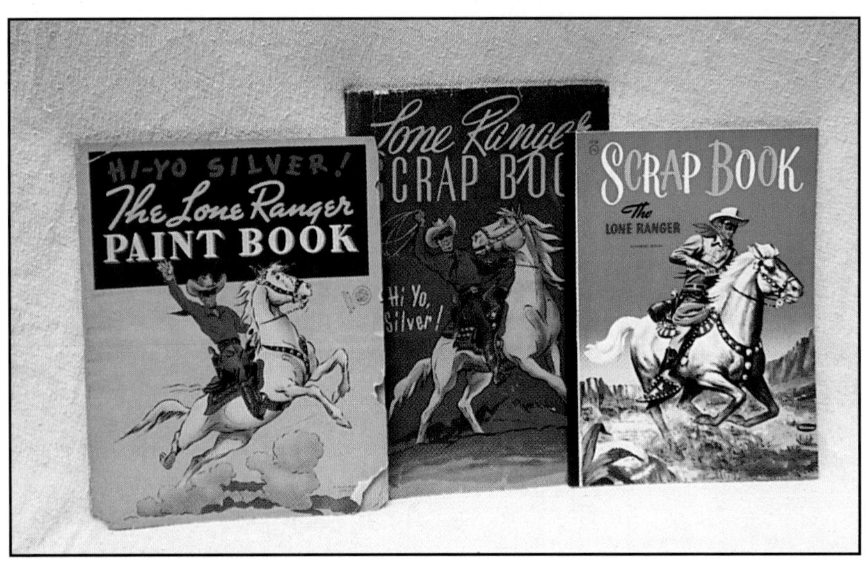

Paint book, 1940, $125.00 – $150.00; Scrapbooks, 1940, $75.00 – 85.00; 1955, $65.00 – 75.00.

Small coloring books, 1960, $125.00 – 150.00.

Lone Ranger to the Rescue and Heigh-Yo Silver books, 1939, $175.00 – 650.00 each.

Pictorial scrapbook, first and second editons, 1979 and 1989, $25.00 – 65.00 each.

English annuals comics and text, 1960s, $45.00 – 75.00.

Tin wind-up, unauthorized, 1960s, $150.00 – 250.00.

English, reprint comics and text, 1950s, $65.00 – 95.00.

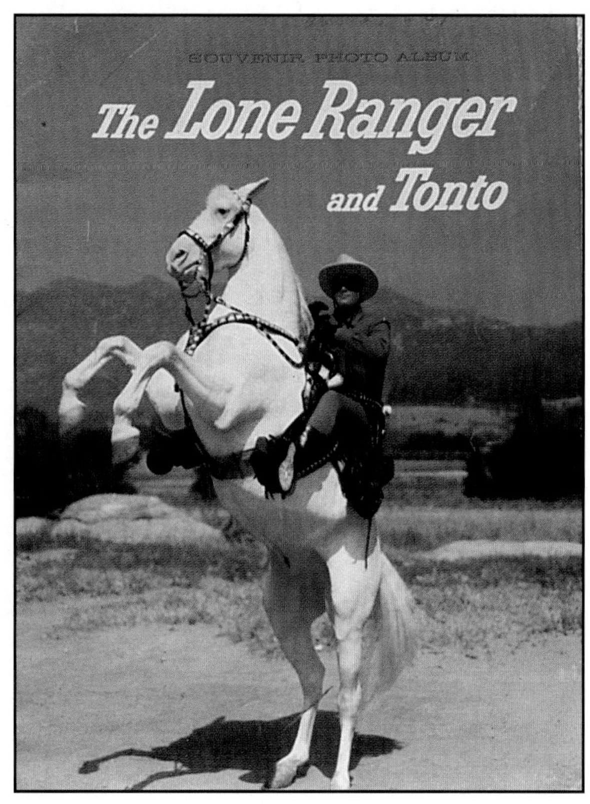

Photo album, 1950s, $110.00 – 135.00.

Lone Ranger and Tonto figures, unauthorized, 1940s, $150.00 – 350.00 pair.

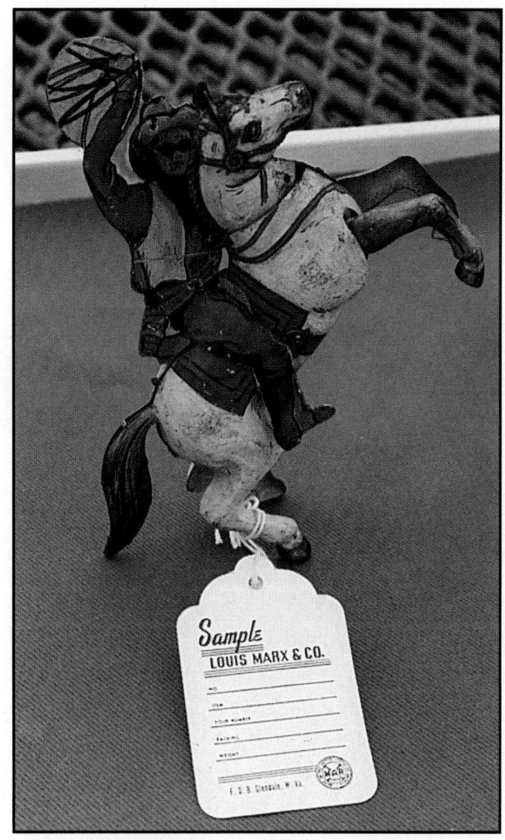

Marx prototype, one of a kind, 1938 – 1940, rare, price unknown.

Sweater, 1950, $125.00 – 175.00.

Magic slate, 1978, $45.00 – 75.00.

Jigsaw puzzles with box, 1940, $75.00 – 125.00.

Printing set, 1938, $175.00 – 225.00.

Hairbrush, 1945, $45.00 – 65.00.

Single holster set with box, 1939, $175.00 – 225.00.

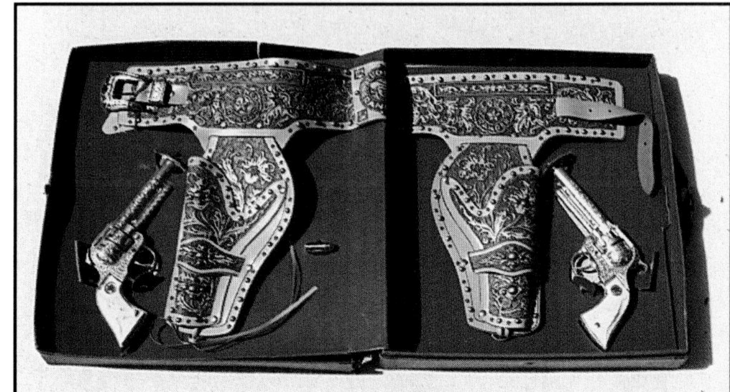

Gun holster suitcase, 1945, rare, $350.00 – 750.00.

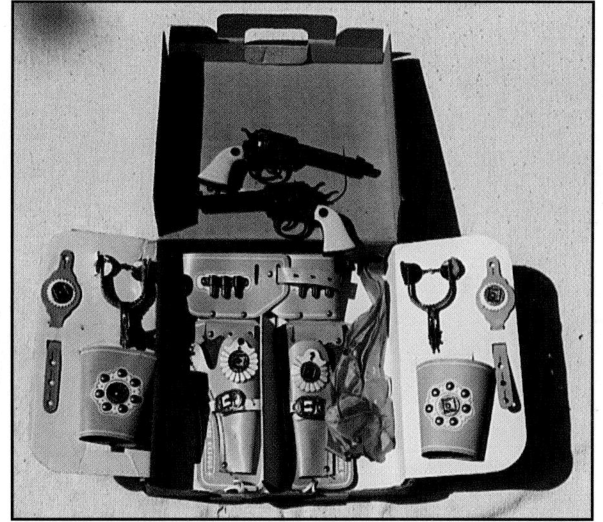

Double holster set, box, 1950, $175.00 – 750.00.

Marx flashlight pistol with box, 1944, $175.00 – 225.00.

Round-up snow dome, 1950, $65.00 – 95.00.

Floor puzzle, 2' x 3', 1980, $125.00 – 175.00.

Left: small tin sign, Bond bread, 1938 – 1940, $150.00 – 250.00; Right: official belt set, 1938, $75.00 – 95.00.

Plastic binoculars, 1950, $75.00 – 125.00.

First aid kits with booklet, 1938, $75.00 – 95.00 small, $125.00 – 225.00 large.

Hand puppets, 1951, $75.00 – 125.00 each.

Pencil box, 1938, rare, $175.00 – 195.00.

Pencil boxes, small, 1938 – 1940, $75.00 – 125.00.

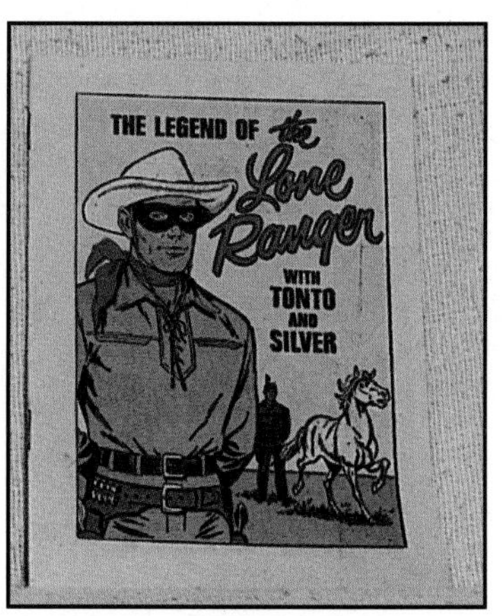

Legend comic, milk premium, 1980, $45.00 – 65.00.

Leather wallet, 1950, $65.00 – 95.00.

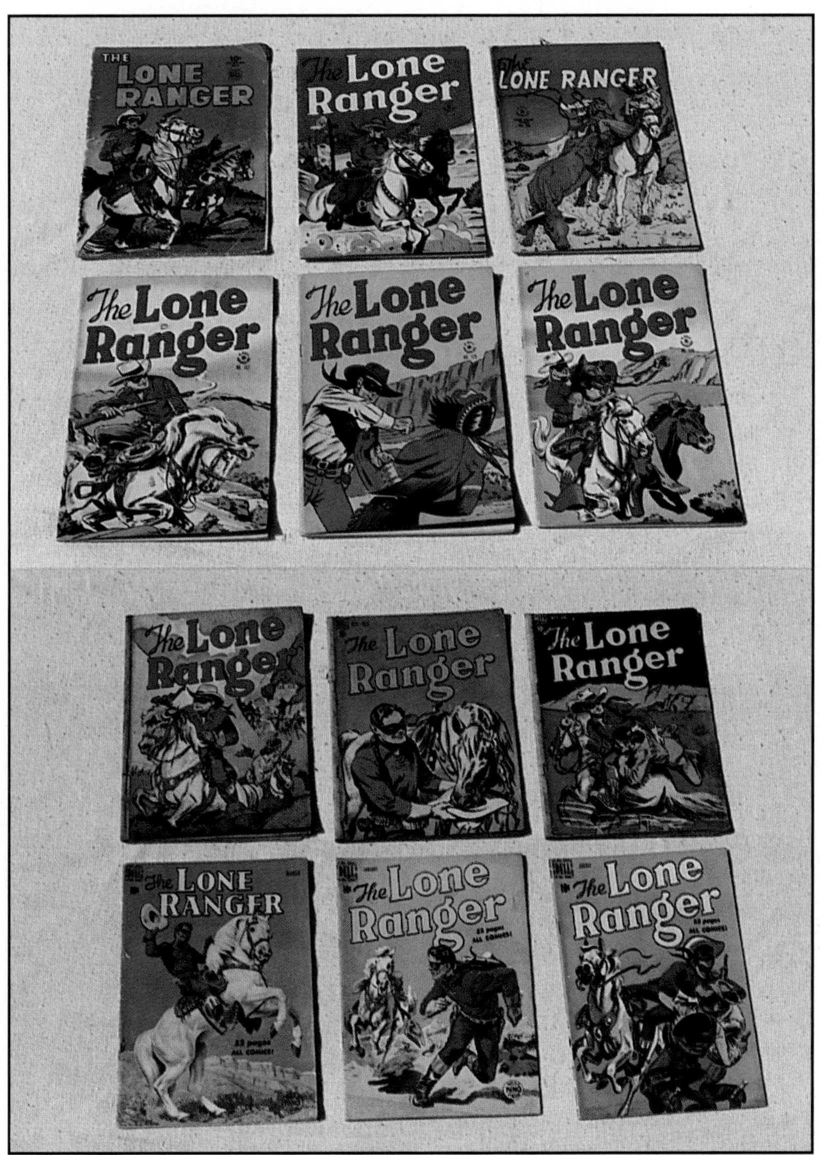

Top: Dell four-color comics, 1945 – 1947, $150.00 – 600.00 each; Bottom: Dell comics, fine condition, 1948 – 1951, #1 $195.00 – 500.00; others $90.00 – 275.00 each.

Dell comics, mask logo, fine condition, 1951 – 1957, $36.00 – 95.00 each.

Dell comics, Clayton Moore covers, fine condition, 1957 – 1962, $60.00 – 125.00 each.

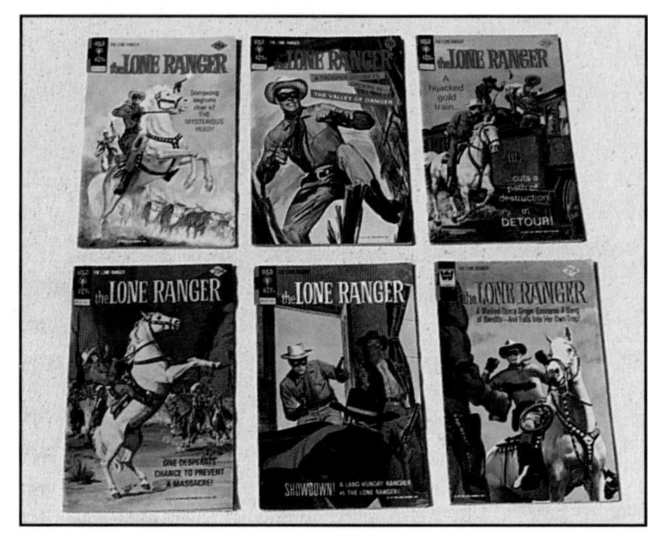

Dell comics, Gold Key, fine condition, 1964 – 1977, $12.00 – 35.00 each.

Lone Ranger's Companion, Tonto, Dell, fine condition, 1951 – 1959, $40.00 – 75.00 each.

Lone Ranger's Horse Silver, Dell, fine condition, 1952 – 1960, $35.00 – 75.00 each.

Comics by Aurora, Dell Topps, Gabriel, etc., 1954 – 1994, $10.00 – 175.00 each.

Serial lobby card, 1938, $325.00 – 450.00.

Lone Ranger Rides Again serial lobby card, 1939, $300.00 – 400.00.

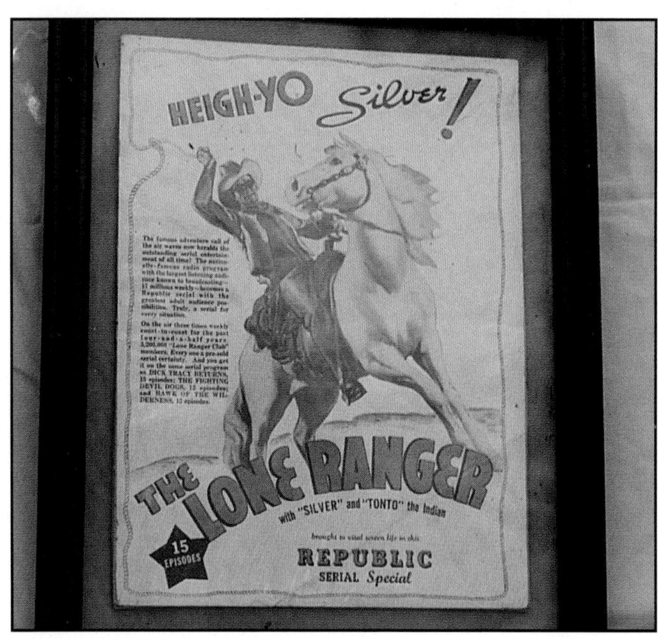

Serial magazine ad, 1938, $75.00 – 150.00.

Serial one-sheet poster, 1938, $650.00 – 1,200.00.

Lone Ranger Rides Again serial lobby care, 1939, $250.00 – 300.00.

Hi-Yo Silver, feature version of serial lobby card, 1939, rare, $300.00 – 450.00.

One-sheet movie poster, 1956, $450.00 – 750.00.

One-sheet poster, Spanish edition, 1958, $150.00 – 200.00.

Lobby cards, 1958, Spanish edition, 1956 and 1958, $75.00 – 150.00 each.

Pressbook, Lone Ranger Rides Again, 1939; pressbook, Lone Ranger, 1938, rare item, $800.00 – 1,200.00 each.

One-sheet poster, features art from comic book, rare, Spanish edition mistakenly gives Tim Holt Lone Ranger credit, 1949, $150.00 – 250.00.

Left: Pressbook, first feature movie facts and ad, 1958, $250.00 – $450.00; Right: Lone Ranger *Lost City of Gold*, second feature movie facts and ad, 1958, $225.00 – 400.00.

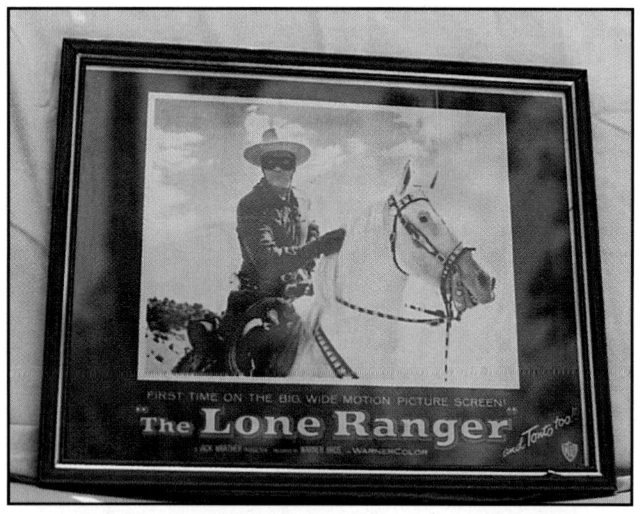

Lobby card, 1956, $125.00 – 175.00.

Double feature movie poster, Spanish, 1958, $175.00 – 275.00.

Color poster, 22" x 28", 1956, $150.00 – 250.00.

Clayton Moore standee, 1956, rare, $1,500.00 – 2,000.00.

Lost City of Gold, **one-sheet movie poster, 1958, $350.00 – 650.00.**

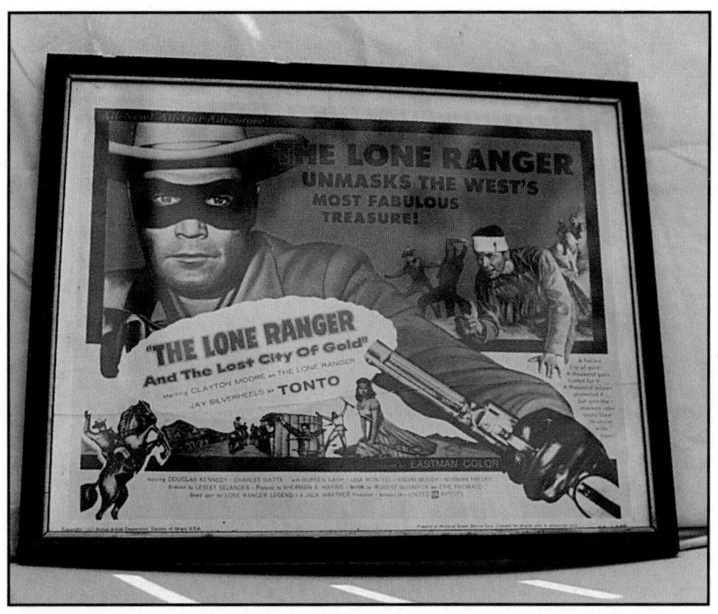

***Lost City of Gold* lobby card, 1958, $125.00 – 175.00.**

One-sheet, Spanish, 1938, $250.00 – 450.00.

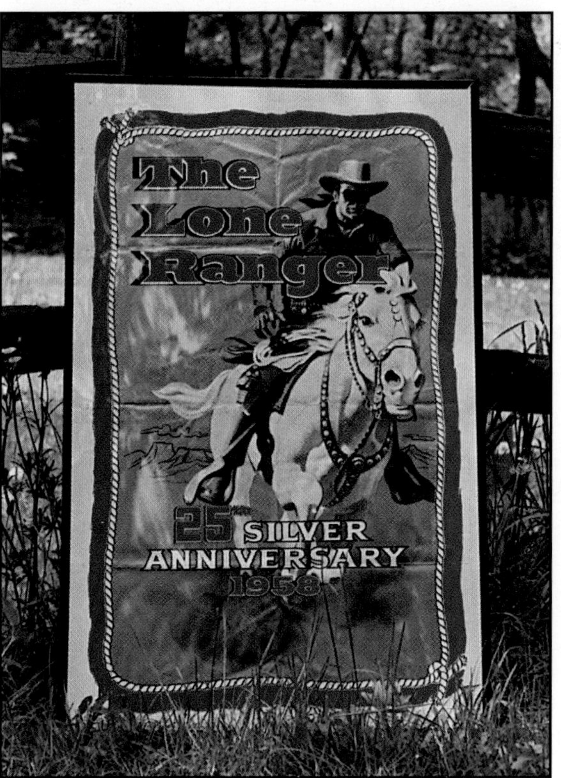

One-sheet poster, 25th anniversary, $1,200.00 – 1,500.00.

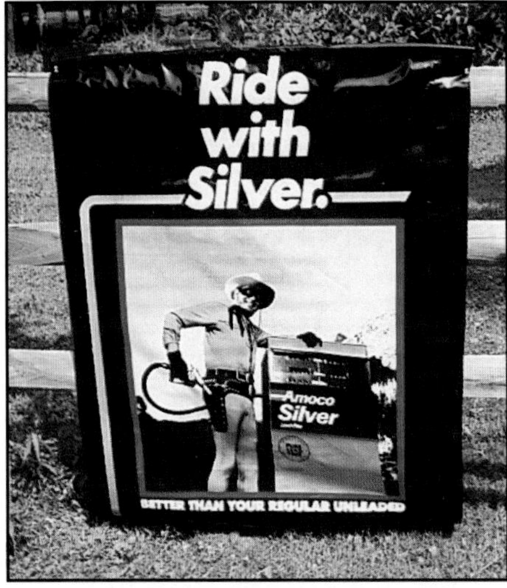

Plastic poster, Amoco ad campaign, 1980, $650.00 – 850.00.

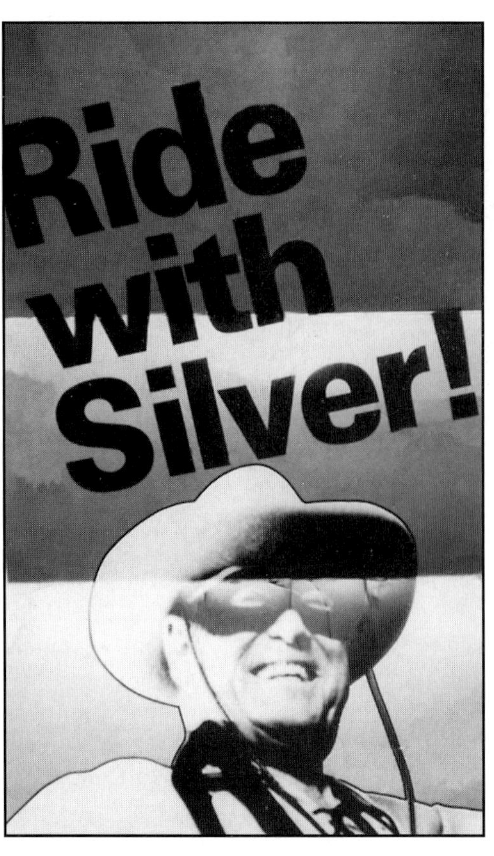

Foam core poster, Amoco ad campaign, 3-sheet size, 1980, $600.00 – 800.00.

10" composition doll with felt hat, 1938 – 1940, $600.00 – 1,500.00.

Compass, straps show Flanders Art, 1950s, $95.00 – 150.00.

Dollcraft dolls in three sizes, 16", 20", 24", 1938 – 1940, $600.00 – 2,500.00.

Playchest card game, 1978, $75.00 – 95.00.

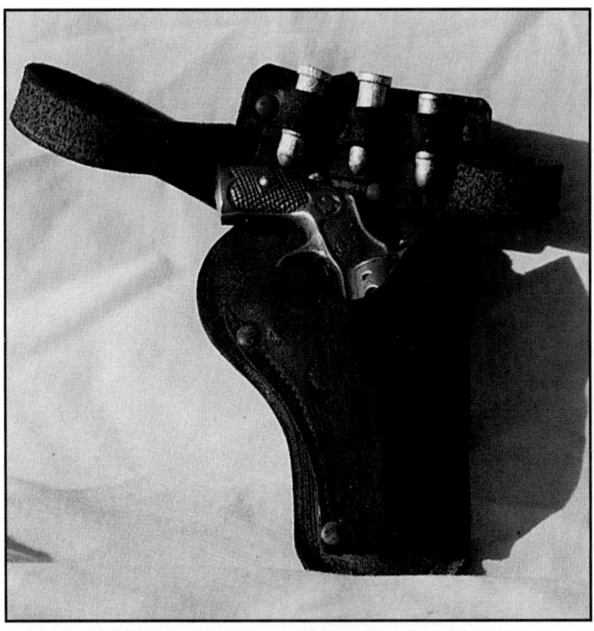

First gun and holster set, gun unmarked, 1936, $350.00 – 650.00 set.

Autographed photo of Jay Silverheels TV's Tonto, 1950s, rare, $125.00 – 350.00.

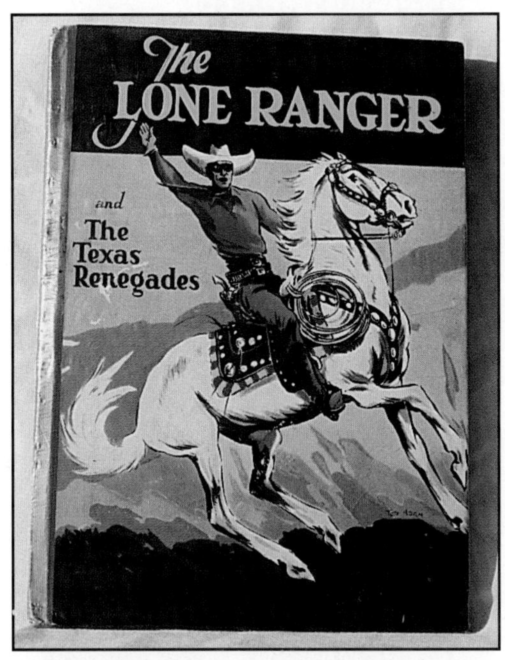

Texas Renegades, based on serial, 1938, $85.00 – 150.00.

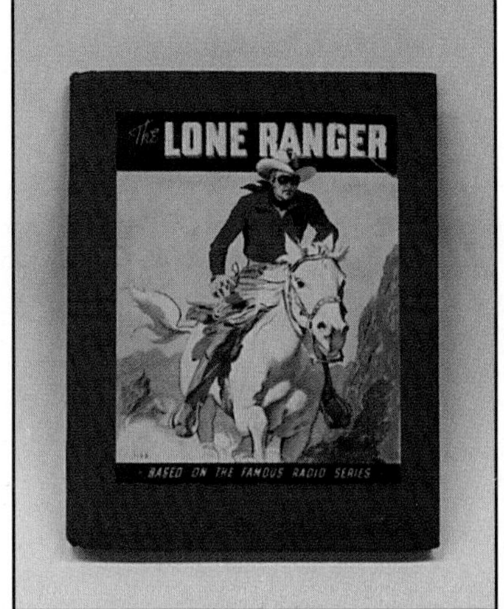

Book, based on radio series, 1940, rare, $150.00 – 200.00.

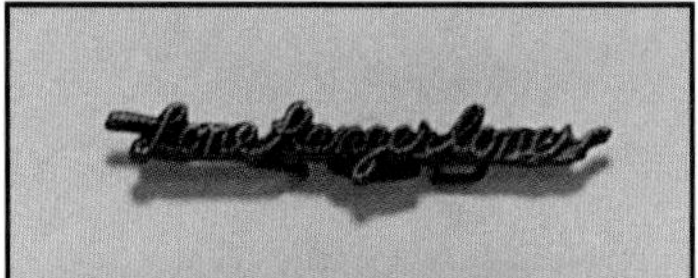

Ice cream pin, worn by employees in ice cream stores, 1938, $75.00 – 125.00.

Charm bracelet featuring Ranger, Tonto, Silver, and silver bullet, 1938, rare $600.00 – 750.00.

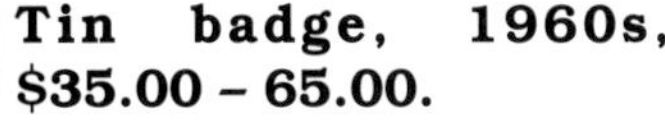

Tin badge, 1960s, $35.00 – 65.00.

Pin, recent, $25.00 – 45.00.

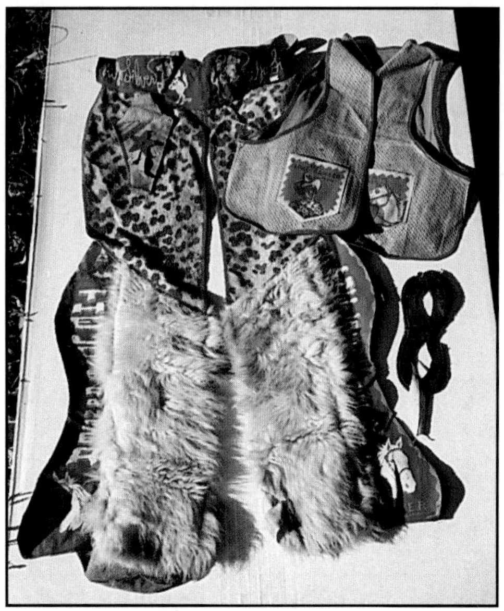

Cowboy outfit, first outfit produced, 1938, $350.00 – 450.00 with box.

Coybow outfit, art work based on Beemer image, 1940s, $250.00 – 350.00 with box.

Gun/holster/knife set, 1950, $195.00 – 250.00.

Fountain pen, 1938 – 1942, $85.00 – 125.00 complete.

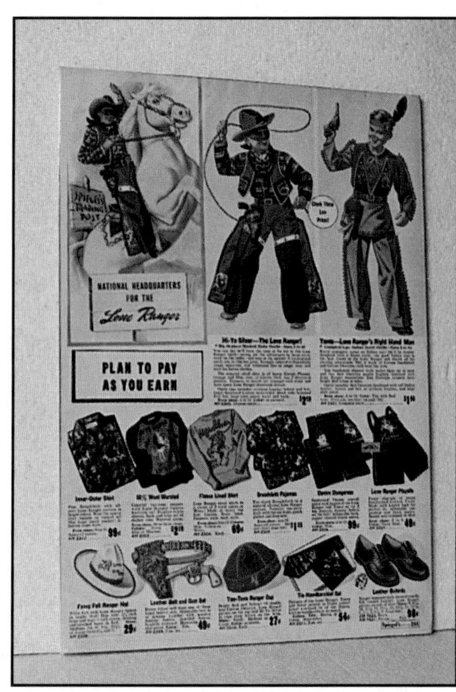

Advertisement, Spiegel catalog page of Ranger toys, 1940, $45.00 – 75.00.

Statue of Brace Beemer and Silver with wooden base and metal plaque, 1980, $250.00 – 750.00.

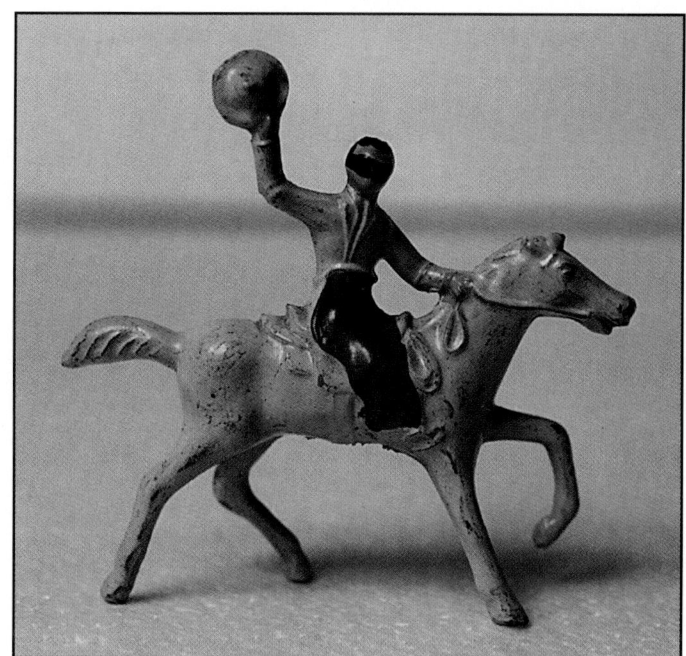

Metal figure, date unknown, $15.00 – 45.00.

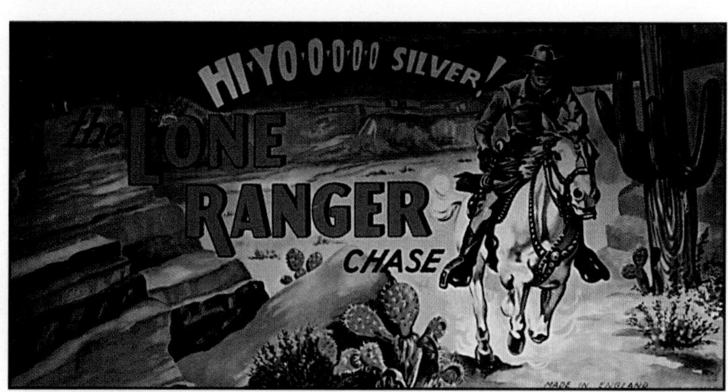

Game, made in England, 1950s, $75.00 – 125.00.

Game, small, 1950s, $75.00 – 95.00.

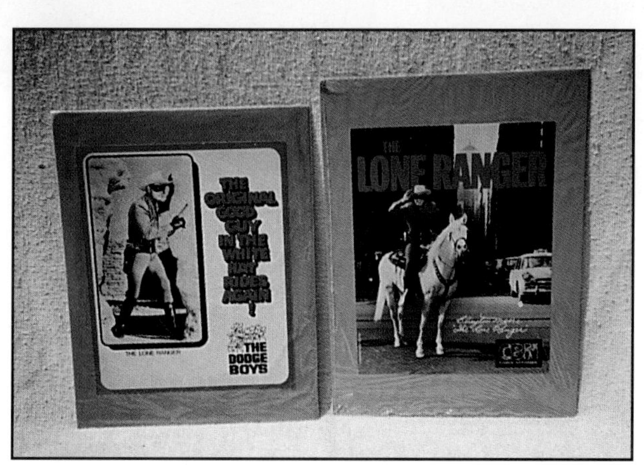

Advertisements, 1960 – 1970, $25.00 – 55.00 each.

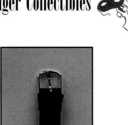

Wrist watch, 1980, $50.00 – 80.00.

Cast iron figure, Clayton Moore item, 1970, $45.00 – 85.00.

50th anniversary medal, silver and gold, 1983, rare, $250.00 – 350.00.

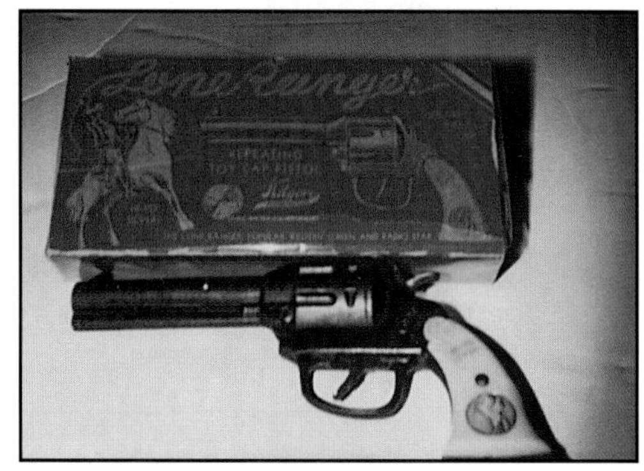

Cap gun with box, Kilgore, 1938, $95.00 – 175.00.

17th anniversary medal, 1950, rare, $125.00 – 250.00.

Plastic figure on Silver, 1970, $65.00 – 95.00.

Tonto figure on Scout, 1970, $65.00 – 95.00.

Lucky coin, 1954, $45.00 – 75.00.

Animation cell, 1965, $150.00 – 250.00.

Animation cell, 1965, $150.00 – 250.00.

Animation cell, 1965, $150.00 – 250.00.

Dell comic cover, 1956, $2,000.00 – 3,000.00.

Original painting WXYZ radio, 1938, $5,000.00.

Original painting WXYZ radio, 1938, $5,000.00.

Original painting, WXYZ radio, 1950, $5,000.00.

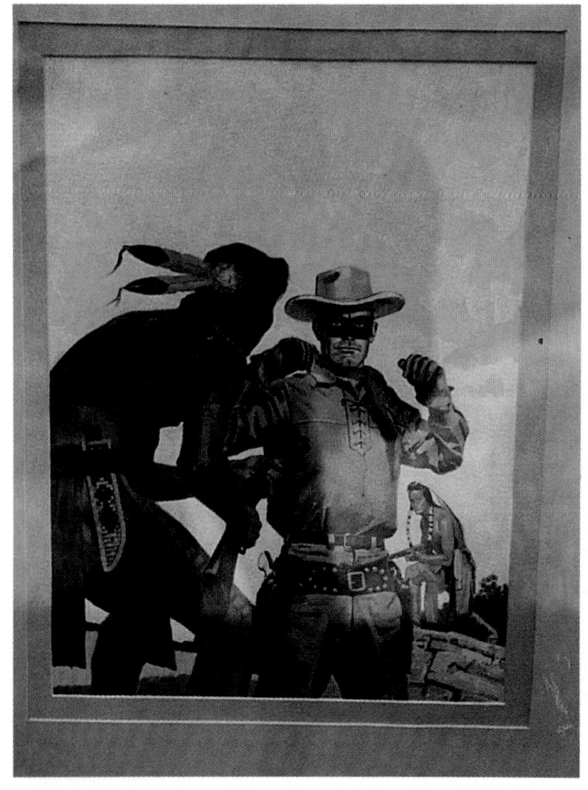

Comic book cover, 1958, $2,000.00 – 3,000.00.

Pop-up book wrap-a-round cover painting, 1980, $1,800.00 – 2,500.00.

Lone Ranger art, date unknown, $750.00 – 1,000.00.

Action figures boxed by Gabriel, 1980, $15.00 – 25.00.

Gabriel, 8-way action saddle, 1980 $75.00 – 95.00.

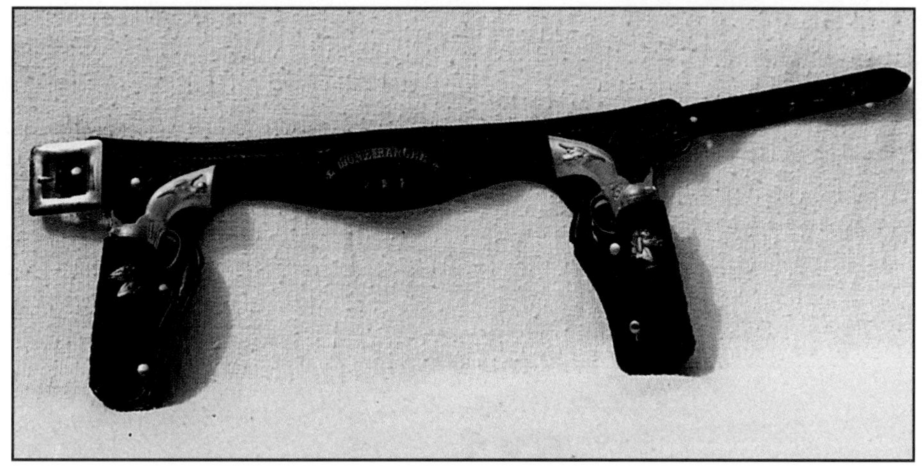

Small double holster set, 1981, $75.00 – 125.00.

Marx action figure outfits, 1980, $25.00 – 35.00 each.

Legend of Lone Ranger, **movie standee, 1981, $250.00 – 600.00.**

***Legend of Lone Ranger*, movie one-sheet poster, 1981, $25.00 – 50.00.**

***Legend of Lone Ranger*, store posters, 1981, $50.00 – 75.00 each.**

***Lend of Lone Ranger* advance movie folder, 1981, $25.00 – 45.00.**

Leather belt, 1981, $35.00 – 65.00.

***Legend of Lone Ranger* storybook, 1981, $12.00 – 18.00.**

Wallpaper, 1981, $45.00 – 65.00 per roll.

Sweatshirt, 1981, $10.00 – 25.00 each.

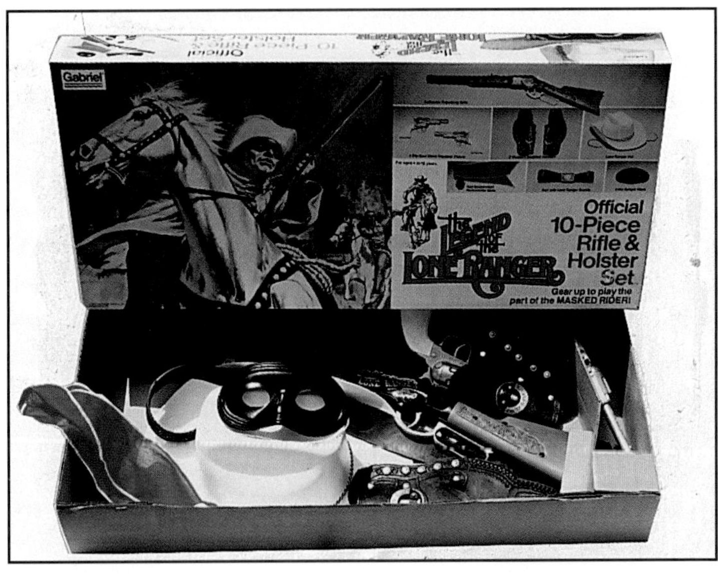

Ten-piece double holster set, 1981, $35.00 – 65.00.

Target sets, 1981, pistol set $25.00 – 45.00; double barrel rifle $35.00 – 55.00.

Four-piece desk set, complete, 1981, $45.00 – 75.00.

Bulletin board/bookends, 1981, $55.00 – 75.00.

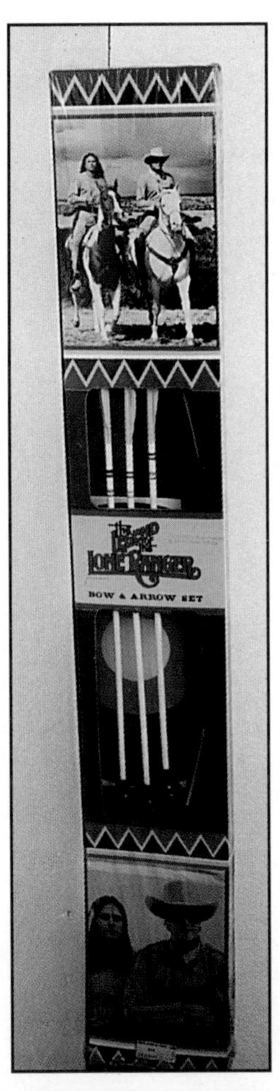
Bow and arrow set, 1981, $12.00 – 18.00.

Tablets, 1981, $12.00 – 25.00 each; rocking horse book (Ranger/Tonto on side), $15.00 – 25.00.

Ranger, Silver, Scout, Gabriel, 1980, $15.00 – 25.00.

Mysterious prospector set, Gabriel, $25.00 – 55.00.

Mask play set, 1981, $12.00 – 25.00.

Metal buckle, given out at Washington D.C. premiere of movie, 1981, rare, $150.00 – 250.00.

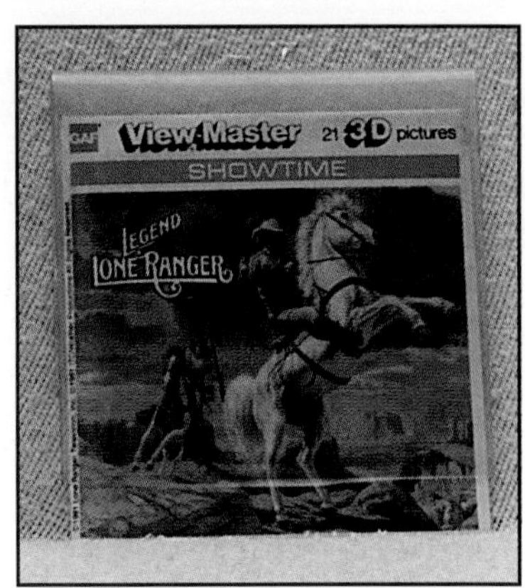

View Master reel, 1981, $25.00 – 35.00.

Leroy Neiman print, 1981, rare, $250.00 – 600.00.

Record, 1981, $25.00 – 35.00.

Paperback book, 1981, $10.00 – 15.00.

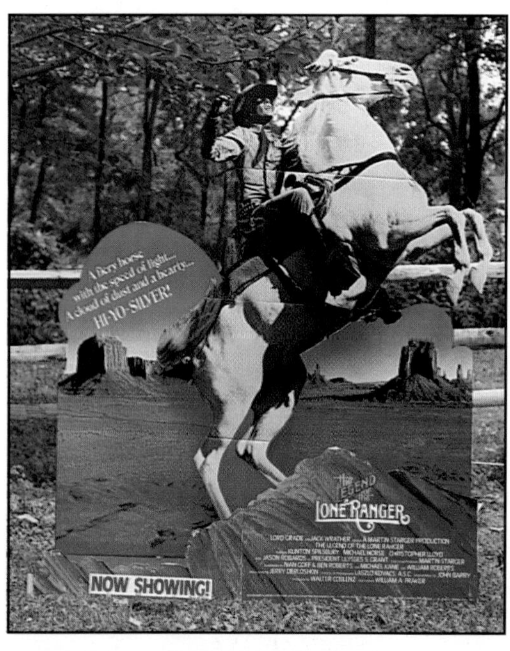

Movie standee, 8' high, 1981, $650.00 – 1,250.00.

Cup set, movie giveaway, complete, 1981, $50.00 – 65.00.

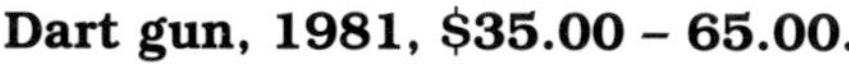

Dart gun, 1981, $35.00 – 65.00.

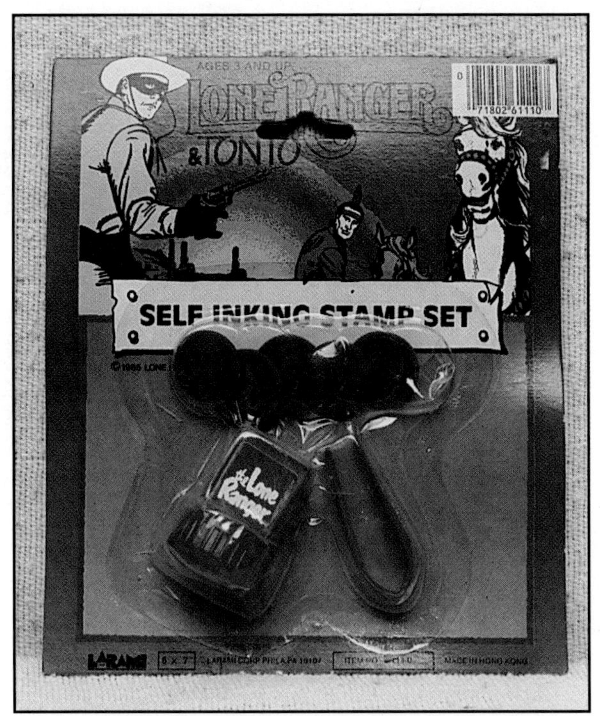

Stamp set, 1981, $12.00 – 25.00.

Beach towel, rare, $35.00 – 65.00.

Authentic story record, 1981, $15.00 – 25.00.

School bag, 1981, $45.00 – 65.00.

Lunch box/thermos, 1981, $45.00 – 75.00.

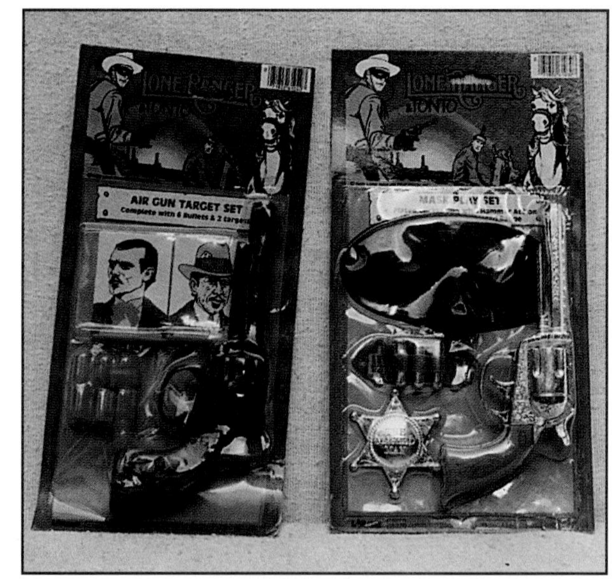

Gun sets, 1981, $12.00 – 25.00.

T-shirts, 1981, $15.00 – 25.00 each.

Frontier playset, 1981, $50.00 – 75.00.

Simplicity Patterns, 1981, $25.00 – 35.00.

Inflatable T.V. chair, 1981, $25.00 – 35.00.

4-1 prairie wagon set, Gabriel, $35.00 – 55.00.

Carson City set, Gabriel, 1980, $35.00 – 55.00.

Gabriel figures, 1980, $75.00 – 125.00 each.

Game, 1981, $65.00 – 95.00.

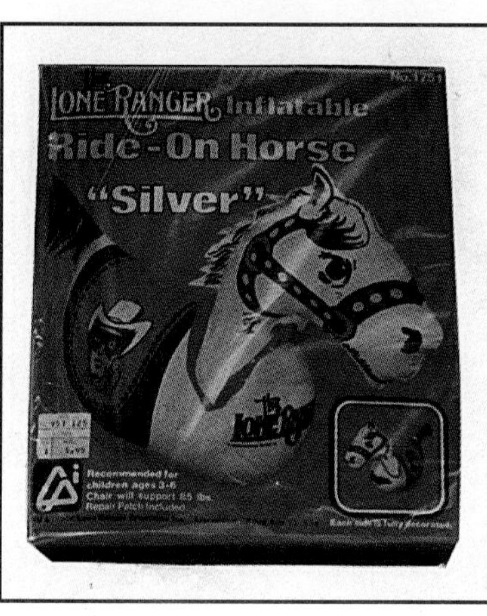

Inflatible Silver, 1980, $45.00 – 75.00.

Movie press kit, saddle bag design, 1981, $125.00 – 225.00.

Bop bag, 1980, $45.00 – 75.00.

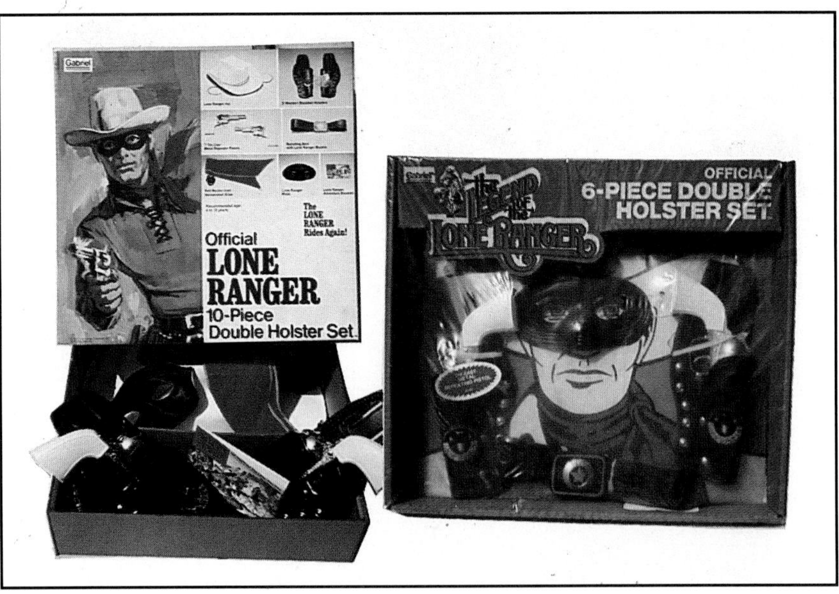

Gun/holster sets, 1980, 6-piece set $35.00 – 65.00; 10-piece $65.00 – 95.00.

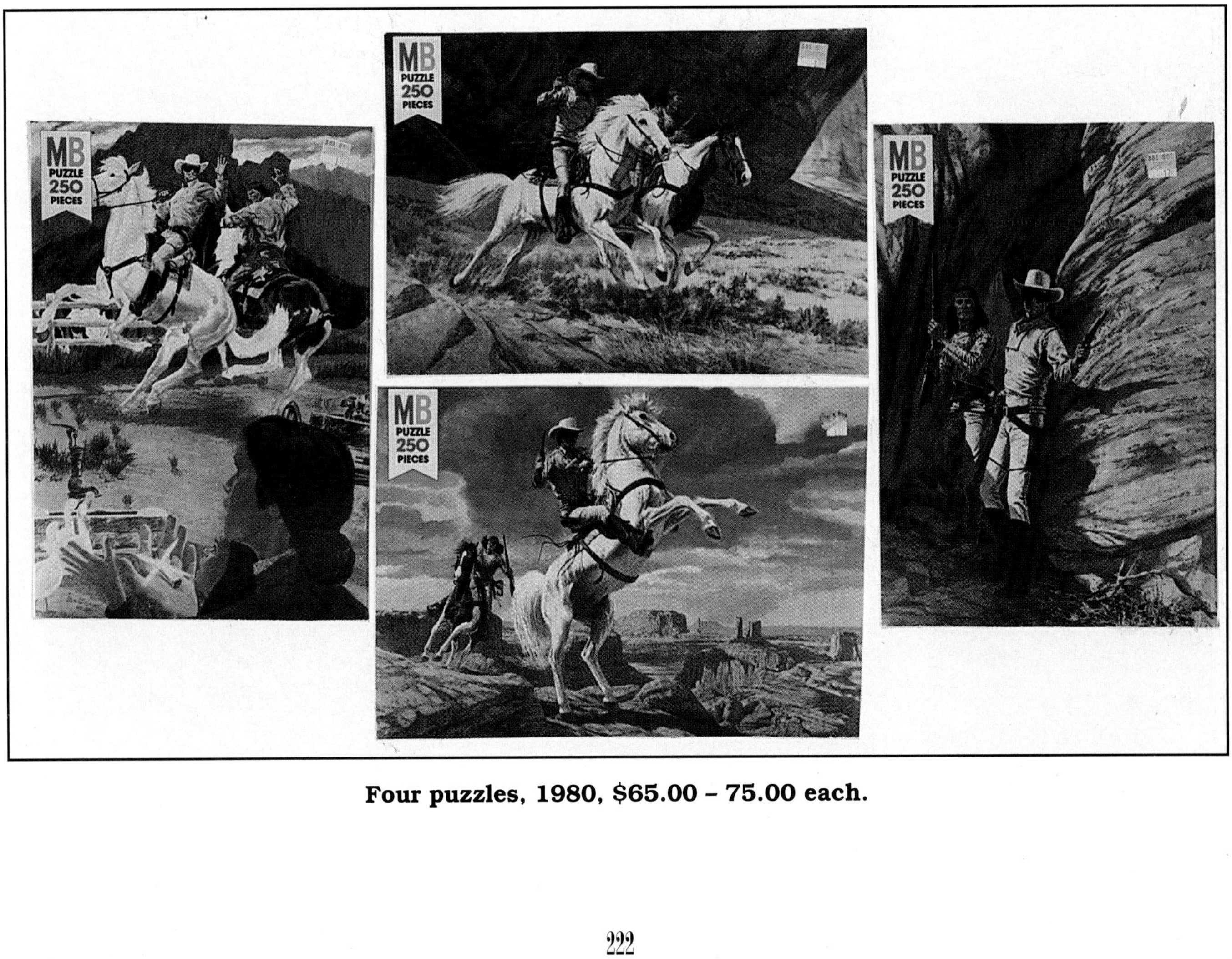

Four puzzles, 1980, $65.00 – 75.00 each.

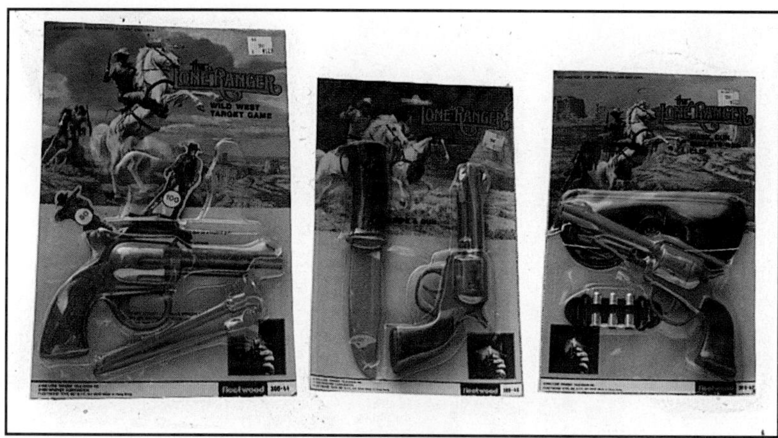

Gun sets, 1981, $25.00 – 45.00 each.

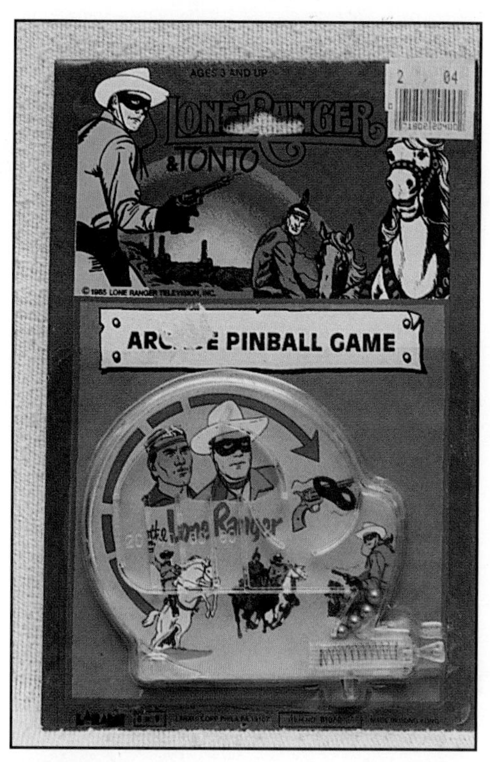

Pinball game, 1981, $12.00 – 25.00.

Suspenders, 1981, $12.00 – 25.00.

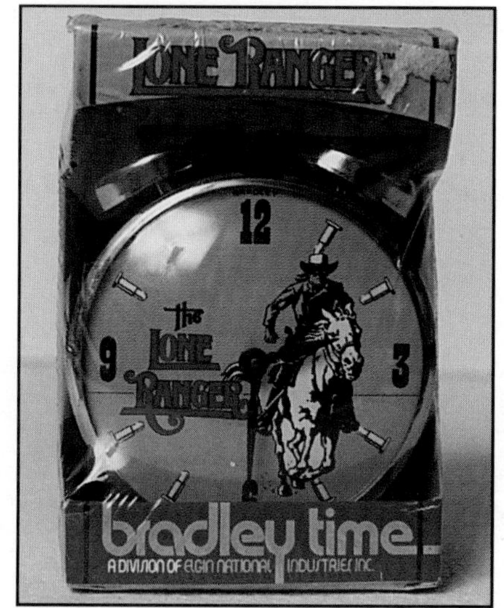

Alarm clock, 1981, $95.00 – 125.00.

Christmas ornament, 1981, $50.00 – 75.00.

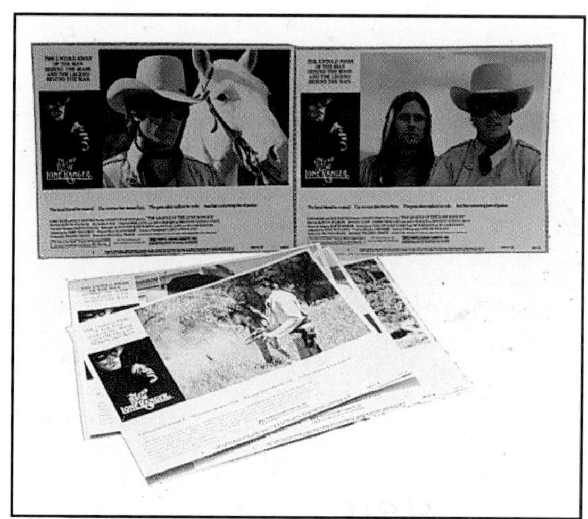

Lobby cards, set of 8 cards, 1981, $10.00 – 12.00 per card.

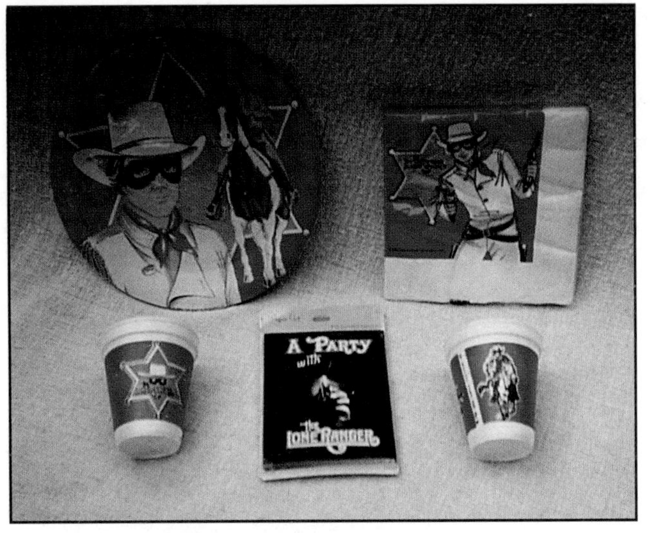

Party set, 1981, $12.00 – 25.00.

Party set, 1981, $12.00 – 25.00.

Sneakers, 1981, $35.00 – 65.00.

Underros, 1981, $15.00 – 35.00.

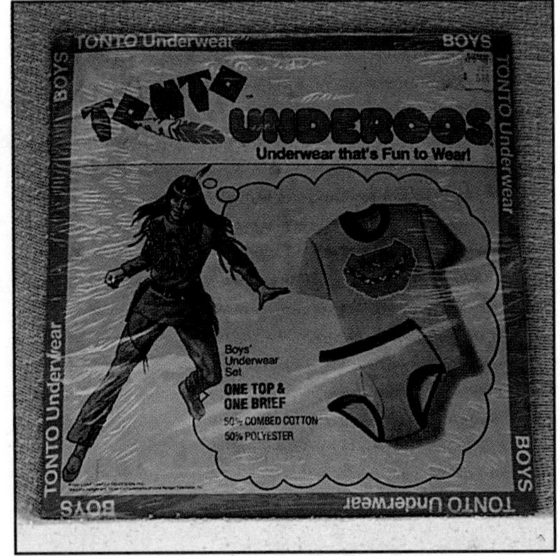

Tonto underros, 1981, $15.00 – 35.00.

Puffy stickers, 1981, $6.00 – 12.00.